Brilliant
Microsoft® Windows Vista
for the Over 50s

Joli Ballew

PEARSON
Prentice
Hall

Harlow, England • London • New York • Boston • San Francisco • Toronto • Sydney • Singapore • Hong Kong
Tokyo • Seoul • Taipei • New Delhi • Cape Town • Madrid • Mexico City • Amsterdam • Munich • Paris • Milan

Pearson Education Limited
Edinburgh Gate
Harlow CM20 2JE
United Kingdom
Tel: +44 (0)1279 623623
Fax: +44 (0)1279 431059
Website: www.pearsoned.co.uk

First edition published in Great Britain in 2009

ISBN: 978-0-273-72056-0

British Library Cataloguing-in-Publication Data
A catalogue record for this book is available from the British Library

Library of Congress Cataloging-in-Publication Data
Ballew, Joli
  Brilliant Microsoft Windows Vista for the over 50s/Joli Ballew.--1st ed.
     p. cm.
  ISBN 978-0-273-72056-0 (pbk.)
  1. Microsoft Windows (Computer file) 2. Operating systems (Computers) I. Title.
   QA76.76.O63B35923 2008
   005.4'46--dc22
                              2008043538

10 9 8 7 6 5 4 3 2 1
12 11 10 09 08

Typeset in 11pt Arial Condensed by 30
Printed and bound in Great Britain by Ashford Colour Press Ltd, Gosport, Hants

The publisher's policy is to use paper manufactured from sustainable forests.

Brilliant guides

What you need to know and how to do it

When you're working on your computer and come up against a problem that you're unsure how to solve, or want to accomplish something in an application that you aren't sure how to do, where do you look? Manuals and traditional training guides are usually too big and unwieldy and are intended to be used as end-to-end training resources, making it hard to get to the info you need right away without having to wade through pages of background information that you just don't need at that moment – and helplines are rarely that helpful!

Brilliant guides have been developed to allow you to find the info you need easily and without fuss and guide you through the task using a highly visual, step-by-step approach – providing exactly what you need to know when you need it!

Brilliant guides provide the quick easy-to-access information that you need, using a table of contents and troubleshooting guide to help you find exactly what you need to know, and then presenting each task in a visual manner. Numbered steps guide you through each task or problem, using numerous screenshots to illustrate each step. Added features include 'See also...' boxes that point you to related tasks and information in the book, while 'Did you know?...' sections alert you to relevant expert tips, tricks and advice to further expand your skills and knowledge.

In addition to covering all major office PC applications, and related computing subjects, the *Brilliant* series also contains titles that will help you in every aspect of your working life, such as writing the perfect CV, answering the toughest interview questions and moving on in your career.

Brilliant guides are the light at the end of the tunnel when you are faced with any minor or major task.

Publisher's acknowledgements

The author and publisher would like to thank the following for permission to reproduce the material in this book:

Microsoft product screen shots reprinted with permission from Microsoft Corporation.

Every effort has been made to obtain necessary permission with reference to copyright material. In some instances we have been unable to trace the owners of copyright material, and we would appreciate any information that would enable us to do so.

About the author

Joli Ballew is a technical author, a technology trainer and website manager in the Dallas area. She holds several certifications including MCSE, A+ and MCDST. In addition to writing, she occasionally teaches computer classes at the local junior college, and works as a network administrator and web designer for North Texas Graphics. She's written over two dozen books, including *Brilliant Laptops for the Over 50s*, *Degunking Windows*, *CNet's Do It Yourself 24 Mac Projects*, *PC Magazine's Office 2007 Solutions*, and *Breakthrough Windows Vista* with Microsoft Press.

Joli can be contacted at www.joliballew.com

Dedication

For all of the over 50s people in the world who have been waiting for a series created just for them.

Contents

Introduction

i

Welcome to *Brilliant Microsoft® Windows Vista for the Over 50s*, a visual quick-reference book that shows you how to master all of the features of the new MS Vista OS. Specifically written for those of you who did not have significant contact with computers in your working lives, but who now have the time to explore the possibilities of the new technology. Fully updated throughout to cover MS Vista SP1 it provides an easy-to-use guide to anyone wanting to get the most out of their computer.

Find what you need to know – when you need it

You don't have to read this book in any particular order. We've designed it so that you can jump in, get the information you need and jump out. To find the information that you need, just look in the table of contents or Troubleshooting guide, and turn to the page listed. Read the main text, follow the step-by-step instructions in the side columns, along with the illustrations, and you're done.

How this book works

Each task is presented with step-by-step instructions in one column and screen illustrations in the other. This arrangement lets you focus on a single task without having to turn the pages too often.

Step-by-step instructions

This book provides concise step-by-step instructions that show you how to accomplish a task. Each set of instructions includes illustrations that directly correspond to the easy-to-read steps. Eye-catching text features provide additional helpful information in bite-sized chunks to help you work more efficiently or to teach you more in-depth information. The 'For your information' and 'Did you know?' features provide tips and techniques to help you work smarter, while the 'See also' cross-references lead you to other parts of the book containing related information about the task. Essential information is highlighted in 'Important' boxes that will ensure you don't miss any vital suggestions and advice.

Troubleshooting guide

This book offers quick and easy ways to diagnose and solve common problems that you might encounter, using the Troubleshooting guide. The problems are grouped into categories.

Spelling

We have used UK spelling conventions throughout this book. You may therefore notice some inconsistencies between the text and the software on your computer which is likely to have been developed in the USA. We have however adopted US spelling for the words 'disk' and 'program' as these are commonly accepted throughout the world.

Instant Vista

Introduction

Windows Vista is the most important software installed on your computer. Although you likely have other software programs (like Microsoft Office or Photoshop Elements), Windows Vista is your computer's *operating system,* and thus, it's what allows *you* to *operate* your computer's *system*. You will use Windows Vista to find things you have stored on your computer, connect to the Internet, send and receive e-mail, and surf the Web, among other things.

You don't need to be a computer guru or have years of experience to use Windows Vista. Its interface is intuitive. The Start button offers a place to access just about everything you'll need, from photos to music to e-mail; the Recycle Bin holds stuff you've deleted; and the Sidebar offers a bar full of *gadgets* that you are likely to want to access, like a clock, the weather and news headlines. In this first chapter you will discover how little you need to know (and learn) to get started with Windows Vista.

! Important

Windows Vista comes in several editions and computer manufacturers often add their own touches. As a result, your screen may not look exactly like what you'll see in the screenshots in this book (but it'll be close).

One of Windows Vista's main jobs is to serve as a liaison between you and your PC. When you physically move the mouse on your desk, Vista helps the PC to virtually move the cursor on the computer's Desktop. When you save a file, Vista interacts with the hard drive to offer a place to save the information and remembers where it is stored. If you want to print a webpage, Windows Vista communicates with the printer and sends the required information to it. And, when you want to burn a CD or DVD, Vista communicates with those drives too, making sure what you want to do is completed successfully. Vista's work is behind the scenes, making sure that you never have to worry about how anything technically works.

Windows Vista also offers applications to help you be more productive and do more things. For instance, Windows Calendar is available for scheduling, Windows DVD Maker helps you create DVDs, Windows Fax and Scan lets you, well, fax and scan, Windows Mail lets you send and receive e-mail, and Windows Photo Gallery, Media Center and Movie Maker will serve all of your media needs. You also get Internet Explorer for surfing the Web and the Sync Center for synching portable players for music, photos, videos, and e-books.

Beyond Vista though, you probably have additional programs installed. You might have Microsoft Office, a Photoshop program or an art program. You may even have applications that were installed by the computer manufacturer, like a PDF reader, firewall, PC update software, music players or anti-virus software.

Now that you know a little about what Windows Vista offers, it's time to do some exploring. If this is your first time to start Vista, and you're on a new PC, you'll be prompted to enter some information. Specifically, you'll type your name as you'd like it to appear on your Start menu (capital letters count), activate Windows Vista and, if desired, register your copy of Windows Vista. It's important to know that while activation is mandatory, registration is not. You'll learn more about both of these things shortly.

Important

To activate and register Windows Vista during the initial setup, you'll have to be connected to the Internet. If no Internet connection is available, a phone number will be provided. Activation is mandatory. You will be prompted to activate Windows every day for 30 days or until Windows is activated, whichever comes first. If you do not activate Windows within the 30-day timeframe, Windows Vista will lose all functionality – except for the activation process. Registering lets you get tips and hints, and creative ideas for using Windows Vista via e-mail and the Web, and is not required.

Start and activate Windows Vista (cont.)

Starting and activating Windows Vista

1 If applicable, open the laptop's lid.

2 Press the Start button on the PC. It's generally on the front of the PC, but is sometimes found on the top of the PC. On a laptop, it's likely to be located somewhere on the keyboard (to keep you from accidentally turning on the PC when the lid is closed).

3 If applicable, press the Start button on the computer monitor.

4 Work through the activation and registration process, if applicable. Just follow the directions, clicking Next to move from one page of the activation wizard to the next.

5 Click your user name and input a password, or, just wait for Windows to start. What happens here is different based on your current setup.

6 Wait a few seconds for Windows Vista to initialise.

7 Click the Start button on the desktop. It's in the bottom left hand corner.

8 Locate your user name in the Start Menu.

When you first start Windows Vista, the Welcome Center opens. There are at least two sections: Get started with Windows and Offers from Microsoft, and perhaps others not included here. Often computer manufacturers add their own listings and links to help you learn about your computer and the applications they've installed on it, as well as links to their own Help files or website.

Using the Welcome Center's Get started with Windows section you can choose:

- View computer details – see what Windows Vista edition is installed (most likely Basic, Home Premium or Ultimate), the processor type and speed, the amount of memory (RAM) and other details.

- Transfer files and settings – learn about and use Windows Easy Transfer, an application included with Windows Vista that helps you transfer user accounts, files and folders, program settings, Internet settings and Favorites, and e-mail settings, contacts and messages from an older computer to your new one. (Don't worry, you can use this any time.) There's more information about this in Appendix A.

- Add new users – learn how to secure your computer with user accounts for each person who will access it. If two people share one PC, each can have his or her own user account, where documents, e-mail, photos and other data are secure. You can also customise settings and set up parental controls here.

- Connect to the Internet – use Windows Vista wizards to help you set up an Internet connection. You can set up a connection using an existing account or choose from a list of Internet Service Providers (ISPs).

- Windows Ultimate Extras – available only on Windows Vista Ultimate edition, this section allows you to access new programs, services and publications aimed directly at Vista Ultimate users.

- What's new in Windows Vista – access information regarding what's been added since Windows XP including but not limited to keeping devices in sync, backing up and

Explore the Welcome Center

1

Explore the Welcome Center (cont.)

encrypting files, faxing and scanning documents, and creating, saving and using Search folders.

■ Personalize Windows – change the picture that appears on your Desktop, change your screen saver, personalise sounds and change fonts.

■ Register Windows online – go online to register your copy of Windows. Registering lets you get tips, hints and ideas for using Windows Vista.

■ Windows Media Center – available in Windows Home Premium and Windows Ultimate editions, this option allows you to set up Windows Media Center where you can: watch, pause and record live television; locate, download and/or listen to music and radio; view, edit and share photos and videos; and play DVDs (among other things).

■ Windows basics – learn how to use the mouse and keyboard, work with files and programs, use e-mail, connect to the Internet, surf the Web, secure your PC and work with digital pictures.

■ Ease of Access Center – make your computer easier to see, hear and use by adjusting the display and other settings.

■ Backup and Restore Center – open the Backup and Restore Center and back up important files once or on a schedule. If you have Windows Vista Ultimate you can also create a copy of your entire PC should anything ever go wrong.

■ Windows Vista demos – watch videos to learn to work with programs, files and folders, use e-mail and the Internet, print documents, secure your PC, set up user accounts and solve problems.

■ Control Panel – access the Control Panel to change computer settings like the clock or time zone, the colour scheme and, if you want to share files with other users, add or remove programs, use Search, configure network and Internet settings, and more.

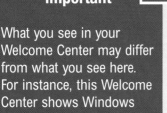

Important

What you see in your Welcome Center may differ from what you see here. For instance, this Welcome Center shows Windows Ultimate Extras, something you'll only see if the edition of Vista you've chosen is Windows Vista Ultimate.

4 Programs
   Welcome Center

Joli
Documents
Pictures
Music
Games
Search
Recent Items ▶
Computer
Network
Connect To
Control Panel
Default Programs
Administrative Tools ▶
Help and Support

See all results
Search the Internet

3 Welcome Center ✕

2

Showing the Welcome Center

1 To show the Welcome Center, turn on the PC.

2 If the Welcome Center does not open automatically, click the Start button.

3 In the Start Search window, type Welcome Center.

4 Under Programs, in the Start Menu, click Welcome Center.

?

Did you know?

In the Welcome Center, you can select Windows Vista Demos, and then click Open Windows Vista Demos to watch videos of the most often-performed tasks in Windows Vista including learning to use the mouse, printing to an installed printer, using the Web and diagnosing computer problems.

Explore the Welcome Center (cont.)

Exploring the Welcome Center

1 With the Welcome Center open, click View computer details.

2 Read the details regarding your computer. For more information about what you see here, refer to the Jargon buster. Make note of what edition of Vista is installed. In the next section you'll learn the difference between the editions and can decide if you want to upgrade to a feistier version.

3 Click Show all <number of> items. (Remember, you might see a different number, depending on your PC's configuration.)

4 Click Personalize Windows.

5 Notice the top pane changes to reflect your choice.

6 Later, you can click Personalize Windows to modify your copy of Vista.

7 If you do not want the Welcome Center to open every time you start Windows Vista, remove the check mark from Run at startup (Welcome Center can be found in Control Panel, System and Maintenance).

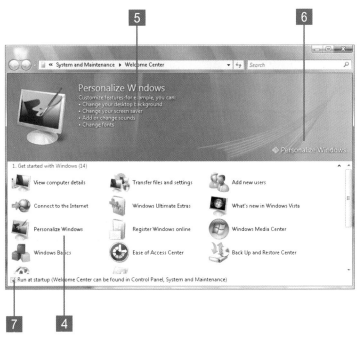

Using the Welcome Center's Offers from Microsoft section allows you to go online to learn about Windows Live, visit the Windows Marketplace, find ways to protect your PC and sign up for online technical support. These are all extras and include things you may want to explore later.

Jargon buster

Processor – short for microprocessor, this is the silicon chip that contains the central processing unit (CPU) inside a computer. Generally, the terms CPU and processor are used interchangeably. CPUs do almost all of the computer's calculations and the CPU is the most important piece of hardware in a computer system.
RAM – short for random access memory, it's the hardware inside your computer that temporarily stores data that are being used by the operating system or programs. Although there are many types of RAM, all you need to know is that the more RAM you have, the faster your computer will (theoretically) run and perform.
GPU – short for graphics processing unit, it's a processor used specifically for rendering graphics. Having a processor just for graphics frees up the main CPU, allowing it to work faster on other tasks.
GHz – short for gigahertz, this term describes how fast a processor can work. One GHz equals 1 billion cycles per second, so a 2.4 GHz computer chip will execute calculations at 240 billion cycles per second. Again, it's only important to know that the faster the chip, the faster the PC.

Explore the Welcome Center (cont.)

As an example, as you acquire and/or begin to use Windows technologies like Hotmail, Messenger, Mail and Photo Gallery, you may begin to want to integrate these technologies. With Windows Live, you can. For instance, Windows Live offers a Windows Live toolbar for searching from any webpage and having immediate access to Hotmail, Windows Live Mail and other Live services like Windows Live Spaces. With Windows Live Spaces you can easily create your own free website, and then use Windows Live Writer for creating your own online blog, complete with photos, videos and any other content. But we're getting ahead of ourselves. For now, let's focus on getting to know Vista!

You saw in the Welcome Center what edition of Vista your PC has installed. This information is available from the View computer details section. Here, the computer is running Windows Home Premium edition.

There are four Windows editions:

■ Windows Vista Basic – this is the most basic edition of Windows Vista. This edition includes necessary security features, network connectivity tools, Internet Explorer and the new Search features. If you have this edition, don't think that you're not appropriately covered PC-wise; you have all you need to perform basic computing tasks like e-mailing, creating documents, storing pictures and videos, and surfing the Web.

■ Windows Vista Home Premium – this is an upgrade to Windows Vista Basic and includes the basic features along with new display features (Aero), mobility and Tablet PC support for laptops and portable PCs, Media Center (for watching and recording television, among other things), the Backup and Restore Center for creating scheduled backups, Windows DVD Maker, more games, Windows Meeting Space (a way to hold virtual meetings from anywhere) and the ability to create your own movies in high definition.

■ Windows Vista Business – this is an upgrade to Windows Vista Basic and includes the basic features along with new display features (Aero), mobility and Tablet PC support, a backup program that you can use to back up your entire PC,

Know your Vista edition (cont.)

Windows Fax and Scan, the ability to access your PC remotely, and business-related tools like Windows Meeting Space. It does not include Windows Media Center, the additional games included in Home Premium, or the ability to create movies in high definition.

■ Windows Vista Ultimate – this is the ultimate in Windows Vista editions. With this edition you get everything in all of the other editions plus the ability to encrypt data (which makes your data more secure), tablet and touch technology (meaning you can touch the screen of compatible hardware to perform computer-related tasks), Windows Ultimate Extras, language packs and a multiple-user language interface, and secure online backup.

Although we haven't mentioned every feature of Windows Vista, the information here can give you an idea whether or not you'd like to upgrade to another edition of Vista. For instance, if you have Windows Basic or Windows Business, and you want to watch, record and pause live TV, you're going to need to upgrade to Vista Home Premium or Ultimate. However, if your PC does not include a TV tuner card and you don't want to purchase one, there's no reason to upgrade based on this criterion alone. (Don't worry, if you choose to upgrade, you'll get a nice, organised report regarding your PC's compatibility, and what you'll need to buy and add on to use the additional features in the upgraded edition.)

Did you know?

Windows Vista Starter is an affordable way for emerging markets to gain access to Windows Vista. Windows Vista Starter is not available in high-income markets like the United States, the European Union, Australia and the Netherlands. This version of Vista is designed for users with little or no computer experience and in countries where PCs have previously been unavailable or unwarranted due to price and/or lack of user experience.

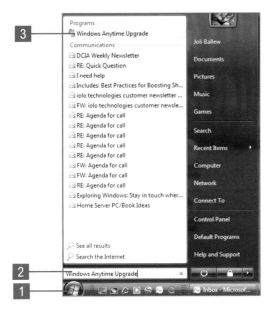

Considering an upgrade

1 Click the Start button.

2 In the Start Search dialogue box, type Windows Anytime Upgrade.

3 Under Programs, click Windows Anytime Upgrade.

4 Click Compare the editions of Windows Vista. You can click Compare just to explore. Nothing will happen to your PC, and your PC won't be upgraded. It doesn't hurt to look!

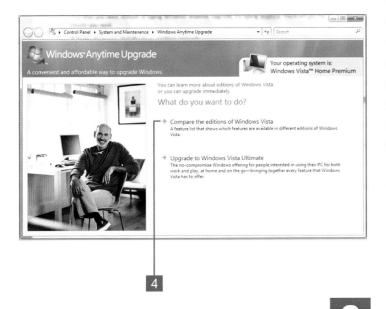

Did you know?

You can type part of what you're looking for in the Start Search dialogue box and usually find what you need. Instead of typing Windows Anytime Upgrade, try typing Anytime. You'll still get the results you need.

Know your Vista edition (cont.)

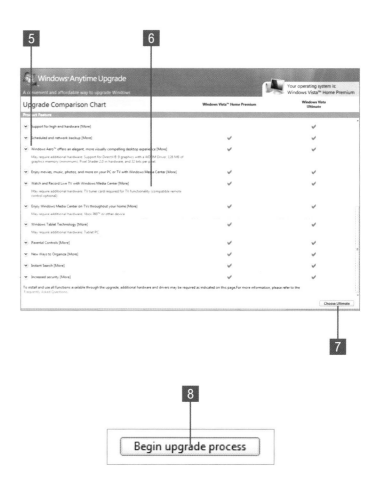

5 Read the information in the comparison chart. Note that you can click any down arrow for more information, or the up arrow to show less.

6 Read the information that details additional hardware you may need to use the feature. On the report for the PC in this example, notice that if we choose to upgrade and we want to watch and record live TV with Windows Media Center, we'd probably need to purchase a TV tuner card. This information is in the report because the Windows Anytime Upgrade feature can't find this hardware installed at this time.

7 To upgrade, click the Choose button.

8 In the next screen, click the Begin upgrade process button.

9 Follow the directions on Microsoft's website to pay for, and download and install, the upgrade.

Did you know?

You won't find Windows Anytime Upgrade on Windows Vista Ultimate edition PCs. That's because there's nothing to upgrade to!

What you see on the desktop will vary depending on how long you've been using your computer. If it's brand new, you may see only the Recycle Bin and the Sidebar. If you've been using Windows Vista for a while, you may see other things, including Computer, Network, Control Panel, or a folder with your name on it (for storing your personal files). You might even see icons with names of applications or ISPs written on them. Here you can see a sample Desktop.

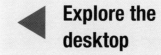

When you double-click any icon, the associated folder, file, or application opens. Windows Vista icons are shown here. You can add or remove icons from the desktop if you desire. You'll learn how to do that in Chapter 4.

Here are just a few of the things you might find on the desktop (remember, you'll learn how to add these icons and more in Chapter 4):

- Recycle Bin – this holds deleted files until you decide to empty it. The Recycle Bin serves as a safeguard, allowing you to recover items accidentally deleted or items you thought you no longer wanted but later decide you need. Note that once you empty the Recycle Bin, the items in it are gone for ever. (You can empty the Recycle Bin by right-clicking it and choosing Empty Recycle Bin.)

Explore the desktop (cont.)

■ Sidebar – this is a desktop component that lies *on top of* the desktop. It's transparent and offers, by default, a calendar, the weather and a clock. You can delete and add Sidebar items, called gadgets, to show the information you want to see. You can also hide the Sidebar. You'll explore the Sidebar in Chapter 2.

■ Network – double-clicking this icon opens the Network window, where you can view the computers on your network. If you are not connected to a network, you'll see something similar to the following.

■ Computer – double-clicking this icon opens the Computer window, shown here. You can see your hard disk drive(s) where the operating system, installed applications and personal data are stored, along with CD or DVD drives and sharing folders. You'll learn more about sharing folders in Chapter 8.

■ Control Panel – double-clicking this icon opens the Control Panel window. In Control Panel, you can change settings related to system and maintenance, user accounts, security, appearance, networks and the Internet, the time, language and region, hardware and sounds, visual displays and accessibility options, programs and additional options.

Explore the desktop (cont.)

■ Your personal folder – the name of this folder is the user name you created when you set up Windows Vista. Every user account has a personal folder. Double-clicking the folder icon opens it, and inside are subfolders named Documents, Music, Saved Games, Pictures, Downloads, Searches, Videos and more. You'll use these folders to store your personal data.

In addition to the icons on the desktop, you'll notice the Start button, Quick Launch area and the Notification area.

- Start Button – you'll use the Start button to locate programs installed and data stored on your computer. Click it once to open the Start menu, right-click it to see additional options.

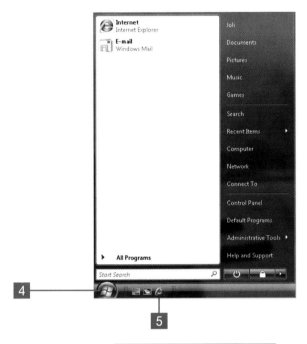

- Quick Launch – you'll use the Quick Launch area to quickly view the desktop (if there are open windows on it, switch between open windows, access Internet Explorer and more).

Exploring the desktop

1. If the Welcome Screen is open, close it by clicking the x in the top right corner.

2. Locate the Recycle Bin.

3. You may see other icons, like the ones shown here, including Network, Computer and Control Panel. The folder named Joli is my personal file folder, and inside it are my saved documents, pictures, e-books and videos. Your folder will have your name (not mine).

4. Locate the Start button. It's located on the bottom left corner.

5. Locate the Quick Launch area.

Explore the desktop (cont.)

6 Locate the clock and volume. (You may see additional icons.)

7 Locate the Sidebar.

■ Notification area – the icons in the Notification differ, depending on your PC's setup and installed programs. However, you will see some Windows icons there, including the Clock and Volume icons.

Just about anything you want to access on your computer can be accessed through the Start menu. You can access office applications, graphics applications, games and even your personal folders. You can access Computer, Network and Control Panel too, as well as Help and Support. In this section though, we'll only look at one part of the Start Menu, and that part is the All Programs menu.

Windows Vista comes with just about everything you need when it comes to applications and software. There's Internet Explorer for surfing the Web, Windows Calendar for keeping track of tasks and appointments, Windows DVD Maker for burning your own DVDs, and Media Player for listening to music. But there are many more features than that. In this section you'll learn a little about many of the available Windows Vista features, and you can decide if it's something you want to explore and use or not. With that out of the way, you can then skip around in the book for the information you need on using and applying the feature, and ignore those you don't need or want to use.

Here are some of the more commonly used Windows Vista features, all available by clicking the Start button and then clicking All Programs.

Discover Windows Vista

1

Important

!

Some features are only available in certain editions. For instance, while Internet Explorer is available in every Vista edition, Windows Media Center is only available in Windows Home Premium and Windows Ultimate editions.

■ Internet Explorer – one software option for accessing and surfing the Web. Internet Explorer offers tabbed browsing, meaning you can have several webpages open at the same time, a place to store links to your favourite pages, a pop-up blocker, and the ability to zoom, change the text size, print and subscribe to RSS feeds among other things. You'll learn more about Internet Explorer in Chapter 10.

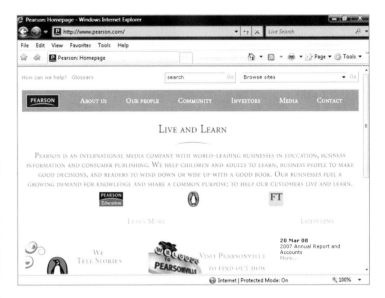

■ Windows Calendar – a software option for creating, editing, saving and publishing a calendar for you, your children or your business. With it you can add tasks and appointments, make notes and even import and export calendar data. You'll learn more about Windows Calendar in Chapter 6.

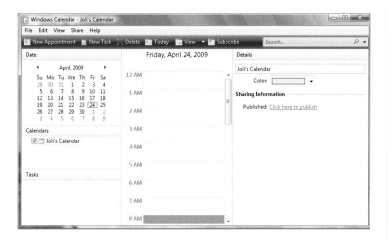

- Windows DVD Maker – an application that lets you create DVDs easily by working through a series of steps, offered by the Windows DVD Maker wizard. You'll learn more about Windows DVD Maker in Chapter 14.

- Windows Fax and Scan – an application that lets you scan and then fax documents or, simply, fax documents created on your PC. Windows Fax and Scan looks a lot like the older Outlook Express, so if you're familiar with that program, using Windows Fax and Scan will be easy. Although you won't find information in this book about using Windows

Discover Windows Vista (cont.)

Fax and Scan, if you learn how to use Windows Mail (Chapter 9) you can easily transfer that knowledge to learn to use Windows Fax and Scan. (Note that you'll need a modem and a phone line to use the program to fax data.)

■ Windows Live Messenger – an application you use to exchange instant messages with others.

■ Windows Mail – a software option for sending, receiving, storing and organising e-mail and e-mail contacts. You'll learn about Windows Mail in Chapter 9.

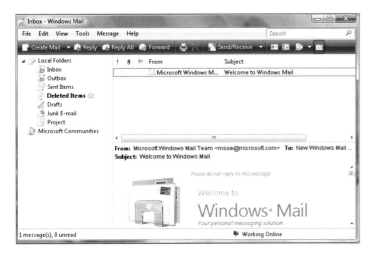

■ Windows Media Center – an application that allows you to watch, record, fast-forward and (after recording or pausing a TV show) rewinding live TV. You can also listen to music stored on your PC, locate and watch sports programmes, view, download and/or purchase online media, burn CDs and DVDs, sync portable music devices, view and organise your personal pictures and videos, and more. To have access to all of Media Center's features though, you'll need a TV tuner, CD and DVD burner, Internet connection, large hard drive and lots of RAM.

Discover Windows Vista (cont.)

■ Windows Media Player – an application that enables you to store, access, play and organise the music stored on your PC. You can also 'rip' music (that means copying music CDs you own to your PC's hard drive), burn CDs, sync portable devices and more. Media Player is covered in Chapter 12.

■ Windows Movie Maker – an application that lets you import videos from a video camera and edit those videos. Using Movie Maker you can add effects, music, transitions, audio and more, as well as edit the video for time and quality.

■ Windows Photo Gallery – an application you can use to import, access, view, send, store and organise pictures and videos. You can create picture galleries that contain only images you want and organise photos easily by year, subject or ratings, among other criteria. You'll learn all about Photo Gallery in Chapter 13.

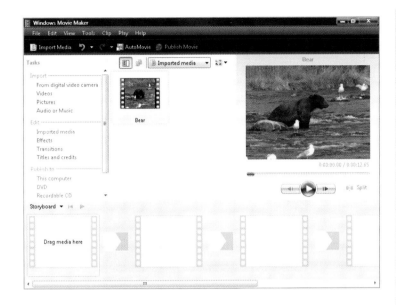

Important

The applications introduced here are not all of the applications that ship with Windows Vista. There are many we did not introduce in the interest of time, space and importance, or because the features (like Windows Update or Windows Defender) are better introduced independently in other chapters.

Discover Windows Vista (cont.)

Discovering Windows Vista applications

1 Click the Start button.

2 Click All Programs.

3 If necessary, use the scroll bar to move to the top of the All Programs list.

4 Locate Internet Explorer. Do not click it or it will open.

5 Locate Windows Calendar. Do not click it or it will open.

6 Continue down the list, noting what programs and applications are available in your edition of Windows Vista.

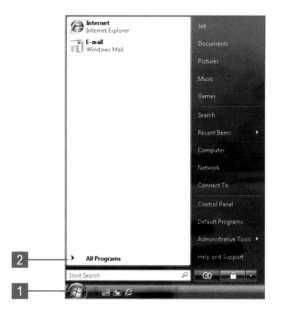

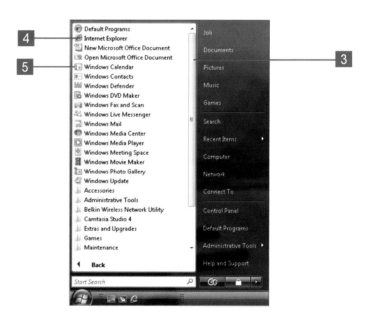

Note: the Accessories folder is located underneath Windows Update in this list. We'll talk about the items in that folder next.

Accessories

Windows Vista also comes with a lot of accessories. These applications are simpler than the applications introduced thus far. Two examples are the calculator and notepad. Accessories are located in the Accessories folder, which you can access from the Start button and the All Programs list.

The accessories in the Accessories folder include:

- Calculator – a standard calculator you can use to perform basic mathematical tasks. Click the View menu and choose Scientific to see the calculator shown here.

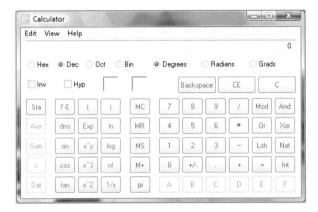

- Command Prompt – opens a command prompt that you can use to communicate with Vista's operating system. This is a task you'll probably never need to do.

- Connect to a Network Projector – enables you to connect to a network project when giving a presentation.

- Notepad – an application that enables you to type notes and save them. Using this application you can also print, cut, copy and paste, find and replace words, and select a font, font size and script.

- Paint – a program you can use to create drawings either on a blank canvas or on top of a picture. You can use the toolbar to draw shapes, lines, curves and input text. You can use additional tools including paint brushes, pencils, airbrushes and the like, as well as choose colours for objects you draw.

Discover
Windows Vista
(cont.)

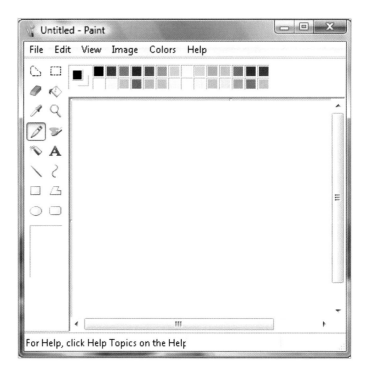

■ Remote Desktop Connection – a program you can use to access your computer from somewhere else, like an office or hotel room.

■ Run – a dialogue box where you can type a command. There are many commands, one example is sfc/scannow, which will cause Vista to find and fix problems with the operating system, and msconfig, which opens a dialogue box where you can control what programs load when you start Windows, among other things.

- Snipping Tool – a tool you can use to copy any part of any screen, including information from a webpage, part of your desktop or even part of a picture.

- Sound Recorder – a recording program that you can use to record your own voice. You can use the voice clips as reminders for tasks and you can add them to Movie Maker files or a webpage, among other things.

- Sync Center – an application that lets you set up partnerships between Windows Vista and external devices like portable media players, e-book readers and portable PCs or phones. After a partnership is set up, each time you connect the device to your PC, the information that has changed is synced per your instructions during setup.

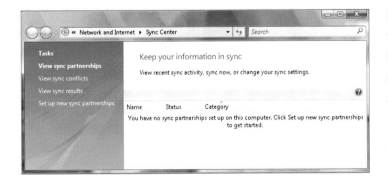

Discover Windows Vista (cont.)

■ Welcome Center – discussed earlier in the chapter, a place for Windows Vista to 'welcome' you by offering quick links to setting up the Internet, viewing computer details and securing your PC, among other things.

■ Windows Explorer – opens an 'explorer' window where you can browse for files, programs, pictures, music, videos and more. However, it's generally easier to locate these items in their respective folders or from the Start menu. Here Public folders are selected. (You'll store items in these folders when you want to share them with others who use your PC or are on your local network.) In the Explorer window you can also change how you share files and burn CDs.

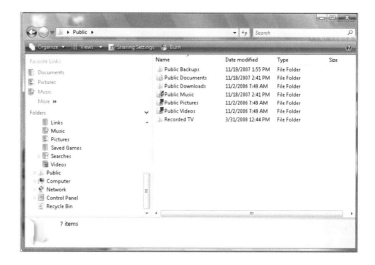

■ Windows Sidebar – opens the Windows Sidebar, detailed earlier in this chapter and again in Chapter 2.

■ WordPad – a word-processing program where you can create, edit, save and print files. Like Notepad, you can cut, copy and paste, find and replace words, and select a font, font size and script. However, you also have access to a formatting toolbar, a ruler and additional options. You can insert the date and time into a document, and an object, like a graph or chart, or a compatible picture. WordPad's toolbars and interface are shown here.

■ Ease of Access folder – allows you to access tools that make using the computer easier for those with disabilities. Items include things like a magnifier and narrator. You'll learn more about Ease of Access tools in Chapter 5.

■ System Tools – allows you to access tools you'll need to maintain your computer's health. These include but are not limited to Disk Cleanup, Disk Defragmenter and System Restore. You'll learn more about these things in Appendix B.

■ Tablet PC – you'll only see this option if you have a laptop with Windows Vista Home Premium or Ultimate, or if your PC runs Vista Ultimate. Accessories include tools related to mobile PCs like the Tablet PC input panel and Windows Journal, among other things.

Discover
Windows Vista
(cont.)

Discovering Windows Vista accessories

1 Click the Start button. Click All Programs.

2 Use the scroll bar to move down the list until you see Accessories.

3 Click Accessories.

4 Click Calculator. Close the Calculator program by clicking the red x in the top right corner.

5 Repeat steps 1–4 and click Paint. Close the Paint program by clicking the red x in the top right corner.

6 Repeat steps 1–4 and click Sound Recorder. Close the program by clicking the red x in the top right corner.

7 Continue as desired, exploring additional features.

By default, Windows Vista will turn off the display and put the computer to sleep after a specific amount of idle time. The amount of time that must elapse before this happens depends on the power settings that you've configured for the PC, the settings configured by the manufacturer or the operating system's settings default. (You'll learn all about power settings in Chapter 2.) It's important to note that when the computer goes to sleep, it uses very little power. Because of this, there's often no need to actually turn off the PC, unless you plan to move it, not use it for a few days or if you're extremely energy conscious.

That being said, if you do want to turn off your PC, don't just hit the power button. You need to let Windows Vista handle the shutting down process. Remember, Vista is an operating system, and is here to help you operate your computer system safely and properly.

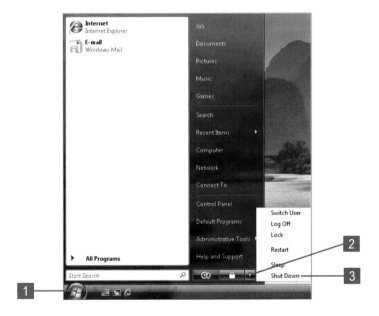

Shut down Windows

1 Click the Start button.

2 Click the arrow in the bottom right corner of the Start menu.

3 Click Shut Down. Note that you can also choose to put the computer to sleep, restart the computer, switch users, log off or lock the computer.

Shut down Windows (cont.)

The options available in the list shown here include the following:

- Switch User – if more than one user account is available on the PC, select Switch User to switch to another user. Switching users is different from logging off. When you choose to switch users, the current user's program, files, folders and open windows remain intact. When you switch back you do not need to reopen these items. Switching users has nothing to do with putting the computer to sleep or turning it off.

- Log Off – choose this option when you want to log off of your computer session. This does not shut down or put the computer to sleep, but will bring up the log-in screen. Once logged off, you'll need to log back on, usually by inputting your user name and/or password.

- Lock – use this option to lock the computer. You'll have to input your password to unlock the PC if one is assigned. If a password is not assigned, you'll simply click your user name.

- Restart – use this option to restart the PC. You should restart your PC any time you're prompted to (usually after a Windows Vista update or the installation of a program), when you know an application has stopped working, or the computer seems slow or unresponsive.

- Sleep – use this option to put the computer to sleep. Vista's Sleep state uses very little energy and is a better option than turning off the computer completely, unless of course you do not plan to use the PC for a couple of days or longer.

- Shut Down – choose this option when you want to shut down the computer completely. Shutting down a computer is harder on the components than simply letting the computer sleep. However, if you do not plan to use the computer for two or more days, turning it off is the best option.

Did you know?

Many computers now come with a Sleep button on the outside of the PC tower or on the inside of a laptop. Clicking the Sleep button puts the computer to sleep immediately.

Vista basics

Introduction

Now that you're a tad more familiar with the Vista desktop and its features, including the Recycle Bin, Start menu and personal folders (as well as many of Vista's applications, including Internet Explorer, Windows Mail and Windows Media Player), let's take a few minutes to dive deeper into Vista's interface. In this chapter we'll focus on the features you'll see, access and use virtually every time you turn on your computer: the Start menu, taskbar and Windows Sidebar. You'll also set up your PC for long-term use by selecting and/or configuring the appropriate power plan for you and your PC, learn how to locate and open the programs installed on your computer, and learn how to use Vista's Instant Search feature.

What you'll do

Explore the Start menu

Configure the Start Menu

Configure the taskbar

Enable the sidebar

Personalise sidebar gadgets

Configure the sidebar

Add and remove gadgets

Find and open a program

Explore the Start menu

The Start menu offers a place to easily access installed programs, Vista features and applications (like Windows Mail and Internet Explorer), recent items you've accessed like programs, pictures or spreadsheets, and your personal folders including Documents, Pictures, Music and Games.

You can open any of the items in the Start menu by clicking once on their name or icon. For instance, clicking Documents opens your personal Documents folder; clicking Pictures opens your personal Pictures folder; clicking Control Panel opens Control Panel. You can also click Recent Items to see a fly-out list of items you've recently worked with. These can be anything from documents to spreadsheets to pictures to folders. Again, clicking once opens the file or folder. In addition, you can click a program in the recent programs list to open it, or click Internet or E-Mail to open the corresponding application.

Did you know?

You can click on anything you want, open it and then close it using the X in the top right corner of the program window. And don't worry – you can't hurt anything!

Note:if you click a folder in the Start menu, a new window will open for the folder and the Start menu will close.

Note: if you click an item in the Recent Items list, the file or folder will open and the Start menu will close.

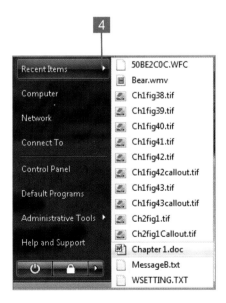

Using the Start menu

1 Click the Start button.

2 Locate your personal folder.

3 Locate the Games folder. If you click Games in the list, the Games window will open. You can close it, leave it open, or click any game to play it.

4 Click Recent Items. You may see items in the list that you've accessed recently.

Explore the Start menu (cont.)

Note: if you click a program in the Start menu, the program will open and the Start menu will close.

5 Locate applications that are 'pinned' to the Start menu. These are located on the top left corner. These do not change based on how often you use them; you must manually change or remove these.

6 Locate programs you've recently opened. These are located in the left pane of the Start menu under the 'pinned' applications. The items in this list change depending on how often you use them.

7 Locate the Start Search window. You'll learn about searching using this window later in this chapter.

Of course, you know you can click All Programs, and drill into the All Programs list. In the All Programs list you'll find applications that ship with Windows Vista as well as any third-party programs you or the computer manufacturer installed.

You may be perfectly happy with the Start menu, including how it looks, what is accessible from it, the fact that recently opened files and programs appear on it, and you may even approve of Vista's new Start menu style. However, if you don't like something about the Start menu, fear not. Like just about every other part of the Windows Vista interface, you can personalise it to suit your desires and needs.

Here are a few of the things you can change on the Start menu:

- The Start menu style – you can use Vista's new Start menu style, the one you've seen so far in this book, or you can use the Classic Start menu. The Classic Start menu gives you the look and functionality of previous Windows versions.

- Privacy – you can choose to show or not show recently opened files and/or programs.
- Customise – you can configure the Start menu to display the items Computer, Control Panel, Documents, Games, Music, Pictures and your personal folder as a link, a menu or not to display the item at all. (A link only displays the icon; clicking the link will open the folder in a new window. A menu displays the items in the folder as a fly-out menu, similar to what you see when you click Recent Items.)

Configure the Start menu

Did you know?

You don't have to configure the Start menu. If you're happy with it the way it is, just skip this section.

Did you know?

You can further customise the Start menu by clicking Customize in the Properties dialogue box. In the Customize dialogue box that opens, you can choose what to show and not show on the Start menu, as well as how to display it. Click Customize if you're curious. Don't worry, you can't mess anything up!

Configure the Start menu (cont.)

Configuring the Start menu

1. Right-click the Start button.

2. Click Properties. The Taskbar and Start Menu Properties dialogue box opens.

3. To change from the Windows Vista Start menu style to the Classic Start menu style, click Classic Start menu.

4. To hide (not show) the list of recently opened files, deselect Store and display a list of recently opened files.

5. To hide (not show) the list of recently opened programs, deselect Store and display a list of recently opened programs.

6. Click Apply. (Apply will be greyed out if you have not made any changes.)

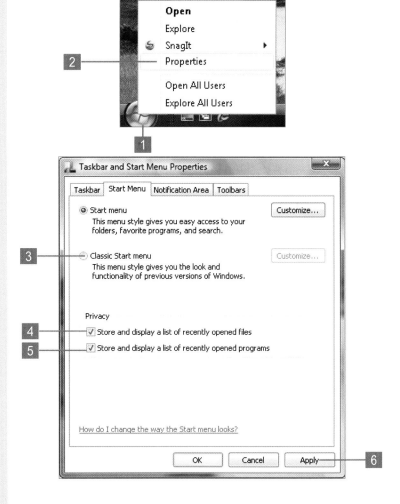

Important

When you open a program from the Start menu, the program opens in a 'window'. When you open a document, it opens in a 'window'. And, when you open a folder, it also opens in a 'window'. Note that the word *window* here is not capitalised. This *window* has nothing to do with Microsoft Windows Vista or any other 'window' term you may have heard. Window, as it's used in this context, is synonymous with an open program, file or folder.

The taskbar is the black bar that runs horizontally across the bottom of your screen. It contains three areas:

- The Quick Launch toolbar – this feature lets you open programs with a single click. The Quick Launch toolbar stores shortcuts to programs so you can easily access and open them. By default three items are stored there, but you can easily add your own. The programs and features with links here include the Show desktop icon, which lets you access the entire desktop immediately no matter how many windows are open; the Switch between Windows icon, which lets you move easily between open windows; and Internet Explorer, for surfing the Internet.

- The *middle section* – this section (aptly called the middle section) displays icons for open programs and documents. When nothing is open, it's blank. When programs and documents are open, you'll see their names here. You can easily open any window by clicking its icon in the taskbar. By default, similar taskbar buttons are grouped.

- The Notification area – this area includes the clock and the volume icons, and also holds icons for applications that are running in the background. You may see icons for your anti-virus software, music players, updates or Windows security alerts.

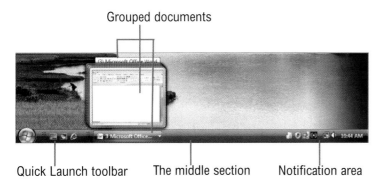

Grouped documents

Quick Launch toolbar   The middle section   Notification area

Note: you'll learn about using the taskbar later in this chapter, specifically in the section **Working with programs**.

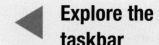

Explore the taskbar

2

Explore the taskbar (cont.)

You can configure the taskbar just as you can configure the other aspects of Windows Vista. There are features specific to the taskbar that you may want to tweak:

■ Lock the taskbar – enabling this will keep the taskbar in its default position, lying horizontally across the bottom of the screen. When unlocked, it is possible to drag the taskbar to other areas of the screen and/or to change how thick the taskbar is, as shown here. (To move or resize the taskbar, just click an empty area of the taskbar and drag it to another area of the desktop.)

■ Auto-hide the taskbar – enabling this will cause the taskbar to disappear when not in use. It will reappear when you move your mouse over the area of the screen where the taskbar lies.

■ Keep the taskbar on top of other windows – enabling this will keep the taskbar on top of any windows that are open. By default this is not selected, as it is generally preferable to keep the taskbar behind open windows so that you have more screen 'real estate'.

- Group similar taskbar buttons – enabling this will allow like programs, documents and folders to be grouped together to save taskbar real estate. When not grouped, the taskbar can become cluttered, as shown here.

Not grouped

- Show Quick Launch – enable this to show the Quick Launch area; disable to hide this feature.

- Show windows previews (thumbnails) – enable this to show thumbnails (small pictures) of items shown on the toolbar. Here you can see that Windows Photo Gallery is open and a thumbnail for it is showing. A thumbnail is a smaller version of the actual open window. Note that the thumbnail only shows when you hover the mouse over the item in the taskbar.

Did you know?

You don't have to configure the taskbar. If you're happy with it the way it is, just skip this section.

Explore the taskbar (cont.)

Configuring the taskbar

1 Right-click an empty area of the taskbar in the middle section.

2 Click Properties.

3 In the Taskbar and Start Menu dialogue box, select or deselect any feature by clicking in its checkbox.

4 Click OK.

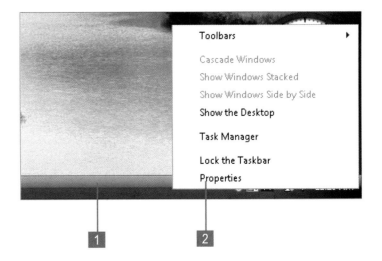

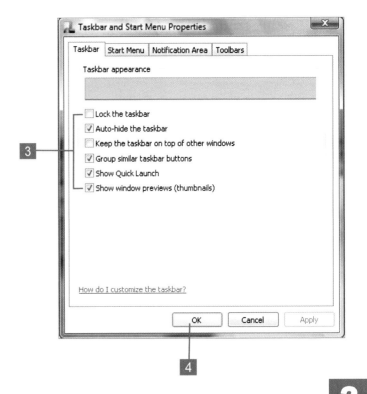

Did you know?

If you can't find an empty area of the taskbar to right-click, you can right-click the Start menu. When the Properties dialogue box opens, choose the Taskbar tab.

Windows Sidebar is a nifty feature that sits on your desktop and offers information on the weather, time and date, as well as access to your contacts, productivity tools and CPU usage. You can even have a slideshow of your favourite pictures. You can customise the Sidebar by hiding it, keeping it on top of or underneath open windows, adding or removing 'gadgets', and even detaching gadgets from the sidebar for use anywhere on the desktop. Here you can see the parts of the Sidebar.

Detached gadget   Windows Sidebar   Add gadget icon

Sidebar gadgets   Windows Sidebar icon

Did you know?

When you detach a gadget it often shows much more information than when it is part of the Sidebar.

Explore the Sidebar (cont.)

You can see what Sidebar gadgets are available here. You access this Sidebar gallery of gadgets by clicking the Add gadget icon shown in the previous screen. There are several default options, including but not limited to a calendar, clock, notes and weather. It's important to understand that much of this data comes from the Internet. Your computer doesn't know what the weather is like outside, but when you're connected to the Internet, that information is automatically retrieved and updated on the Sidebar. The same is true of feed headlines (news headlines) and stock prices. If you're not always connected to the Internet, you won't always have up-to-date information.

You can add additional gadgets by clicking Get more gadgets online. If you're connected to the Internet when you click the link, you'll be taken to the Windows Vista Sidebar webpage, where you can review, choose, download and install just about any gadget imaginable. Gadgets are categorised by their function, and you can search for gadgets that involve games, mail, instant messaging, music, movies, TV, news, feeds, safety, security, search tools, utilities and more.

Did you know?

The Stocks gadget runs about 15 minutes behind real-time stock data, so don't start buying and selling based on what you see here!

Important

Make sure you read the reviews of the gadgets you want prior to downloading and installing them. Although the gadgets you'll find here are almost always harmless, you might run across one or two that don't work or cause computer problems. Don't be afraid to get gadgets online, just be careful and read the reviews before installing.

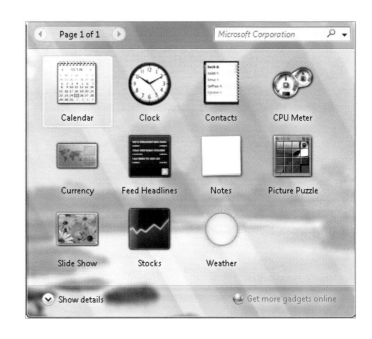

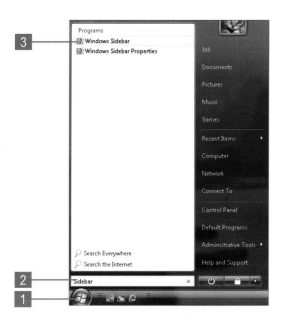

Enabling the Sidebar

1. If the Sidebar is not on the desktop, click Start.

2. In the Start Search window, type Sidebar.

3. Under Programs, click Windows Sidebar.

Explore the
Sidebar (cont.)

Personalising Sidebar gadgets

1 Position the mouse pointer over the clock in the Sidebar. Look for the small x and the wrench to appear.

2 Click the arrow in the Time zone window and select your time zone from the list.

Did you know?

Clicking the x will remove the gadget from the Sidebar. Clicking the wrench will open the gadget's properties, if properties are available.

Important

To get the most out of Windows Sidebar, connect to the Internet.

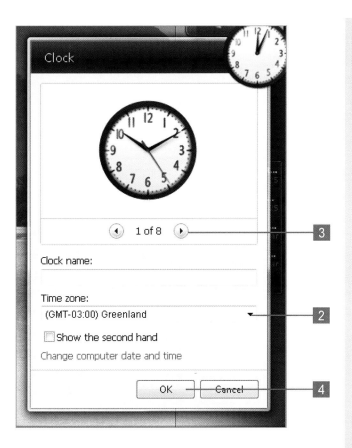

3 Click the right arrow underneath the clock to change the clock type. You might choose the one shown here.

4 Click OK.

5 Drag the weather sidebar to the desktop. Notice the gadget gets bigger.

Note: if the weather gadget is not on the Sidebar, skip these steps. You will learn how to add a gadget shortly.

Explore the
Sidebar (cont.)

6. Hover the mouse over the weather gadget and click the wrench icon.

7. In the Weather dialogue box, type your location. Click the Search button (it looks like a magnifying glass).

8. Choose Fahrenheit or Celsius.

9. Click OK.

10. If desired, drag the weather gadget back to the Sidebar.

11. Repeat these steps to personalise additional gadgets as desired.

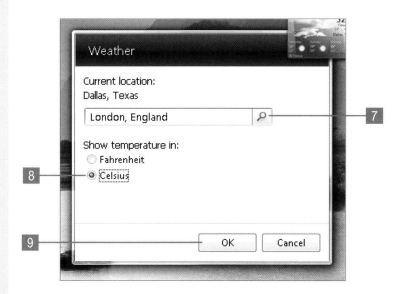

Did you know?

You don't have to configure the Sidebar. If you're happy with it the way it is, just skip this section.

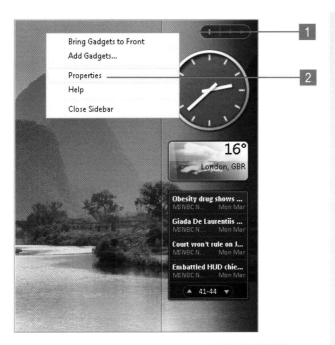

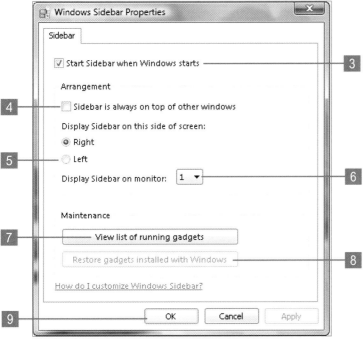

2

Configuring the Sidebar

1 Right-click an empty area of the Sidebar. (Try the area to the left of the Add gadgets icon.)

2 Click Properties.

3 In the Windows Sidebar Properties dialogue box, make changes as desired. For instance, if you do not want the Sidebar to start each time you start your PC, deselect Start Sidebar when Windows starts.

4 To keep the Sidebar on top of other windows, select Sidebar so it is always on top.

5 To reposition the Sidebar to the left or right side of the screen, make the appropriate selection as shown here.

6 If you have multiple monitors, choose which monitor to display the Sidebar on.

7 To view a list of running gadgets, click View list of running gadgets.

8 If you've deleted gadgets in the past, select Restore gadgets installed with Windows. (This will be greyed out if not applicable.)

9 Click OK.

Did you know?

To remove a gadget from the Sidebar, click the x beside it.

Explore the Sidebar (cont.)

Adding and removing gadgets

1 To add a gadget, click the Add gadget icon on the Sidebar.

2 In the gadget gallery, drag the gadget you want to add to the Sidebar and drop it there. (Repeat as desired.)

3 Click the x in the Gadget Gallery to close it.

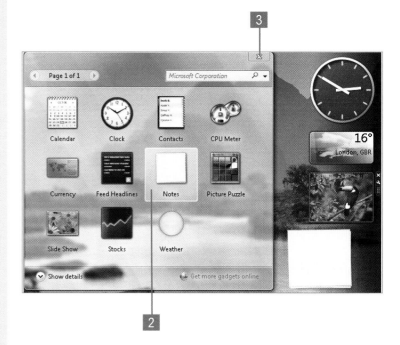

4 Click the x in any gadget to remove it from the Sidebar. This does not remove it from the computer. Remember the x will not appear until you hover the mouse over it.

5 If you add more gadgets than you have space for on the desktop, click the forward arrow (or the back arrow) to move to the next batch of added gadgets.

2

Did you know?

You can close the Sidebar by right-clicking an empty area of the Sidebar and selecting Close Sidebar. You can do the same by right-clicking the Sidebar icon in the Notification area.

Work with programs

Programs (also called applications or software) offer computer users, like you, an interface to easily perform computer tasks. You already have a word-processing program that enables you to write letters and print them (WordPad), an image-editing program that lets you fix red-eye problems in photos as well as crop them or change brightness or contrast (Windows Photo Gallery), and a mail program that lets you receive, organise and send e-mail (Windows Mail). These all come with Windows Vista. You can buy additional computer programs though, either from Microsoft or any of the thousands of third-party software companies, if you find you need more than what Windows Vista offers.

You open programs that are installed on your computer from the Start menu. Sometimes, you'll find shortcuts to the programs you want right on the desktop. You can move shortcuts to the desktop too, if there's a program you use often and want easy access to. You'll learn about customising the desktop, including adding shortcuts for programs, in Chapter 4.

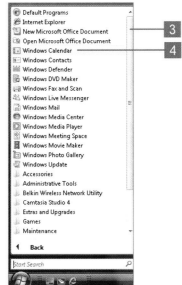

1 Click Start.

2 Click All Programs.

3 Use the scroll bar to move to the top of the All Programs list (if applicable).

4 Click Windows Calendar. The program Windows Calendar opens.

To use a program you must first open it. This is almost always achieved from the Start menu, although you can open a program from Quick Launch and other areas. Once a program is open, you can access its tools to perform tasks. For instance, if you open Windows Photo Gallery, you can use the interface options to view photos, fix problems with photos, place photos in categories, rate them, and delete them (among other things).

Work with programs (cont.)

5 Close Windows Calendar by clicking the red x in the top right corner of the window.

6 Repeat steps 1, 2, 3, 4 and 5 to open and close the following programs:

a. Windows DVD Maker

b. Windows Media Player

c. Windows Movie Maker

d. Windows Photo Gallery.

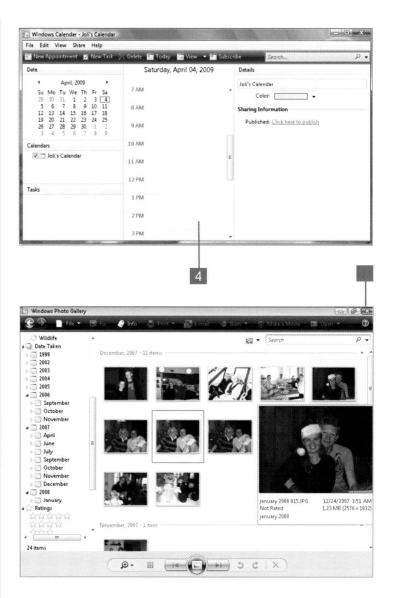

Note: throughout this book you'll learn more about working with programs; for now, it's only important you know how to open and close them.

Computing essentials

3

Introduction

To get the most out of your computer you need to understand some basic computing essentials. For example, it's important to understand what a 'window' is and how to resize, move or arrange open windows on your desktop. This is essential because each time you open a program, file, folder, picture or anything else, a new window almost always opens. You might have 10 open windows to sort through, depending on how well you multitask! Windows can also contain menus, tabs or toolbars, and you'll use all of these to access features inside the window, from importing video to printing a document. Beyond understanding windows though, you'll need to know how to get help when you need it, and be able to find your way around Vista's Control Panel and the Computer feature.

Work in Windows frames

Many options and features are common to almost all open windows. Menus offer drop-down lists that allow you to access additional features pertinent to the open window. In the case of an open program, for instance, you might use the Edit menu to cut, copy or paste information, or the File menu to print a document. Here you can see the Edit menu from inside Windows Movie Maker.

Some newer programs are starting to offer tabs instead of menus, and one notable example is the newest Microsoft Office suite. To access the items under a tab, simply click it. Here you can see the Home tab of Microsoft Office Word 2007. From the Home tab you can change formatting, among other things. Notice the other tabs: Insert, Page Layout, References, Mailing, Review, View and Add-Ins.

Application and folder windows usually also offer some sort of toolbar. Most windows offer multiple toolbars, which you can hide or show according to your preference. Here you can see Windows Internet Explorer, with one toolbar showing, the Menu bar. Here the Menu bar offers options for opening menu lists for the following: File, Edit, View, Favorites, Tools and Help. Click any menu title to see the menu choices. Toolbars can also offer tabs or icons, another option for accessing additional features.

Menu bar

3

Common options in Vista's Windows

Vista's application windows also have their own features, including toolbars, menus and icons. In a Vista operating system window, you might click the Burn icon to write data to a CD or use the View menu to change the size of the icons in the window. In the Network window, shown here, you can even add a printer or wireless device (using an icon).

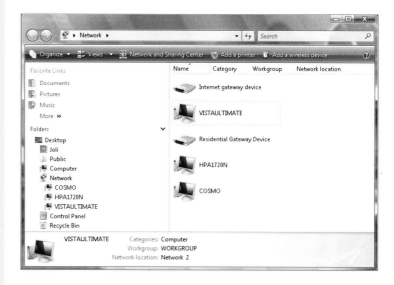

There are characteristics and features common to most Vista-related windows. This list includes a few you'll run across often:

▦ Organize – use this option to perform editing tasks like cut, copy and paste, or undo, redo, select all, delete or rename, or to change the layout or view properties for a selected item.

▦ Views – use this menu or icon to change how the items in the window look. The options are shown here.

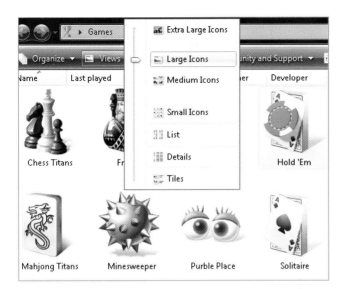

■ Burn (or Burn to Disk) – use this icon to copy files you've already selected to a CD or DVD. More on this in Chapter 14.

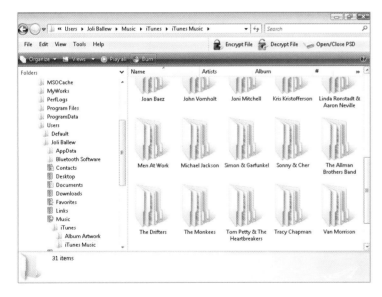

■ Tools – use this icon or menu to change the properties of the items in the application window.

Common options in Vista's Windows (cont.)

Changing the view in a window

1 Click Start.

2 Click Games.

3 In the Games window, click Views. Click Views three more times. Notice how the view changes each time you click the Views icon.

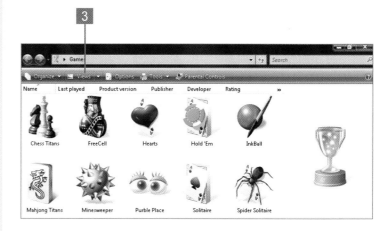

Did you know?

You can also click the arrow next to Views and select the view you want from the drop-down list.

Exploring the contents of a folder window

1 Click Start.

2 Click your user name.

3 Your personal folder opens. Note the items at the top of the window: Organize, Views, and Burn.

4 Click the Pictures folder once. Notice that two new icons appear: Explore and Share.

5 Click Explore to see the contents of the Pictures folder.

3

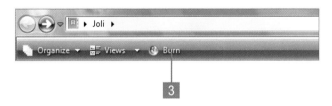

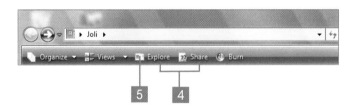

Common options in Vista's Windows (cont.)

6 Click the Back button to return to your personal folder.

7 Click Organize.

8 Click Close.

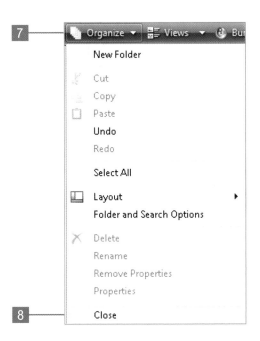

Did you know?

You can close any window by clicking the red x in the top right corner of the window.

When you first begin working with programs, files, folders and the like, you'll probably have only a few windows open on the desktop at one time. However, as you get more adept with the computer, you'll find that you often have more and more windows open at once. For example, you may have iTunes open and playing music while you edit a movie in Movie Maker. Along with that, you may have Windows Mail open and Internet Explorer. You may even have a Word document open where you keep a to-do list. With this many windows open at the same time, it becomes important to be able to move among them quickly.

Note: before working through this part of the chapter, open a few programs from the Start menu.

There are several ways to move among open windows:

- Click the icon that represents the window you want to access from the taskbar.

- Use Windows Flip. Windows Flip offers a quick way to choose a window using the graphical option shown here.

- Use Windows Flip 3-D. Windows Flip 3-D offers a different option for accessing open windows and is used in conjunction with the Aero interface.

Working with multiple open windows

3

Working with multiple open windows (cont.)

■ Minimise, restore or close windows until the one you want to view appears. (To minimise a window, you must click the small dash in the top right of the window.) When you minimise a window, it is placed on the taskbar so that you can see the open window that was 'underneath' it.

Accessing a window from the taskbar

1. Locate the taskbar.

2. Locate the icon for the window you want to bring to the front of the other open windows. (Multiple windows can be open, but one is always on top, or in front of, other windows.)

3. Items may be grouped, as shown here. If items are grouped, they will have a number by them to denote how many similar windows are open. Click the arrow in the window.

4. Select the item to show by clicking it once.

3

Important !

You won't see any items in the middle of the taskbar unless you have at least one window open.

Working with multiple open windows (cont.)

Using Flip and Flip 3-D

To use Flip:

1. With multiple windows open, on the keyboard, hold down the Alt key with one finger (or thumb).

2. Press and hold the Tab key.

3. Press the Tab key again (making sure that the Alt key is still depressed).

4. When the item you want to bring to the front is selected let go of the Tab key and then let go of the Alt key.

To use Flip 3-D:

1. With multiple windows open, on the keyboard, hold down the Windows key (which may have Start written on it) with one finger (or thumb).

2. Click the Tab key once, while keeping the Alt key depressed.

3. Press the Tab key again (making sure that the Alt key is still depressed) to scroll through the open windows.

4. When the item you want to bring to the front is selected let go of the Tab key and then let go of the Alt key.

You can also minimise and maximise windows, or click the Restore button so you can resize or move the window. A minimised window only appears on the taskbar and is not on the desktop. A maximised window is as large as it can be and takes up the entire screen. When the window is in *restore mode*, you can resize or move the window as desired. You can't resize a window that is maximised or minimised.

Note: there are no screen shots associated with using Flip or Flip 3-D here.

Important

If Flip 3-D doesn't work, or if you get only Flip and not Flip 3-D, either your PC does not support Aero or is not configured to use it. We'll talk about this in Chapter 4.

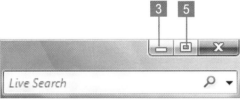

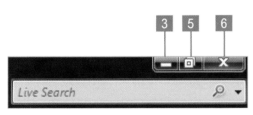

Working with multiple open windows (cont.)

Minimising, restoring and maximising windows

1. Click Start, and click Internet. (It's OK if you aren't connected to the Internet; we're only focusing on the actual window here, not its content.)

2. You will see one of two things in the top right corner of the window. Both are shown here.

3. To minimise the window (remove it from the desktop and relegate it to the taskbar), click the minimise button.

4. On the taskbar, locate the Internet Explorer icon and click it once to bring it back onto the desktop.

5. Click the single square in the top right corner if shown. If you see overlapping squares instead, click those. The single square 'maximises' the window. The two overlapping squares 'restore' the window. Repeat this step.

6. If you want to close Internet Explorer, click the x in the top right corner.

3

Moving and resizing windows

2 The maximise button should be showing

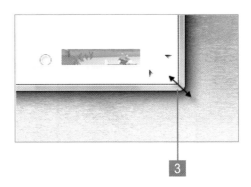

3

Click and drag here

1 Click Start, and click Internet.

2 If you see the maximise button in the top right corner, do nothing. If you see the restore button (the two overlapping squares) in the top right corner, click it. You want the maximise button to show.

3 Position the mouse at one of the window corners, so that the mouse pointer becomes a four-pointed arrow.

4 Hold down the mouse button and drag the arrow to resize the window.

5 Repeat Steps 3 and 4 to drag from the top, sides or any other corner of the window to resize it.

6 To move a window, click at the top of the window and drag. In Internet Explorer, click just above the Live Search window.

Important

!

You can move and resize windows only if they are in 'restore' mode, meaning the maximise button is showing in the top right corner of the window.

Windows often contain menus and sometimes those menu choices offer dialogue boxes. Menus enable you to access features of a program, edit the contents of a folder, document or picture, access help and support, and access tools for the program or folder (to name a few). Menu names differ depending on the window or program that's open. When you click a menu on a toolbar, a drop-down list appears. Here you can see the Format menu choices in WordPad.

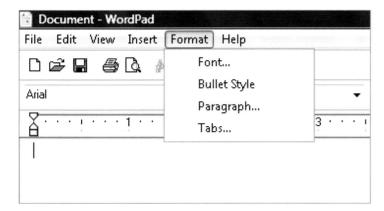

When you select a menu option, sometimes a change is made automatically (like when you use cut, copy or paste in a word-processing program), but sometimes a *dialogue box* opens. In WordPad, clicking Format and then clicking Font offers up the dialogue box shown here. You use a dialogue box to make desired changes to whatever it is you're working on.

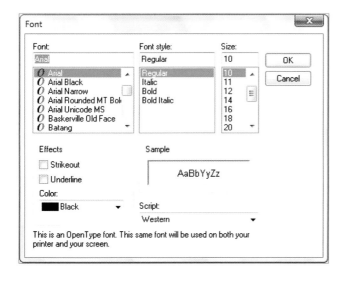

3

Understand menus and dialogue boxes (cont.)

As you might imagine, dialogue boxes can differ dramatically. Some have tabs, while some do not. This is the Games folder options dialogue box. It does not offer tabs, only configuration options.

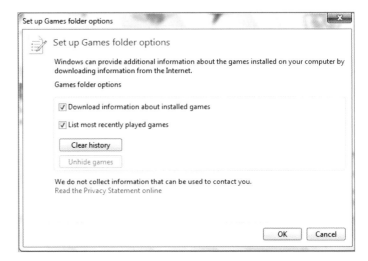

And here is Internet Explorer's Options dialogue box. It does have tabs; in fact, it has quite a few of them. You click on the tab's title to access the information under that tab.

Sometimes, clicking inside a dialogue box will open a second dialogue box! Here, clicking the Language button in the Internet Options dialogue box opens the Language Preference dialogue box. When this happens, you have to click OK in the last dialogue box opened before you can return to the previous dialogue box. Whew.

3

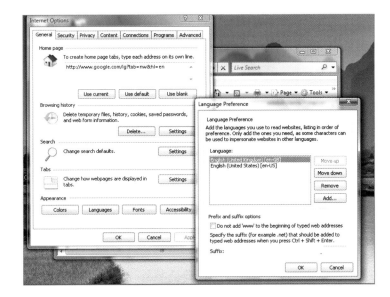

For your information

You'll be using menus and dialogue boxes throughout the book, but for now, you need only be familiar with their names and what you might expect when accessing them.

Understand menus and dialogue boxes (cont.)

Accessing menus and dialogue boxes

1 Click the Start button.

2 In the Start Search window, type WordPad.

3 Under Programs, click WordPad.

4 If you have a printer installed:

a. Click File.

b. Click Print.

c. Review the options in the Print dialogue box and then click Cancel. (Your Print dialogue box will not look exactly like this one.)

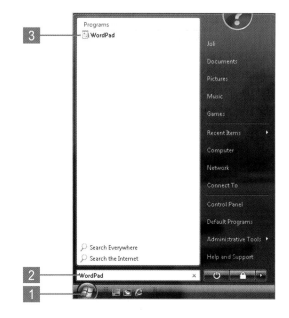

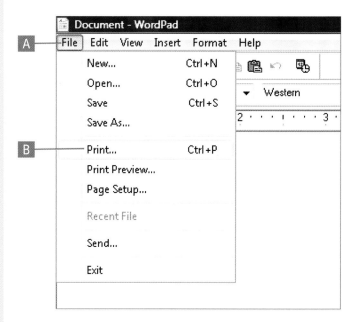

List of printers

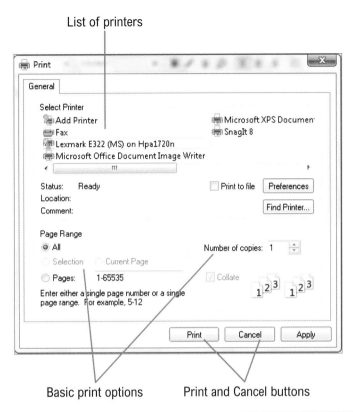

Basic print options   Print and Cancel buttons

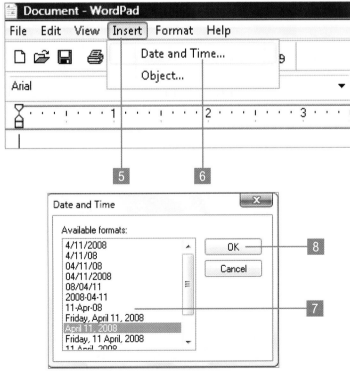

5 Click Insert.

6 Click Date and Time.

7 In the Date and Time dialogue box, click any date format.

8 Click OK. Note that the date is inserted into the document.

3

Understand menus and dialogue boxes (cont.)

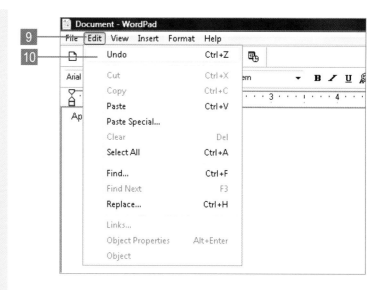

9 Click Edit.

10 Click Undo. Note that the date is removed from the document.

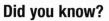

Did you know?

If a menu choice has a tick by it, it's currently being displayed. If there is no tick by it, it is not being displayed.

If toolbars are a feature of a window, you can configure what toolbars, if any, should appear in that window. Sometimes, you add and remove toolbars using the View menu, as shown here, but most of the time you use a different method.

For most windows, you'll *right-click* somewhere on a toolbar to select the toolbars you want to show or to remove toolbars you want to hide. Here, in Internet Explorer, we've right-clicked to the left of the Tools icon to show the toolbar options. Note that the Menu bar is selected and is showing. The Menu bar is the one that lists File, Edit, View, Favorites, Tools and Help. Your Menu bar might not be activated; it isn't by default.

Important

If you right-click a toolbar and nothing happens, try right-clicking in an empty area of the toolbar. If nothing happens then, there are no toolbar configuration options.

3

Understand menus and dialogue boxes (cont.)

Configuring toolbars

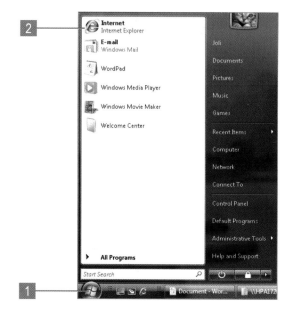

1 Click Start.

2 Click Internet.

3 Right-click on the Home icon, or any other icon on the toolbar.

4 To show any toolbar in the list, tick it. (If there's a tick by it, it's already showing.)

5 To hide any toolbar in the list, tick it. (If there's a tick by it, it's showing; if there's not, it's already hidden.)

Did you know?

You can also click the Internet Explorer icon in the Quick Launch area (if you enabled it in Chapter 2) to open Internet Explorer.

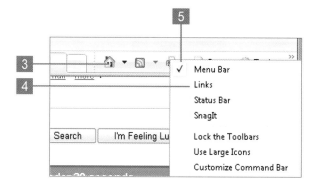

Sometimes you'll find toolbars even further in the menu structure. Here, in Internet Explorer, we've clicked Tools and then clicked Toolbars, to show even more toolbars to add. You'll learn more about these toolbars in Chapter 10.

Understand the Control Panel

Throughout this book you'll use the features located in Control Panel to perform such tasks as configuring and checking for Windows updates, configuring security settings, optimising appearance and adding new users. You'll also use Control Panel to add printers, uninstall programs and perform routine maintenance on your PC, among other things. For now though, you only need to know where Control Panel is, and what you can use it for.

Control Panel offers access to the features, tools and windows you'll need to configure your computer. For instance, under Network and Internet, you can choose to set up file sharing. Under User Accounts and Family Safety, you can choose to set up parental controls. And under Appearance and Personalization, you can change the desktop background, adjust screen resolution and more. Additionally, from the Ease of Access centre, you can optimise the display, change how your mouse works, start speech-recognition software and even change how your keyboard works.

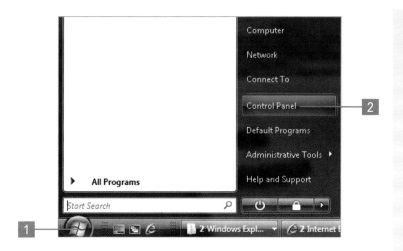

Understand the Control Panel (cont.)

Working with Control Panel

1 Click Start.

2 Click Control Panel.

3 Click System and Maintenance.

3

Understand the Control Panel (cont.)

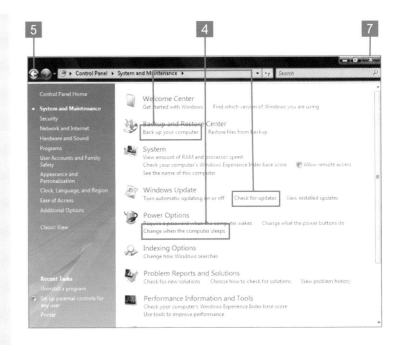

4 Note the available items in the System and Maintenance window. Here is where you will back up your computer, check for updates, change power options and more.

5 Click the Back button to return to Control Panel.

6 Repeat Steps 3, 4 and 5 for the following:

a. Security

b. Network and Internet

c. Hardware and Sound

d. Programs

e. User Accounts and Family Safety

f. Appearance and Personalization

g. Clock, Language, and Region

h. Ease of Access

i. Additional Options.

7 Close the Control Panel by clicking the x in the top right of the window.

Computer is a window that you can access from the Start menu. The Computer window is shown here. The Computer window, like many of Vista's windows, is partitioned into panes. The Favorite Links pane offers links to places you'll visit often, like your Documents, Pictures, Music, Recently Changed, Searches and Public folders.

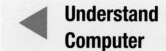

Favourite Links pane

Folders pane

There's also a Folders pane, where you can explore and locate virtually anything on the PC. The largest pane, on the right, shows your computer's hard disk drives, CD and DVD drives, and Sharing folders. The area across the bottom of the window shows information regarding your computer, including what version of Windows Vista is installed, processor type and speed, and the amount of memory installed.

You may need to maximise the Computer window to see everything here. Remember, to maximise a window, click the

3

Understand
Computer (cont.)

square in the top right corner. (If you see overlapping squares, the window is already maximised or as large as it can be.) You can also drag the divider between the panes to reposition them. Here you can see where you can position the mouse to reposition the panes. Move the mouse until you see the two-headed arrow, and then drag.

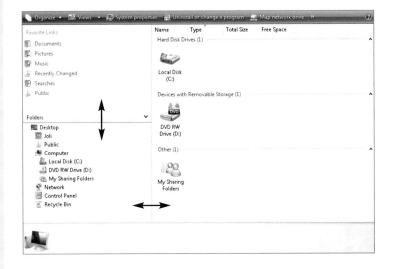

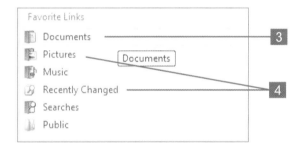

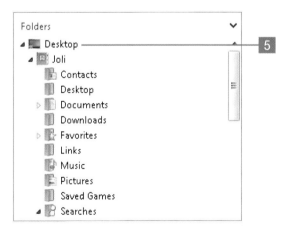

Understand Computer (cont.)

Working in My Computer

1 Click Start.

2 Click Computer.

3 In the Favorite Links pane, select Documents. Note the items in the Computer window change to show what's in that folder.

4 Repeat Step 3 to select Pictures and Recently Changed. You may have to reposition the pane to see these items. (Position the mouse between the panes until you see a two-headed arrow, then click and drag.)

5 In the Folders pane, select Desktop. (You may have to use the scroll bars or reposition the pane to see this.)

3

Understand Computer (cont.)

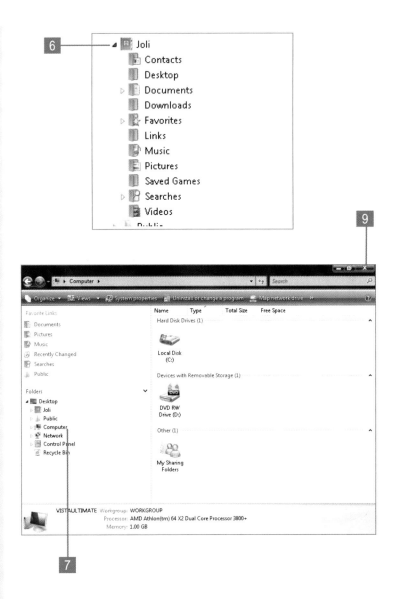

6 In the Folders pane, click all downward-pointing triangles to compress expanded folders.

7 With the Folders pane decompressed, click Computer.

8 Hover your mouse over your Hard Disk Drives icon. If more than one exists, perform this step on both. Notice the information that appears. Space free tells you how many gigabytes of hard drive space you have left; Total size tells you the size of the hard drive itself.

9 Click the x in the top right corner to close Control Panel.

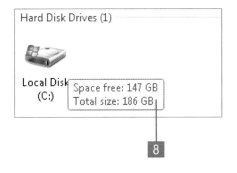

Sometimes you need a little bit more than a book can give you. When that happens, you'll need to access Windows Vista's Help and Support feature. You can access Help and Support from the Start menu.

When you open the Help and Support Center you'll have several options, all shown here. If you have time, click each option to see what it offers. You'll be surprised how much information is available. For instance, Windows Basics offers helpful articles on everything from using your mouse to setting up a wireless network. If you want help on something in particular, like Internet Explorer or Windows Mail, type what you're looking for in the Search Help window and the articles that apply to that will appear.

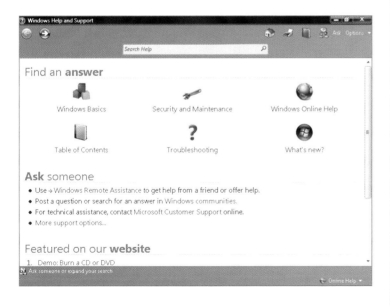

Did you know?

The Help and Support window offers an Options icon, where you can print help topics and change the text size.

3

Access Help and Support (cont.)

If you're looking for something in particular, click Table of Contents. From the Contents page, just click the option that most closely matches what you're looking for. If you don't find what you want on the new page, just click the Back button to try again. Additionally, you can type anything in the Search Help window if you'd rather go that route.

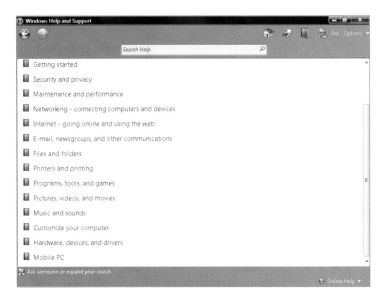

Additionally, know that you can access the Help and Support Center from virtually anywhere in Windows Vista. You only need to locate the round blue question mark shown here, which you'll find in almost all windows and dialogue boxes.

Finally, almost all programs offer a Help menu option. For help regarding an open program, click Help and select an option in the drop-down list.

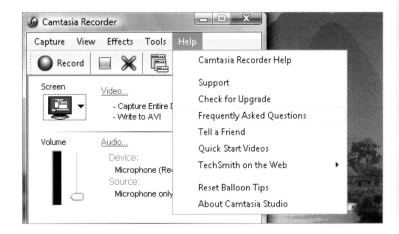

3

Access Help and Support (cont.)

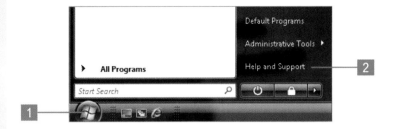

1. Click Start.

2. Click Help and Support.

3. Click Windows Basics.

4. Use the scroll bar to browse through the topics.

5. Select any topic to read more about it.

6. Click the Back button to return to the previous screen.

7. Repeat Steps 4–6 as desired.

8. Click the Home icon in the Help and Support Center to return to the first page of Help and Support.

Note: if you have a printer installed, you can click the Printer icon to print any help topic.

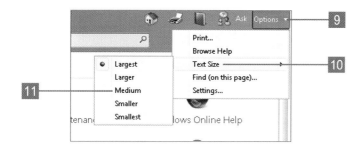

9 Click Options.

10 Click Text Size.

11 Select the desired text size.

12 Click the x in the top right of the Help and Support Center to close it.

3

Access Help and Support (cont.)

Locating and watching a Windows Vista demonstrating video

1 Click Start.

2 In the Start Search window, type Welcome.

3 Under Programs, click Welcome Center.

4 In the Welcome Center, under Get started with Windows, click Show all ___ items...

5 Double-click Windows Vista Demos.

6 Maximise the Windows Vista Demos screen if necessary.

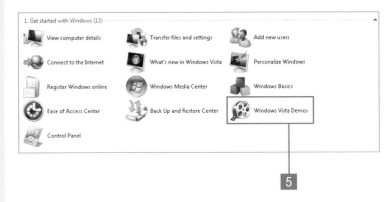

Note: you may need to turn up your speakers to hear the demo!

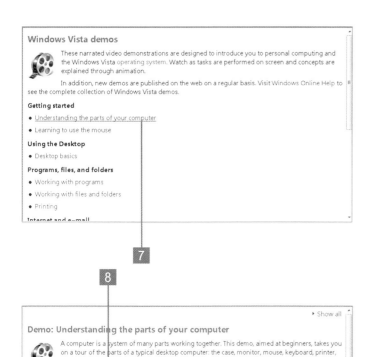

7 Note that you can select any video title, but in this exercise, click Understanding the parts of your computer.

8 Click Watch the demo.

9 To stop the demo, or to close Windows Media Player, click the x in Windows Media Player.

Personalising Windows Vista

Introduction

One of the first things many people like to do when they get a new PC or upgrade an older one is to personalise the picture on the desktop, select a screen saver and create shortcuts to their favourite programs or folders so they are easily accessible. You may also want to enable Aero, Vista's new interface feature, or change the screen resolution, colour or appearance. That's what we'll do here. This isn't a must-read chapter, though; either you want to change how Vista looks or you like it just the way it is. You can always come back here if you decide you want to apply a theme or change the desktop background. However, if you're ready to explore personalisation options, read on!

What you'll do

Enable Windows Aero (note Flip 3-D)

Change the background

Change the screen saver

Change the Windows Vista icons on the desktop

Create desktop shortcuts for programs, files, and folders

Remove icons and shortcuts from the desktop

Change the screen resolution

Choose a new mouse pointer

Use the Windows Classic theme

Adjust font size

Personalise the desktop

Did you know?

You don't have to use Aero. If you prefer the basic Vista experience, you can turn this feature off.

Aero is a new interface feature you can enable for a cleaner, sleeker interface and Vista experience. You can only use Aero if your computer hardware supports it, meaning that the hardware installed on your computer meets Aero's minimum requirements and that you are running something other than Windows Vista Basic (i.e. Home Premium, Ultimate or Business). Windows Aero builds on the basic Windows Vista interface and offers a high-performing desktop experience that includes (among other things) the translucent effect of Aero Glass. Aero Glass offers visual reflections and soft animations too, making the interface quite 'comfortable'.

You can see Aero in action here. Note that you can see 'underneath' the Start menu to view the Control Panel and Media Player below.

Look underneath the translucent glass to see the open windows below.

Another new Aero feature we'll discuss is Windows Flip 3-D, which offers a new way to switch among the windows on your desktop. As you saw in Chapter 3, there are new graphical options that give you another way to work and access open windows, including Flip 3-D and Flip (in case you don't have Aero). Here you can see Flip 3-D.

Instead of spelling out what is actually required to run
Windows Aero, let's just see if you can enable it. If you can,
your hardware supports it; if you can't, it doesn't. Once
enabled, you'll learn how to use Flip and Flip 3-D.

4

Personalise the desktop (cont.)

Note

Enabling Windows Aero

1 Right-click an empty area of the desktop.

2 Click Personalize.

Note: you may see items in this list that are not shown here or vice versa.

3 Click Window Color and Appearance.

4 If you're currently using Windows Vista Basic, you'll see the Appearance Settings dialogue box.

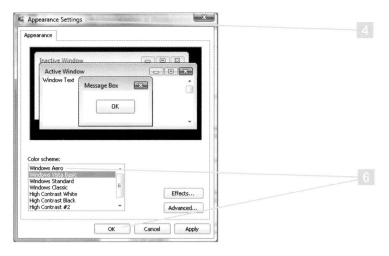

5 If you're currently using Windows Aero, you'll see the Aero options, where you can select a different colour scheme, enable transparency, make changes to the colour intensity or show the colour mixer.

6 To change from Windows Vista Basic to Windows Aero, click Windows Aero in the Color scheme options and then click OK.

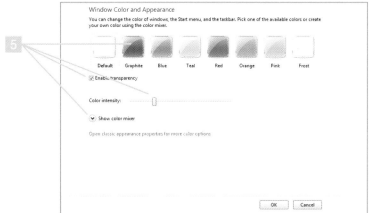

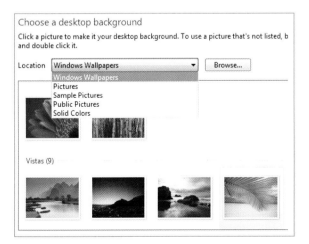

Window Color and Appearance

You can change the color of windows, the Start menu, and the taskbar. Pick one of the available colors or create your own color using the color mixer.

Default   Graphite   Blue   Teal   Red   Orange   Pink   Frost

☑ Enable transparency

Color intensity:

⌃ Hide color mixer

Hue:

Saturation:

Brightness:

Open classic appearance properties for more color options

OK   Cancel

A
B
C
D
E

Personalise the desktop (cont.)

7 To change the Aero defaults:

a. Select a new colour by clicking once on the desired colour.

b. Disable transparency (that's disabling the Aero Glass feature) by deselecting the box.

c. Change the colour intensity by moving the slider to the right or left (moving the slider to the right enhances colour by darkening it).

d. Show the Color Mixer to access sliders for changing hue, saturation or brightness.

e. Open classic appearance properties for more color options (this opens the window shown in Step 4).

Did you know?

You can't use Flip 3-D unless Aero is enabled.

Using Flip and Flip 3-D was detailed in Chapter 3, so if you missed it, return there for more information. Basically, both use a key combination Alt + Tab or Windows + Tab.

The background is the picture you see on the desktop when no windows are on top of it. Vista comes with lots of backgrounds to choose from and you can access them from the Personalization window that you accessed earlier by right-clicking the Desktop.

Choose a desktop background

Click a picture to make it your desktop background. To use a picture that's not listed, b and double click it.

Location   Windows Wallpapers   ▼   Browse...

Windows Wallpapers
Pictures
Sample Pictures
Public Pictures
Solid Colors

Vistas (9)

4

?

Personalise the desktop (cont.)

There are many kinds of backgrounds including:

- Windows Wallpapers – the images included with Windows Vista categorised into Black and White, Light Auras, Paintings, Textures, Vistas and Widescreen.

- Pictures – this folder is empty, but you can click the Browse button to locate a picture you've taken, acquired or otherwise saved to your computer.

- Sample Pictures – the pictures included with Windows Vista including Autumn Leaves, Desert Landscape, Forest and others.

- Public Pictures – this folder is empty by default, but as pictures are added to the Public Pictures folder, they also appear here.

- Solid Colors – solid backgrounds of a single colour are the only options here.

If you use Windows Vista Ultimate, and have downloaded the Windows Vista Ultimate Extras, you'll see many more options for backgrounds. As shown here, there are Windows DreamScene Content, Videos, Sample Videos and Public Videos. More options are sure to come.

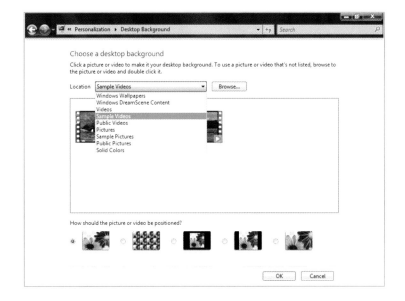

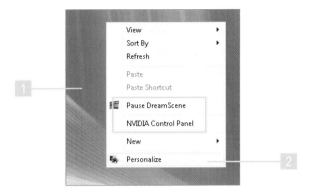

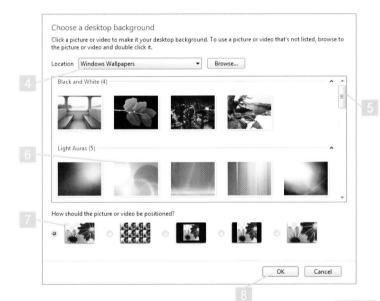

Changing the background

1. Right-click an empty area of the desktop.

2. Click Personalize.

3. Click Desktop Background.

4. For Location, select Windows Wallpapers. You can repeat these steps and the remaining ones using other options, if desired.

5. Use the scroll bars to locate the wallpaper to use as your desktop background.

6. Select a background to use.

7. Select a positioning option (the default is the most common).

8. Click OK.

Did you know?

If you don't find what you want in the Desktop Background options, you can click Browse in any option to locate and find a file stored on your computer. You'll learn more about browsing for data in Chapter 8.

Personalise the desktop (cont.)

A screen saver is a picture or animation that covers your screen and appears after your computer has been idle for a specific amount of time that you set. It used to be that screen savers 'saved' your computer screen from image burn-in, but that is no longer the case. Now, screen savers are used for either visual enhancement or as a security feature. As an extra measure of security, you can configure your screen saver to require a password on waking up, which happens when you move the mouse or hit a key on the keyboard. Requiring a password means that once the screen saver is running, no one can log onto your computer but you, by typing in your password when prompted.

Screen savers come in many flavours and Windows Vista comes with several; the Bubbles screensaver is one of my favourites. As with the enabling Aero or changing the desktop background, you access the settings by right-clicking an empty area of the desktop and selecting Personalize, and then Screen saver.

You can also get screen savers online and from third-party retailers. However, screen savers from these places are notorious for containing, at the very least, annoying pop-ups or purchasing ads and, at worst, malicious code and even viruses. Before you download and install a screen saver from a third party, make sure you've read the reviews and are positive it's from a worthy and reliable source. One screen saver I particularly like is called MarineAquarium2 from **www.serenescreen.com**. Get the full version or you'll be prompted to buy it each time it runs.

4

Personalise the desktop (cont.)

Changing the screen saver

1. Right-click an empty area of the desktop.

2. Click Personalize.

3. Click Screen Saver.

4. Click the arrow to see the available screen savers.

5. Select any screen saver from the list.

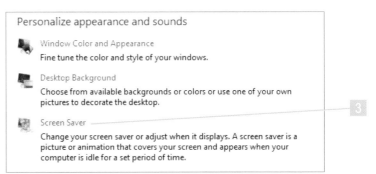

Personalize appearance and sounds

Window Color and Appearance
Fine tune the color and style of your windows.

Desktop Background
Choose from available backgrounds or colors or use one of your own pictures to decorate the desktop.

Screen Saver
Change your screen saver or adjust when it displays. A screen saver is a picture or animation that covers your screen and appears when your computer is idle for a set period of time.

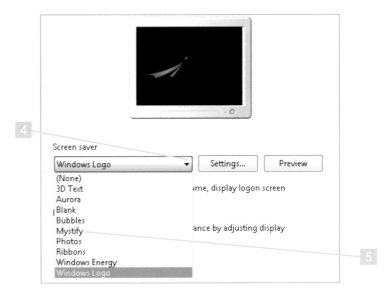

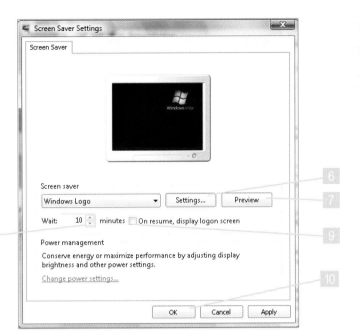

Personalise the desktop (cont.)

6 Click Settings. A few screen savers have settings, including 3-D text, but most do not. If settings are available, accept the defaults or make changes as desired.

7 Click Preview to see what the screen saver will look like. Press any key on the keyboard to disable the preview.

8 Use the arrows to change how long to wait before the screen saver is enabled.

9 If desired, click On resume, display logon screen to require a password to log back into the computer.

10 Click OK.

Tweak the desktop

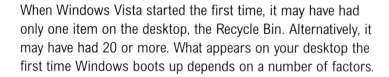

When Windows Vista started the first time, it may have had only one item on the desktop, the Recycle Bin. Alternatively, it may have had 20 or more. What appears on your desktop the first time Windows boots up depends on a number of factors.

If you installed Windows Vista yourself, and you chose not to upgrade from another version of Windows but instead to perform a 'clean' installation, you will probably see only one icon, the Recycle Bin. If you installed Windows Vista as an upgrade from another operating system version, like Windows XP, then you'll see the Vista-related icons you had on your computer prior to the upgrade. These may include Documents, Pictures or even shortcuts to your favourite programs. If you purchased a new PC with Windows Vista installed, you could have icons on your desktop for Internet Service Providers (ISPs) like AOL, Verizon, Time Warner or any number of others. You may also see icons for anti-virus software like McAfee or Semantic. There may also be any number of links to what's called OEM software, or software that comes preinstalled on your PC that you may or may not want, including image-editing applications, music players and word-processing or database applications. Whatever the case, it's likely the desktop doesn't match your needs exactly, and needs to be tweaked. Thus, adding and deleting desktop icons is a pretty common task, and will be discussed in depth.

Besides the icons that are on the desktop by default depending on the installation configuration, there are Windows Vista icons you can add or remove. You can choose to view or hide Computer, Recycle Bin, Control Panel, Network and your personal user folder.

You can also choose to add shortcuts to programs you use often. You can add shortcuts to the Quick Launch area, but you may not know that you can also add shortcuts directly to the desktop. Often, people add shortcuts to the desktop for folders they create, programs they use often, or network places, such as folders stored on other computers. You can even add a shortcut to a public folder, or a single file or picture!

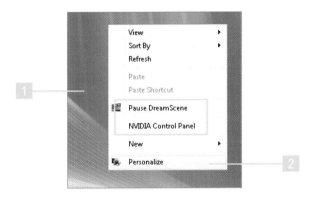

Tweak the
desktop (cont.)

Changing the Windows Vista icons on the desktop

1 Right-click an empty area of the desktop.

2 Click Personalize.

3 Click Change desktop icons.

4 Select the desktop icons you want to appear on your desktop.

5 Click OK.

Did you know?

If you have more than one user account on your computer, each user can configure his or her desktop as desired.

Tweak the desktop (cont.)

A shortcut always appears with an arrow beside it (or on it, actually). Shortcuts enable you to access folders, files, programs and other items stored on your PC without the hassle of drilling into the Start menu or using the Start Search dialogue box. In this figure there are three shortcuts and five Windows icons. Sometimes, a shortcut will even have the word 'Shortcut' in its name!

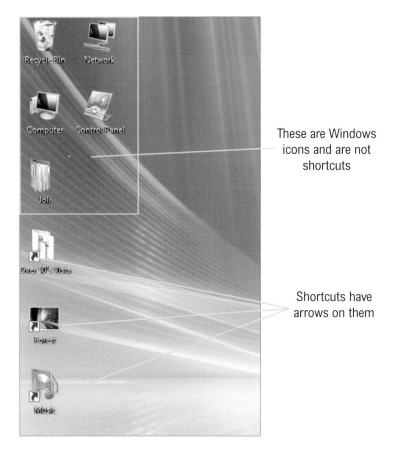

These are Windows icons and are not shortcuts

Shortcuts have arrows on them

There are several ways to create a shortcut. One is to right-click an empty area of the desktop, click New, and then Shortcut. Performing these steps will result in the opening of a dialogue box where you can 'browse' to the location of the file, folder or program for which you want to create the shortcut.

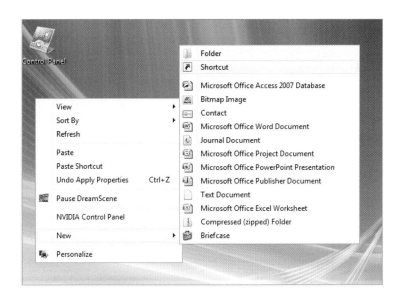

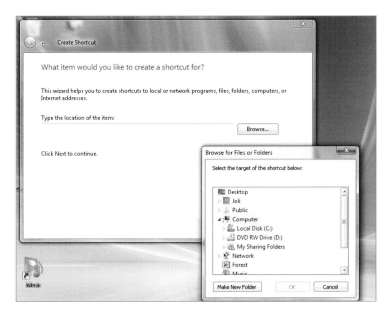

However, this method requires you to understand a bit more than you probably currently do about how files and folders are managed and stored in Windows Vista, as well as where program files are located and what file actually starts the program. Although we cover this in depth in Chapter 8, this is really the long way around the issue of creating a shortcut. There's a better way, and that involves finding the item to create a shortcut for in the Start menu, and dragging it to the desktop, or locating the item and right-clicking it.

Tweak the desktop (cont.)

Creating desktop shortcuts for programs, files and folders

1 Click Start.

2 If you see the item for which you want to create a shortcut, click it and drag it to the desktop. Here, we create a shortcut for the Games folder. Note that as you drag a shortcut an arrow appears.

3 To add a shortcut for a program, in the Start menu, click All Programs.

Important

This is the only time you should use the drag and drop method for creating a shortcut on the desktop. Most of the time, you'll right-click the item, as noted next.

Tweak the desktop (cont.)

4   In the All Programs list, locate the program for which to create a shortcut.

5   Right-click the program name.

6   Click Send To.

7   Click Desktop (create shortcut).

Important

For some reason known only to Microsoft, if you drag and drop a program from the All Programs menu, the actual program files will be moved. You don't want to do that. You want the program files to stay where they are. Additionally, when you drag and drop a file from inside a folder, such as a file, picture, video or song, those files are moved out of the folder and onto the desktop too. If you see Move to Desktop when you drag and drop as shown here, drag the mouse right back to where you started, and use the right-click method instead. You don't want to move the file; you only want to create a shortcut for it.

Tweak the desktop (cont.)

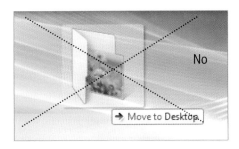

So, to repeat – when you are in the All Programs menu, and in all other instances (with the exception of the Start menu items), to create a shortcut, always right-click the file, folder or program (versus dragging and dropping).

When you're ready to remove items from the desktop, you'll use the right-click method again. The options you'll have when you right-click an item on the desktop will differ depending on what type of icon you select.

When you right-click the Windows Vista icon for Control Panel, you are given four choices: Open, Explore, Create Shortcut, and Delete. When you click Delete, you are prompted about how to add the icon again, if desired. Note that nothing is actually deleted when you do this; all of the Windows Vista files, icons and data are still on your computer and can be easily added to the desktop again at any time.

When you right-click the Games shortcut you created earlier, you'll see many more choices. One is to create a shortcut, interestingly. A shortcut of a shortcut! When you click Delete here, you are prompted to move the file to the Recycle Bin.

Since it's a shortcut, that's just fine. You're not going to delete the Games folder or the games in it; you are simply deleting the shortcut. No worries here.

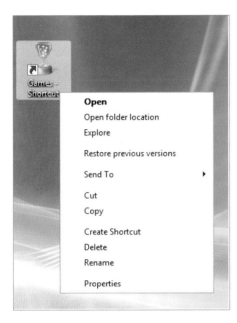

Right-clicking a shortcut to picture (or video, song or file) offers even more choices. Again, clicking Delete simply removes the shortcut. You don't actually delete the picture itself. (Now, if this was an actual picture and not a shortcut to one, you'd delete the picture, but as long as you're deleting a shortcut, you're good to go.)

4

Here's an actual picture file. Note that there is no shortcut arrow beside it. Right-clicking this picture and choosing Delete offers up this dire warning: Are you sure you want to move this file to the Recycle Bin? If you click Yes, the file is gone for good. Well, unless you 'restore' it from the Recycle Bin. You'll learn about the Recycle Bin in Chapter 7.

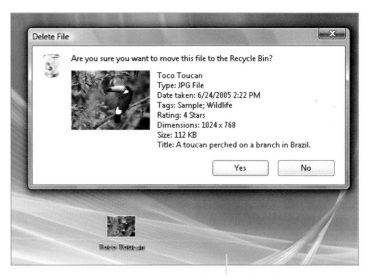

Actual picture file

Removing icons and shortcuts from the desktop

1 Right-click the icon to remove.

2 Click Delete.

3 Carefully read the information in the resulting dialogue box. Click Yes to delete or No to cancel.

For your information

If you are deleting a shortcut, you might still see a warning that you are moving a file to the Recycle Bin, when in reality you are not. Remember, you can always delete a shortcut, even if prompted that it's a file.

4

Configure desktop and monitor settings

There are even more ways to change how Windows Vista looks. One is to change the screen resolution. While the science behind resolution is rather complex, suffice it to say that the lower the resolution, the larger your stuff appears on the monitor; the higher the resolution, the smaller your stuff appears on the monitor. With a higher resolution, you can have more items on your screen. With a lower resolution, fewer.

Here's what my screen looks like at the lowest resolution offered, 800 by 600 pixels.

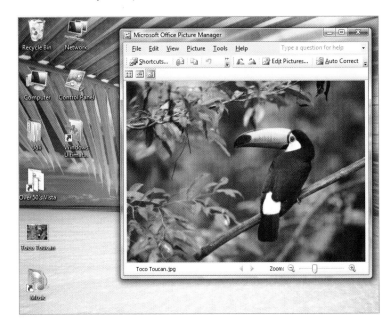

And here's what my screen looks like at its highest available resolution, 1280 by 1024 pixels.

As you can see, the higher resolution settings make it much harder to see what's on the screen, and that includes what you see in dialogue boxes, windows and menus. Note how small the desktop icons are. With the lower resolution setting everything is bigger, including the icons, and what you'll see in dialogue boxes, windows and menus. For your 50+ eyes, you may be most comfortable with one of the lower resolution settings.

If you're interested, technically, choosing 800 by 600 pixels means that the desktop is shown to you with 800 pixels across and 600 pixels down. A pixel is the smallest unit of data that can be displayed on a computer. So, when you increase the resolution, you increase the number of pixels on the screen. This makes items on the screen appear smaller and allows you to have more items on the screen.

Configure desktop and monitor settings (cont.)

Changing the screen resolution

1. Right-click an empty area of the desktop.

2. Click Personalize.

3. Click Display Settings.

4. Move the Resolution slider to the far left position (unless it's already there).

5. Click Apply.

6. If prompted to keep these settings, click Yes. Note how the appearance of the screen changes.

7. Move the Resolution slider one position to the right and click Apply.

8. If prompted to keep these settings, click Yes. Note how the appearance of the screen changes.

9. Repeat these steps as desired, and select the resolution that is best for you.

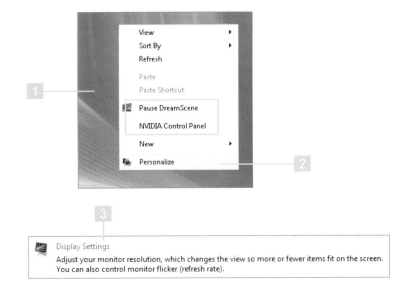

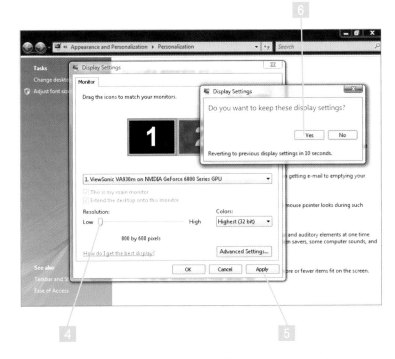

> **Important**
>
> There may be a delay in applying the new resolution as higher resolutions are selected.

You have the option of choosing a different mouse pointer. As you can probably guess, the Mouse Pointers settings are located in the all-familiar Personalization window. Clicking Mouse Pointers opens the Mouse Properties dialogue box, where you can select the pointers you prefer.

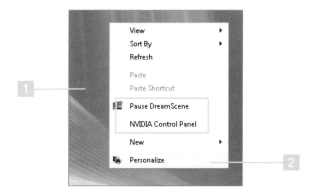

Configure desktop and monitor settings (cont.)

Choosing a new mouse pointer

1 Right-click an empty area of the desktop.

2 Click Personalize.

3 Click Mouse Pointers.

4 Click the down arrow to list additional schemes.

5 Select Windows Black (extra large) (system scheme).

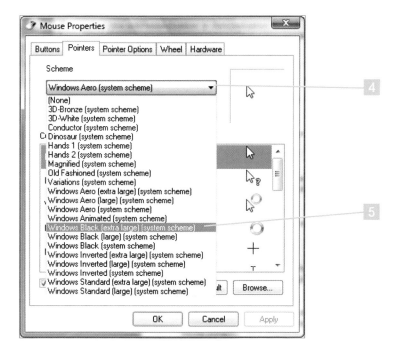

Configure desktop and monitor settings (cont.)

6 Click Apply to apply the new mouse pointer.

7 Select and apply additional mouse pointer schemes by repeating steps 4, 5 and 6. Try Magnified, Conductor and Variations.

8 Click OK.

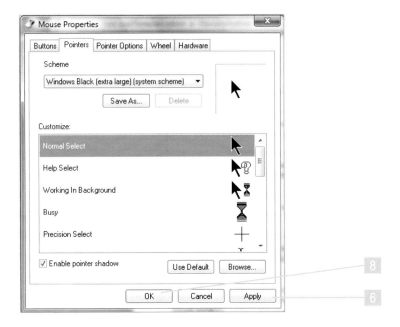

If you prefer the look and feel of an older operating system and the Windows Vista interface and all of its fancy graphics don't do anything for you, you can use the Windows Classic theme. This theme looks and feels like the good old days, back in 2000 or so, when the interface was blue and white, and menu bars were grey. You really can go back in time. This screen shot shows the Windows Classic theme in conjunction with the Classic Start menu.

Configure desktop and monitor settings (cont.)

Using the Windows Classic theme

1. Right-click an empty area of the desktop.

2. Click Personalize.

3. Click Theme.

4. Click the down arrow to show the available themes.

5. Click Windows Classic.

6. Click OK.

Configure desktop and monitor settings (cont.)

7 Right-click the Start button.

8 Select Properties.

9 Select Classic Start Menu.

10 Click OK.

Although Windows Vista includes many features to make the computer more easily accessible for those with disabilities, including applications like Magnifier, Narrator and On-Screen Keyboard (all of which will be covered in Chapter 5), there is a way to simply increase the system font size if need be. If you've changed the screen resolution to 800 by 600 and still have to wear reading glasses to make out what's on the monitor, including desktop icons, increasing the font size may just fit the bill.

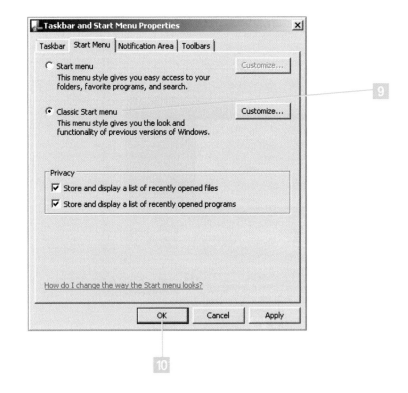

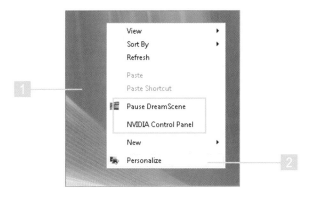

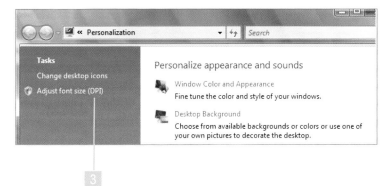

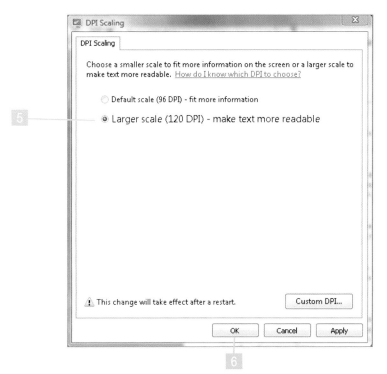

Configure desktop and monitor settings (cont.)

Adjusting font size

1. Right-click an empty area of the desktop.

2. Click Personalize.

3. Click Adjust font size (DPI).

4. You'll be prompted to enter administrator's credentials or click Continue if you're signed in as an administrator. Input the proper credentials.

5. Select Larger scale (120 DPI) to make the text more readable.

6. Click OK.

Configure desktop and monitor settings (cont.)

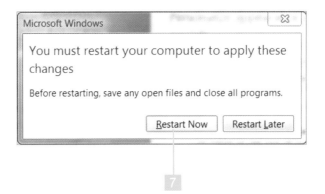

7 Click Restart Now when prompted.

8 After restarting, look how much larger everything appears when 120 DPI is selected.

Configuring accessibility options

Introduction

Windows Vista offers the Ease of Access Center to help you turn on and configure settings that will make using the computer easier if you have any disabilities. You can optimise the display for blindness or just make the items on the screen easier to see. You can use the computer without a mouse or keyboard by using an on-screen keyboard or the built-in speech-recognition program. You can make the keyboard easier to use by configuring sticky keys, toggle keys, filter keys and more. And you can use the built-in Narrator application to read what's on the screen out loud, so you don't have to squint to read it yourself. If you're having trouble accessing your computer, this chapter is for you.

?

Did you know?

After turning 50, two-thirds of us experience vision, hearing or dexterity problems that affect how well we use our computers. Getting older doesn't mean the end of using a computer though; PCs can be customised to meet the needs of those who are blind, deaf and quadriplegic, as well as those with the usual over-50 vision and hearing, as well as manual deftness, problems.

What you'll do

Configure the Narrator

Work with the Magnifier

Make the keyboard easier to use

Explore keyboard shortcuts

Explore additional ease of access options

Configure the Narrator

The Narrator is a basic screen reader. That means that the application will read text that appears on the screen to you, while you navigate using the keyboard and mouse. You can choose what text Narrator reads, change the Narrator's voice, and even configure it to describe events, such as error messages (or not). There isn't much to configuring Narrator; the art of Narrator lies in learning to use it properly. Here you see the Microsoft Narrator dialogue box, where you can have Narrator put voice to your keystrokes, announce system messages, announce when you scroll, and whether or not you want to start Narrator minimised (that means Narrator will appear on the taskbar and not on the screen when you boot up Windows).

Narrator is not a cure-all for those who want to have everything read to them. It's not designed to read content in every program you have; it's really just a *screen reader*. Additionally, Narrator may not pronounce all words correctly, cannot read text that appears below collapsed headings in Help topics, and has various other limitations. However, in the absence of a third-party accessibility program, Narrator will do in a pinch.

Although Narrator is part of the Ease of Access group of applications, you can open Narrator by searching for it from the Start menu. As soon as you click the Narrator link, it starts reading to you. In fact, it talks, and talks, and talks. It first announces that Microsoft Narrator is running and then continues by reading the entire dialogue box shown earlier. Once it stops reading that, it announces each thing you do with the mouse or keyboard. For instance, if you hover the mouse over the Internet Explorer icon, it says 'Launch Internet Explorer Browser. Finds and displays information and Web sites on the Internet. Tooltip.' It may also say things like 'Window opened' or 'Window closed'. Now all of this is great, except that you might not need every little thing read to you. That's what keyboard shortcuts are for. Clicking Ctrl will cause the reading to stop, at least for the current event.

Narrator reads the following items displayed on your screen:

- contents of the open window

- menus and menu options

- text you have typed

- tooltips

- events such as minimising and maximising windows.

5

Configure the Narrator (cont.)

Narrator doesn't read e-mail, although it might read the subject line. It doesn't read webpages, although it will read what appears on the Internet Explorer tab. When you hover over a folder on the desktop, it will read the tooltip that appears describing what it is. It won't read a document, but it will read the title of the document, as it appears on the screen.

To use Narrator effectively then, you need to understand the keyboard shortcuts associated with it. Table 5.1 shows these shortcuts.

Table 5.1 Narrator keyboard shortcuts	
Keyboard shortcut	**Result**
CTRL+SHIFT+ENTER	Get information about the current item
CTRL+SHIFT+SPACEBAR	Read the entire selected window
CTRL+ALT+SPACEBAR	Read the selected window layout
ALT+HOME	Get information about the current item
ALT+END	Get a summary of the current item
INSERT+SHIFT+G	Read a description of the dependent elements of the currently selected element
INSERT+CTRL+G	Read a description of the non-dependent elements adjacent to the currently selected element
INSERT+CTRL+HOME	Enter Virtual Menu navigation mode, which allows you to access Narrator commands without switching from the program that you're currently working with
CTRL	Stop Narrator from reading text
INSERT+Q	Move the text selection to the start of the previous text pattern
INSERT+W	Move the text selection to the start of the next text pattern
INSERT+E	Move the text selection to the start of the current text pattern
INSERT+R	Move the text selection to the end of the current text pattern

INSERT+F2	Select all of the text with the current text pattern
INSERT+F3	Read the current character
INSERT+F4	Read the current word
INSERT+F5	Read the current line
INSERT+F6	Read the current paragraph
INSERT+F7	Read the current page
INSERT+F8	Read the current document

If you learn these shortcuts you'll be much happier with
Narrator than you would be if you don't.

Important

According to Microsoft, the Narrator will read
documents, PDFs, webpages and more. But I can't get it
to work that way. Sure, it will read anything regarding
what I'm clicking on, what I'm doing to the windows,
and if I'm scrolling or not, but getting it to read
documents is another story. Lots of people have
difficulties with it, too, not just you and me. If you find
you're having problems making Narrator work, consider
Dspeech. It's free and you can download it at:
http://www.tucows.com/preview/500654.

Did you know?

Microsoft offers help for those with disabilities at
www.microsoft.com/enable

5

Configure the
Narrator (cont.)

Using the Narrator

1 Click Start.

2 In the Start Search dialogue box, type Narrator.

3 Select or deselect options to configure Narrator to your needs. The default, shown here, is a good place to start.

4 Click the Start button. If you can't hear the Narrator say 'Start. Tooltip', turn up or plug in your speakers.

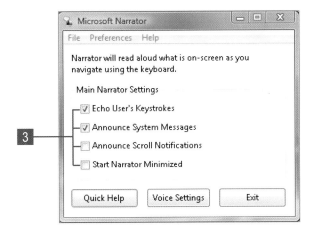

5, 6

8

Configure the Narrator (cont.)

5 Click inside the Start Search dialogue box while Narrator reads what's on the Start menu.

6 Type Internet Explorer.

7 Click the Ctrl key to stop Narrator from continuing to read.

8 Click Exit to turn Narrator off and exit the program.

5

Work with the Magnifier

The Magnifier is another tool in the Ease of Access suite of applications. As with Narrator, you can access Magnifier from the Start Search dialogue box, by typing Magnifier. However, you can open Magnifier from the Ease of Access Center too. This is located in Control Panel. For the sake of exploring these features and controls, here we've opened our accessibility program from the Ease of Access Center. Note that Narrator is here too.

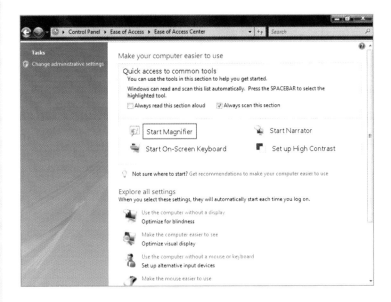

There isn't anything to configure in Magnifier. As with Narrator, the art of Magnifier lies in your ability to use it. When you click Start Magnifier, you'll see a large rectangular box at the top of the page. What you see in this box is a magnification of the area of the screen where your mouse is currently positioned. As you move the mouse around, different parts of the screen are magnified.

You can move this rectangular box around on the screen using the four-headed arrow that appears when you position the mouse inside the rectangle.

This application works much better than Narrator. You are in complete control of the mouse and thus what is magnified in the magnification window. Although you can't enlarge the window, you can at least move it around. Here you can see an open window and Magnifier in action.

5

Work with the Magnifier (cont.)

Notice in this figure how the Network window is positioned, above the Magnifier. If you maximise the open window, the Magnifier sits 'underneath it', and you can't see the Magnifier! A small glitch in the system, but at least there's a way around it. Just position the open window above or below the Magnifier window, and you'll be good to go.

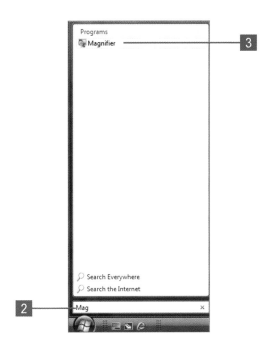

Programs
Magnifier ——— **3**

Search Everywhere
Search the Internet

2 —— Mag ×

6

Magnifier

Work with the Magnifier (cont.)

Using the Magnifier

1 Click Start.

2 In the Start Search dialogue box, type Mag. Note that you do not have to type the entire name.

3 Click Magnifier.

4 Position the mouse inside the Magnifier window. When you see a four-headed arrow, drag the window to the bottom of the screen.

5 Move the mouse around the desktop to explore Magnifier.

6 To close Magnifier, click the x in the Magnifier window.

5

Make the keyboard easier to use

There are several ways to make the keyboard easier to use, including options like Mouse Keys, Sticky Keys, Toggle Keys and Filter Keys. Each of these offer different accessibility options.

- ■ Mouse Keys let you forgo using the mouse; instead, you can use the arrow keys on your keyboard or the numeric keypad to move the mouse pointer on the desktop or inside programs or documents.

- ■ Sticky Keys allow you to configure the keyboard so that you never have to press three keys at once (such as when you must press the CTRL, ALT and DELETE keys together to restart Windows). With Sticky Keys, you can use one key to perform these tasks. You configure the key to use for three-key tasks.

- ■ Toggle can be configured to sound an alert when you press the CAPS LOCK, NUM LOCK or SCROLL LOCK keys. These alerts can help prevent the aggravation of unintentionally pressing a key and not realising it.

- ■ Filter Keys let you configure Windows to ignore keystrokes that occur in rapid succession, such as when you accidentally leave your finger on a key for too long.

- ■ Underline keyboard shortcuts and access keys. This option makes dialogue boxes easier to work with by highlighting the access keys used to control them.

You enable these features in the Ease of Access Center, under Make the keyboard easier to use.

5

Make the keyboard easier to use (cont.)

Making the keyboard easier to use

1 Click Start.

2 In the Start Search dialogue box, type Ease of Access.

3 Select Ease of Access Center from the results.

4 In the Ease of Access Center, use the scroll bar to locate Make the keyboard easier to use. Click it.

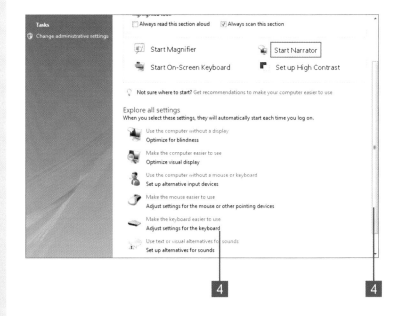

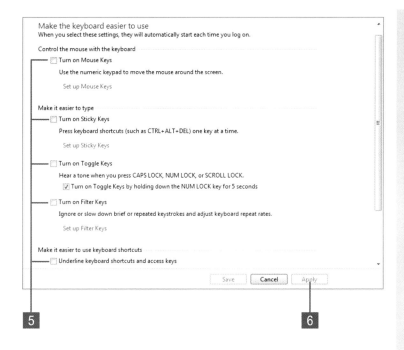

5 Place a tick in the accessibility options to enable.

6 Click Apply.

7 Each item you select can be configured. For now, the defaults are fine. However, note that you can return to the Ease of Access Center to refine how these features perform. There's more on this later in the chapter.

There are keyboard shortcuts that go along with these options. They include:

■ Left ALT + Left SHIFT + NUM LOCK – turn mouse keys on or off

■ NUM LOCK for five seconds – turn toggle keys on or off

■ Right SHIFT for eight seconds – turn filter keys on and off

■ SHIFT five times – turn Sticky Keys on or off.

Explore keyboard shortcuts

It doesn't matter if you're over 50, disabled, have arthritis in your hands or are just a little lazy, learning and using keyboard shortcuts can be one of the best ways to spend your time. Keyboard shortcuts let you do things more quickly than you could with multiple keystrokes. For instance, to open Help and Support you could click Start, and then Help and Support, or you can do it with one movement by clicking the F1 key on the keyboard. Instead of highlighting text in a document and searching for the menu or button that makes that text bold, just click Ctrl + B. And there's more where this came from. In the following sections I'll list my favourite keyboard shortcuts, but if you want more, just search the Internet for 'Windows keyboard shortcuts'.

General keyboard shortcuts

ALT+ESC – cycle through items in the order in which they were opened.

ALT+F4 – close the active item, or exit the active program.

ALT+PRINT SCREEN – copy an image of the selected window to the clipboard.

ALT+TAB – switch between open items.

CTRL+A – select all items in a document or window.

CTRL+ALT+DEL – display options for: Lock This Computer, Switch User, LogOff, Change a Password and Start Task Manager.

CTRL+ALT+TAB – use the arrow keys to switch between open items.

CTRL+C – copy the selected item.

CTRL+ESC – open the Start menu (the Windows Logo key works too).

CTRL+V – paste the selected item.

CTRL+X – cut the selected item.

CTRL+Y – redo an action.

CTRL+Z – undo an action.

DELETE – delete the selected item and move it to the Recycle Bin.

ESC – cancel the current task.

F1 – display Help.

F5 – refresh the active window.

PRINT SCREEN – copy an image of the entire screen to the clipboard.

SHIFT+F10 – display the shortcut menu for the selected item.

Dialogue box shortcuts

ALT+underlined letter – perform the command (or select the option) that goes with that letter.

Arrow keys – select a button if the active option is a group of option buttons.

BACKSPACE – open a folder one level up if a folder is selected in the Save As or Open dialogue box.

CTRL+SHIFT+TAB – move back through tabs.

CTRL+TAB – move forward through tabs.

ENTER – replaces clicking the mouse for many selected commands.

SHIFT+TAB – move back through options.

SPACEBAR – select or clear the check box if the active option is a check box.

TAB – move forward through options.

Explore keyboard shortcuts (cont.)

5

Explore keyboard shortcuts (cont.)

Exploring keyboard shortcuts

1 Click the Windows key on the keyboard. If you don't see a Windows key, click the Start key. The Start menu opens.

2 Click the Tab key on the keyboard. Notice what is selected in the Start menu.

3 Use the arrow keys on the keyboard to move through the Start menu items.

4 Press the Enter key to open the selected item.

There are far too many accessibility options in Windows Vista to cover each and every one. But now that you're familiar with some of them, configuring and using the features we haven't covered will be a little more intuitive.

One of the options in the Ease of Access Center is Make the mouse easier to use. If you click that, you see the settings shown here. You can see that it is easy to select a different colour or size for your mouse. Note that you can also turn on Mouse Keys and set up mouse keys.

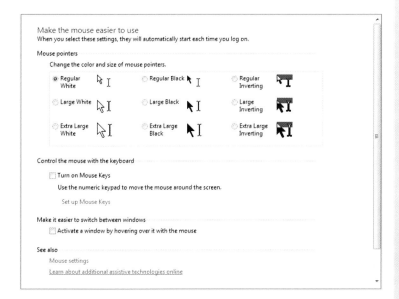

Another option is to Use text or visual alternatives for sounds. Here, you can turn on visual notifications of sounds that play on your computer as well as text captions for spoken dialogue.

Explore additional ease of access options

5

Explore additional ease of access options (cont.)

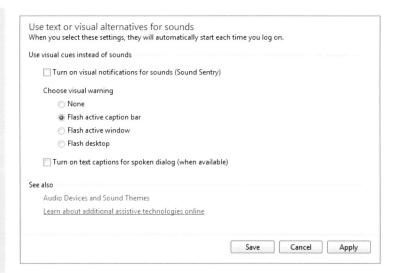

You can also select Use the computer without a display. Here, you can turn on Narrator and Audio Description. The latter lets you hear descriptions of what's happening in the videos you watch, if it's available.

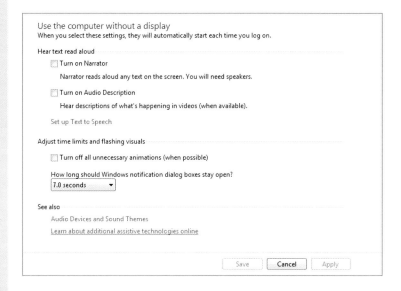

Although there are many other options, perhaps the most helpful is the option Get recommendations to make your computer easier to use. Clicking this option opens a wizard that asks questions about your current abilities (and disabilities), and helps you decide what accessibility options are best for you.

Statements you can select include but are not limited to the following:

- I am blind.
- I have another type of vision impairment (even if glasses correct it).
- A physical condition affects the use of my arms, wrists, hands or fingers.
- Pens and pencils are difficult to use.
- Conversations are difficult to hear (even with a hearing aid).
- I am deaf.
- I have a speech impairment.
- It is often difficult for me to concentrate.
- It is often difficult for me to remember things.
- I have a learning disability, such as dyslexia.

After filling out the questionnaire, you'll receive information regarding the settings recommended for you.

5

Using Vista applications: Part 1

Introduction

Windows comes with a lot of applications, many of which you may already be familiar with, like WordPad and Calculator, and some of which you may not, like the Snipping Tool and the Sound Recorder. These applications, like so many others, can help you work faster and be more productive. Other applications including Solitaire and FreeCell, found in the Games folder, can entertain you when you're not busy. And finally, Paint, Windows Calendar and Windows DVD Maker can help in your daily life, by enabling you to create (perhaps a garage sale or lost dog sign) with Paint, and keep up with appointments and dates with Windows Calendar.

Note: in this chapter you'll learn just enough about each program to use it effectively, but we suggest you spend extra time experimenting with the applications you think you'll use often, perhaps accessing the Help files and viewing Help videos. For more information on Help, refer to Chapter 3.

What you'll do

Use WordPad

Create an appointment in Windows Calendar

Create a task in Windows Calendar

Publish a calendar

Subscribe to a calendar

Use the calculator

Play games

Notepad and Wordpad

If your word-processing tasks only involve creating a quick memo, note or letter and printing it out, or putting together a weekly newsletter that you send via e-mail, there's no reason to purchase a large office suite like Microsoft Office (and learn how to use it) when Notepad and WordPad will do just fine. You can't create and insert tables, endnotes, footnotes, WordArt, text boxes and the like with either, but you may not need to. WordPad and Notepad are quite functional and easy to use, and will suit the needs of many of you quite well. Notepad is a simple program with only a few features; WordPad is a kind of upgrade to it, and probably better for what you'll be doing, as it contains more formatting options and features than Notepad does.

Note: we won't talk any more about Notepad here. WordPad has a lot more features and both are equally simple to use. However, Notepad is worth noting, as it is an application included with Windows Vista.

WordPad has six menus, including File, Edit, View, Insert, Format and Help. After you become familiar with the application and its menus, what you learn will carry over to almost any other program you'll use. Just about every program we've seen has a File menu, Edit menu, Insert menu and Help menu, and many contain the same menu options.

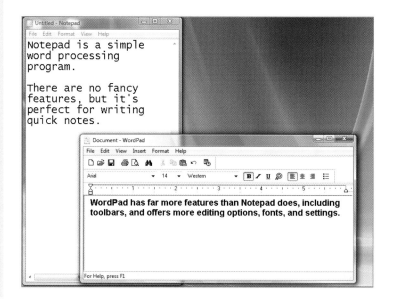

WordPad has far more features than Notepad does, including toolbars, and offers more editing options, fonts, and settings.

Some menu options are always available, like File>New and File>Open. (The > symbol means that you should click the File menu and then select the command that follows, in this case New or Open.) The New command creates a new (blank) document, while Open lets you open a document you created earlier. Of course, there's Save for saving your document and Print for printing it.

Some menu options like Edit>Cut and Edit>Copy are only available in specific instances. For instance, Edit>Copy and Edit>Cut will be available only if you've highlighted text you want to edit (like cutting the text or copying it). When menu options aren't available, they appear to be 'greyed' out.

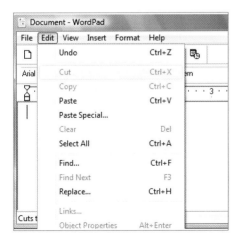

Notepad and Wordpad (cont.)

The View menu options are always available; this is because this is where you decide which toolbars you want to view and which you do not. By default, all are selected. As with other menu options, you select a toolbar name to remove or add a tick. If a tick is beside an option, that toolbar is showing.

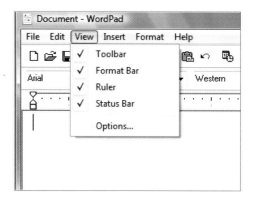

In WordPad you can insert the date and time, or an object. Date and time are self-explanatory, but an object is something else entirely. You can insert all kinds of 'objects', from Excel worksheets, to PowerPoint slides, to Microsoft Office Word documents, to other WordPad documents.

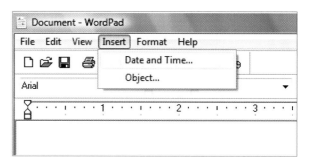

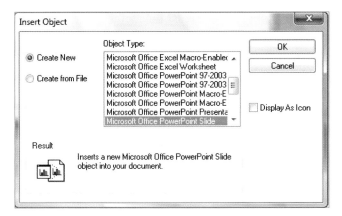

The Format menu, like the Format menu in other programs, includes options for setting the Font, Bullet Style, Paragraph style and Tabs. However, like many applications, these tools can be found on the Formatting toolbar too.

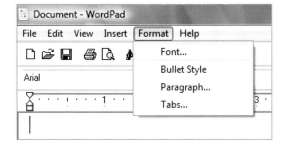

And finally, there's Help. There are only two choices, View Help and About WordPad. When you need help just click Help, and select View Help.

In order to get the most from WordPad, you need to understand not only the menu options but also what's on the toolbars. Here's a quick rundown:

■ The Menu bar is the bar that runs across the top of WordPad with the menus File, Edit, View, Insert, Format and Help.

■ The Standard toolbar is the bar underneath the Menu bar that contains icons, or pictures, of common commands. In order they are New, Open, Save, Print, Print Preview, Find, Cut, Copy, Paste, Undo and Date/Time. Hover your mouse over each icon to see its name.

Notepad and Wordpad (cont.)

■ The Formatting toolbar is just below the Standard toolbar and offers drop-down lists for the font, font size and language, as well as options to configure the font (or any selected text) as bold, italic or underlined. There's a Color option for assigning a colour to a font too, as well as alignment tools for Align Left, Center, Align Right and finally Bullets.

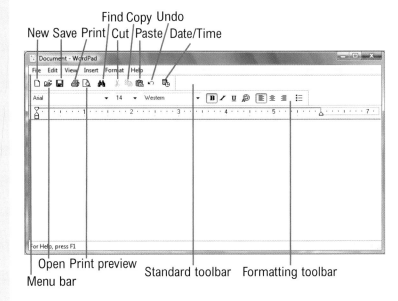

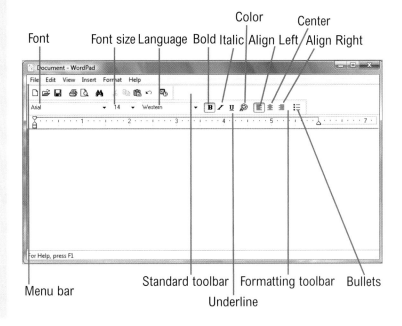

- The Ruler is – well – a ruler. It can be configured in the View>Options dialogue box to show measurements in inches, centimetres, points or picas.

- The Status bar offers information about what you are doing at the moment. If you aren't doing anything, it offers the helpful words 'For Help, press F1', otherwise it offers information regarding the tool you've selected from a toolbar, or information about the task you're performing.

Ruler

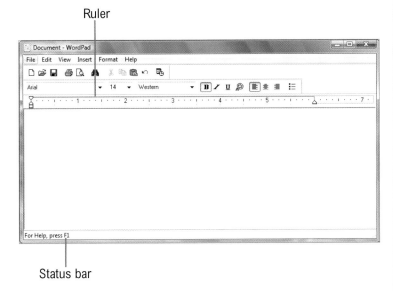

Status bar

Did you know?

When you see something like View>Options in this book it means you should first click the View menu and then the Options choice in the drop-down list to see the desired dialogue box.

Notepad and Wordpad (cont.)

Using Wordpad

1 Click Start.

2 Click WordPad.

3 Select WordPad from the program results. A new, blank document will open.

4 Type the following: 'I am using WordPad.'

5 Click the Edit menu, and choose Select All.

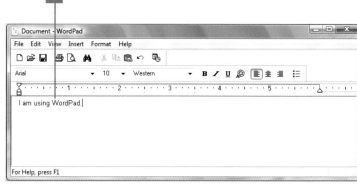

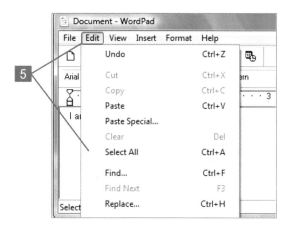

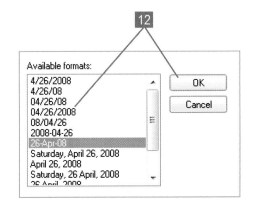

6 Click the B on the Formatting toolbar. This will embolden the selected text.

7 Click the slanted I on the Formatting toolbar. This will italicise the bold text.

8 Click Bullets on the Formatting toolbar. This will make the selected text a bullet.

9 Deselect the text by clicking at the end of the sentence. The cursor should be blinking after the word WordPad.

10 Click Enter to create a new bullet.

11 Click Insert, and then Date and Time (i.e. Insert>Date and Time).

12 Select any format from the list and click OK.

Notepad and Wordpad (cont.)

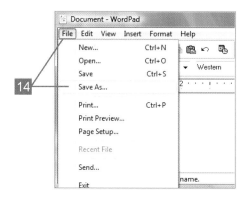

13 Continue working with WordPad, selecting text and experimenting with menu options. Make sure to try out Undo, and Cut, Copy and Paste. For more information, click Help>View Help.

14 To close the program and save your work, click File, and click Save As.

15 Note that the file will be saved in your Documents folder in Rich Text Format (RTF). Type a name for the file and click Save.

16 Click the x in the top right corner to close WordPad.

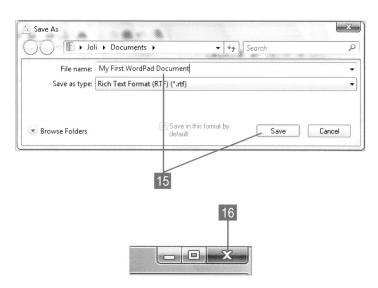

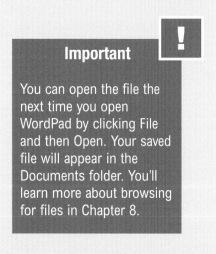

Important

You can open the file the next time you open WordPad by clicking File and then Open. Your saved file will appear in the Documents folder. You'll learn more about browsing for files in Chapter 8.

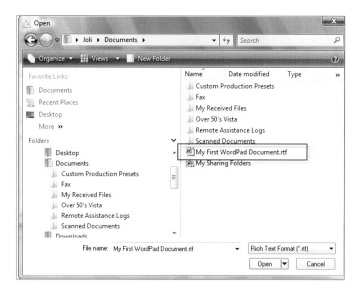

Windows Calendar is a full-featured calendar application that lets you manage your own affairs as well as the affairs of others, using a familiar calendar interface. You can easily create appointments and tasks, and import or export calendar data. You can view the calendar by the current day, work week, week or month, and you can share your calendar with others (and them with you). Sharing is a neat feature in which Windows Calendar lets you subscribe to web calendars from participating organisations' websites and allows you to share your calendar with others in the same manner. If you have a website you keep for family or friends (or even a group you belong to), you can 'publish' your calendar to that website. Take a look at Windows Calendar.

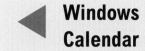

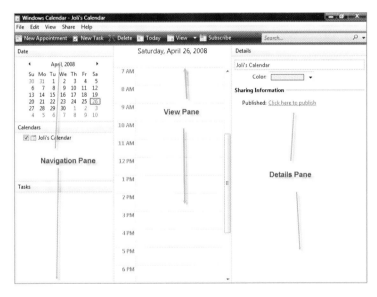

Here you can see the Navigation pane, the View pane and the Details pane. You can also see the menu bar, with some familiar options: File, Edit and View. As noted in the section on WordPad, you'll see these menu titles often, and you'll see many of the same options under them too! Look at Windows Calendar's File menu.

Windows
Calendar (cont.)

In the File menu, although New and Open aren't around as they were in WordPad, there's New Appointment, New Task, New Calendar and New Group. You can use these options to create a new item in the calendar or a new group of people. You can also select Print to make a hard copy of your calendar, or configure options for Windows Calendar including playing a sound to remind you of an upcoming appointment or displaying time-zone information.

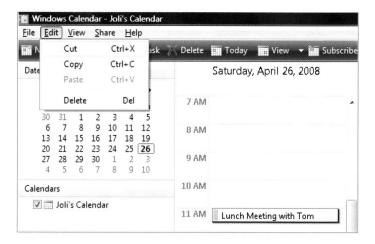

The Edit menu contains familiar options too, including Cut, Copy and Paste, and after data have been entered, Delete. As with other programs' Edit menus, options are greyed out unless something is selected.

The View menu lets you choose how to view your calendar. You can view the calendar in Day mode, meaning one day is shown in the Calendar interface. That's the default. There are others though, including Work Week (Monday through Friday), Week (Sunday through Saturday) and Month. Here we've selected Month from the View menu and removed the Details pane using View>Details.

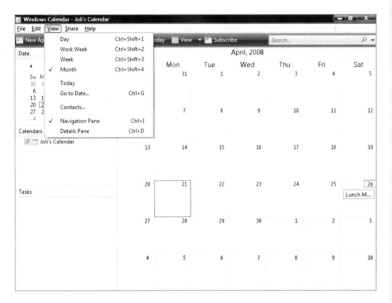

Did you know?

Once you publish a calendar, Stop Publishing will no longer be greyed out in the Share menu.

The Share menu is where you share a calendar or subscribe to someone else's published calendar. Many sports teams, TV and radio shows, universities, schools and companies offer a calendar you can subscribe to. You can share your calendar by publishing it to a webpage or sending it via e-mail. Note that you can sync calendars too, if you have more than one calendar you work with.

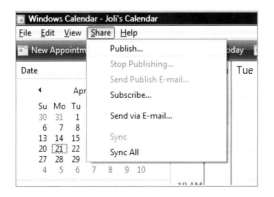

Windows Calendar (cont.)

As you might expect, the Help menu offers Windows Calendar Help, which offers myriad Help files in Vista's Help and Support. (Of course you can always press the F1 key on your keyboard.)

Table 6.1 defines the terms you need to know.

Table 6.1 Definitions	
Windows Calendar item	**Definition**
Calendar	A collection of appointments that makes up your schedule. You can have multiple calendars and combine them if desired.
Group	A collection of related calendars.
Appointment	A meeting or other event. Appointments can have start and end times or they can be all-day events. Appointments can also be configured to span multiple days, weeks or months.
Task	A to-do item. Generally this is a task that needs to be completed by a specific day and time.
Publish	A way to distribute a calendar electronically so that it is shared with others. The calendar can be shared via an online source like a webpage, or on the user's own network.
Subscribe	A method used to access a calendar created by someone else. The calendar is displayed in Windows Calendar and is updated automatically as changes are made to the original. You can choose how often to update the calendar.

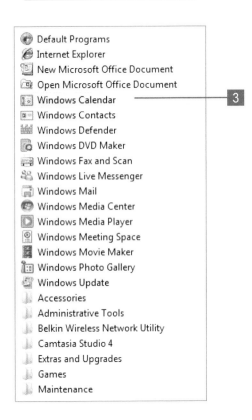

Creating an appointment in Windows Calendar

1 Click Start.

2 Click All Programs. (You can hover the mouse over All Programs and wait a second as well. Either way, the All Programs menu will appear.)

3 Click Windows Calendar.

!

Important

Remember that the > sign means to click the menu title, in this case File, and then click the menu option, in this case New Appointment.

Windows Calendar (cont.)

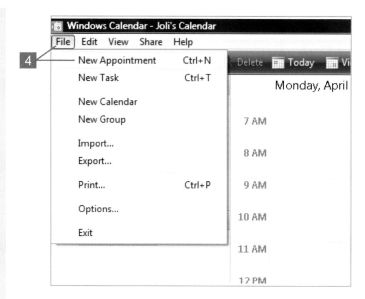

4 Think of something you need to do, such as an appointment or a football game, and then click File>New Appointment. Note that there is also a New Appointment button on the toolbar; you can click this button if you prefer.

5 Type a name for the new appointment. What you type will also appear in the Details pane.

6 In the Details pane, under Appointment Information, for the Start time and date, click the calendar icon.

7 Click the right-arrow or left-arrow in the calendar to locate the date for which to create the appointment.

8 Repeat steps 6 and 7 for the End date, if necessary. By default, the appointment will end the same day it was created for. If desired, click All-day appointment.

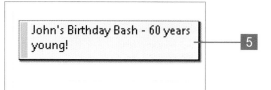

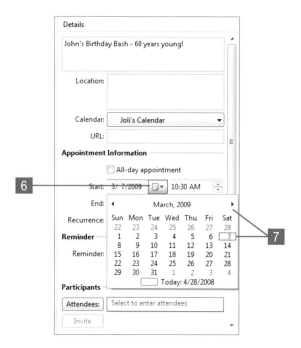

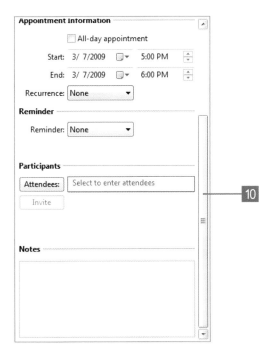

Saturday, March 07, 2009

8 AM	
9 AM	
10 AM	
11 AM	
12 PM	
1 PM	
2 PM	
3 PM	
4 PM	
5 PM	John's Birthday Bash - 60 years young!
6 PM	
7 PM	

9 Drag and drop

9 Although you could select a start and end time using the up and down arrows next to the Start and End dates, it is much easier to drag and drop the appointment in the View pane – that's the middle pane – to the desired time.

10 If necessary, use the slider bar in the Details pane to see the additional options: Recurrence, Reminder, Attendees and Notes.

Appointment Information

☐ All-day appointment

Start: 3/ 7/2009 ▢▾ 5:00 PM ⬍

End: 3/ 7/2009 ▢▾ 6:00 PM ⬍

Recurrence: None ▾

Reminder

Reminder: None ▾

Participants

Attendees: Select to enter attendees

Invite

10

Notes

Windows
Calendar (cont.)

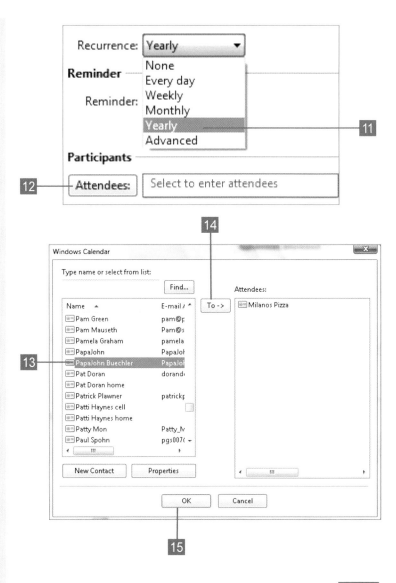

11 To create a recurring appointment, click None for Recurrence, and select how often the appointment will occur. Choices are Every day, Weekly, Monthly, Yearly or Advanced. (Advanced lets you set the number of times to recur and create a stop date.)

12 Click Attendees, if desired, to add names of people who will also be attending the appointment.

13 Select an attendee from the list.

14 Click To ->.

15 After adding all attendees, click OK.

16 If desired, click inside the Notes area and type a note to yourself regarding the event.

Did you know?

You can also double-click a name in the list instead of selecting name and clicking To ->.

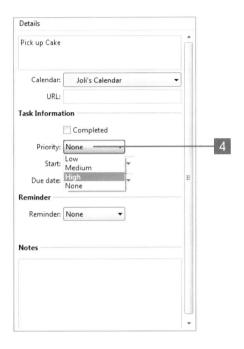

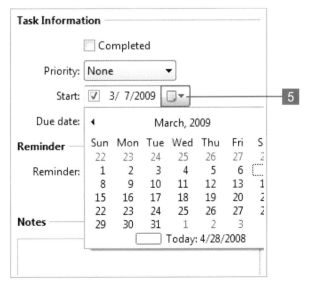

Creating a task in Windows Calendar

1 With Windows Calendar open, on the keyboard, click Ctrl + T. This creates a new task, just as File>New Task would.

2 Type a name for the task.

3 In the Details pane, under Task Information, for the Start date, click the calendar icon.

4 Under Task Information, in the Details pane, click None next to Priority. Select a priority.

5 Click the arrow next to the Start date to open the calendar.

Windows Calendar (cont.)

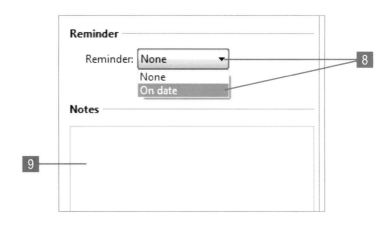

6　Click the right-arrow or left-arrow in the calendar to locate the date for which to create the appointment.

7　Repeat Steps 5 and 6 to create a due date, if desired.

8　To add a reminder, click None next to Reminder and select On date.

9　Add notes if desired.

Did you know?

You can edit any appointment or task by double-clicking it.

Before you can publish a calendar, you need to know where to publish it. If you are part of a company, that may be a company server. If that's the case, contact your network administrator and ask for the server name. You'll type this information when prompted. If you want to publish your calendar to the Web, you'll need to know the server name for your website. That's a little trickier. Your ISP or webhost may require a user name and password, and you must be able to get someone on the line or via e-mail to obtain the information. A web address starts with http:// and is followed by the name of the website. To obtain this information, call your ISP and ask them for help. Tell them you want to publish a calendar to a URL and ask if they can offer you one. After you click the Publish button, Windows Calendar will ask for the information you've acquired. You can also publish information to a shared computer on your network, even if it's a workgroup.

Did you know?

There are places on the Web that allow you to publish your calendars if you don't have a place of your own. Once such place is **http://www.calendardata.com**. Create an account to get started. CalendarData.com is 100 per cent free.

Publishing a calendar

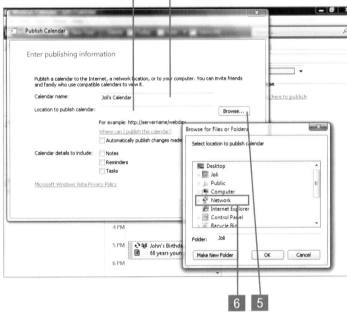

1 Click Share.

2 Click Publish.

3 Type a calendar name.

4 If you know the URL for your ISP, type it in the Location to publish calendar window. Skip to Step 11.

5 If not, click Browse to publish to a computer on your personal network.

6 Click Network.

7 Click the down-arrow to expand the computer to publish to.

8 Click the down-arrow to expand the folder to publish to.

9 Select the folder to publish to.

10 Click OK.

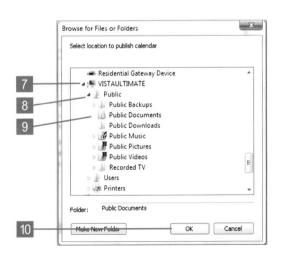

Windows
Calendar (cont.)

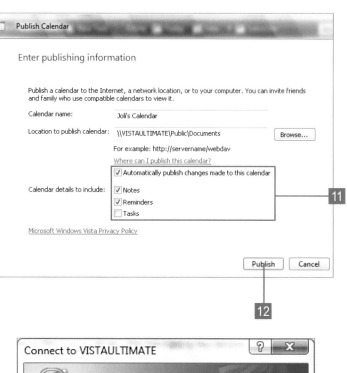

11 Select the desired options, including Automatically publish changes made to this calendar, and Calendar details to include: Notes, Reminders, Tasks.

12 Click Publish.

13 If prompted for credentials, type them in and click OK.

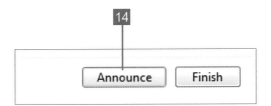

Subscribing to a calendar that belongs to someone else requires you to have the web address of the calendar. This may come to you via an e-mail, from a website's information or calendar page, or from a number of other sources. You must have the address of the calendar to subscribe to it.

If you'd like to see some of the calendars you can subscribe to for free, visit www.calendardata.com. There you can peruse a section called Most Popular Calendars, or search for a specific calendar. You'll now learn here how to subscribe to CalendarData's UK Holidays calendar.

14 When your calendar has been successfully published, click Announce. This will open an e-mail message that includes information for others to access the calendar. If you do not want to send an e-mail, click Finish.

Windows Calendar (cont.)

Subscribing to a calendar

1. In Windows Calendar, click the Subscribe button.

2. In the Calendar to subscribe to window, type webcal://www.calendardata.com/ics/19/UK Holidays. Make sure to type it exactly as shown here.

3. Click Next.

4. Wait while the subscription is created.

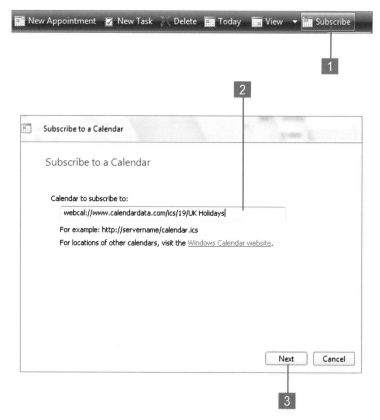

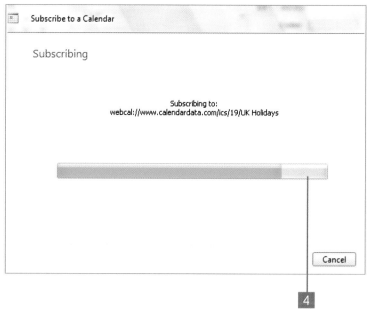

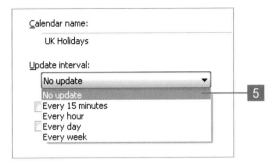

5 Configure settings as desired. Because this is a calendar of holidays, I will choose No update.

6 As desired, select Include reminders and/or include tasks.

7 Click Finish.

8 In Windows Calendar, in the Navigation pane, select the UK Holidays calendar.

9 In the Date window, use the arrows to locate January 1.

10 Note that New Years Day (Bank Holiday) appears on that calendar day.

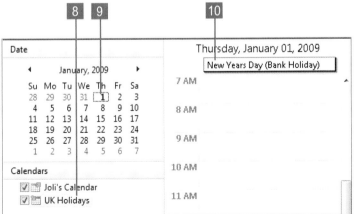

Calculator

Let's take a little breather from the complexity of Windows Calendar and talk about the Calculator. I'm guessing you've used a calculator before, and using Vista's calculator is not different, except that you input numbers with a mouse click, keyboard or number pad. There are two calculator options: Standard and Scientific. The Standard calculator is shown here and is a bare-bones version. The Scientific calculator, also shown, offers many more features.

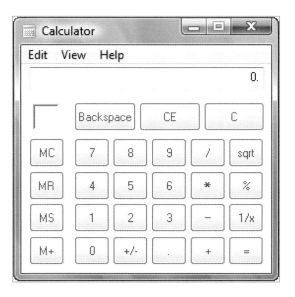

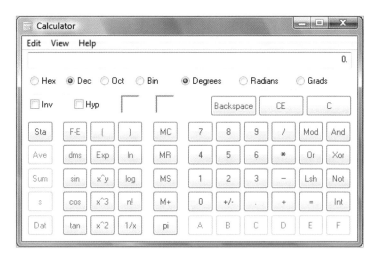

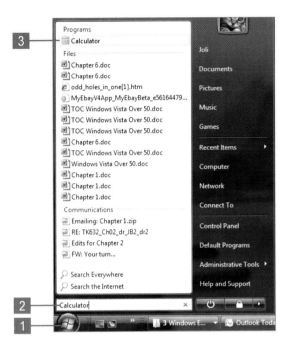

Using the Calculator

1 Click Start.

2 In the Start Search dialogue box, type Calculator.

3 In the Programs results, click Calculator.

4 Input numbers using the keypad, or input numbers by clicking the on-screen calculator with the mouse.

5 Input operations using the keypad, or input numbers by clicking the on-screen calculator with the mouse.

6 Click View to change from Standard to Scientific or vice versa.

7 Close Calculator by clicking the x in the top right corner.

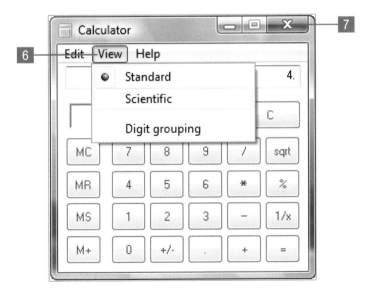

Games

Windows Vista comes with lots of games, but we're not here to teach you how to play them; that'll be up to you. What we want to impart here is how to access the games, learn to play a game, start a game, and save a game when duty calls, so that you can come back to it later.

You access the available games from the Games folder on the Start menu. Clicking the Games icon opens the Games window. While there are lots of games to choose from, the games you see are dependent on what edition of Windows Vista you have. Ultimate has the most games, Home Premium is second in line, and Home Basic is last.

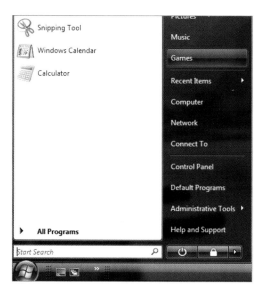

To see how well any game will perform on your computer, click the game's icon one time. Since the games included with Windows Vista don't require much computing power, chances are the games will play just fine.

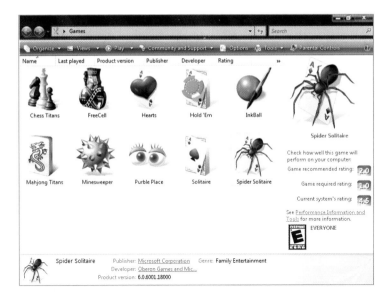

Read the results on the right side of the Games interface. Here, the game's recommended rating is 2.0, and a required rating is 1.0. The system's rating is 4.5, which is certainly above even the recommended rating. This game will play just fine.

To start a game, double-click the icon. Some games will ask you a question or two before you start. Here in Chess Titans, you have to choose if you're a Beginner, Intermediate or Advanced player.

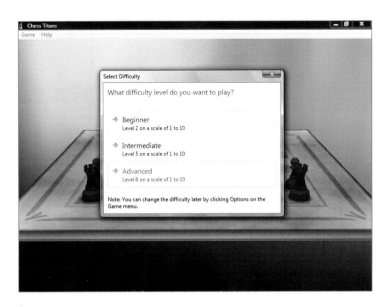

Games (cont.)

Once you've started a game, there will usually be information about playing the game on the screen, and a Help menu where you can get additional information about playing the game. For the most part, moving a player, tile or card, dealing a card, or otherwise moving around the screen, in these games at least, is performed using the mouse. Third-party games require more, often a game pad, remote, keyboard or joystick. Upon exiting the game, either from the Game menu or the x in the top right corner of the screen, you'll be prompted to save the game in progress (if applicable). Note that in this instance you can choose to always save an open game when exiting.

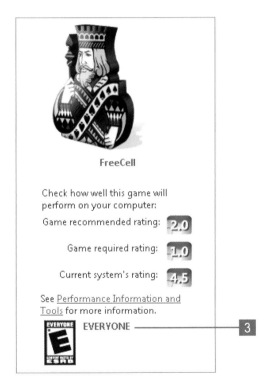

FreeCell

Check how well this game will perform on your computer:

Game recommended rating: **2.0**

Game required rating: **1.0**

Current system's rating: **4.5**

See Performance Information and Tools for more information.

EVERYONE

Playing games

1 Click Start.

2 Click Games.

3 Click any game icon one time to see the associated performance ratings. Notice this game is rated E for Everyone.

4 Double-click a game to open it.

Games (cont.)

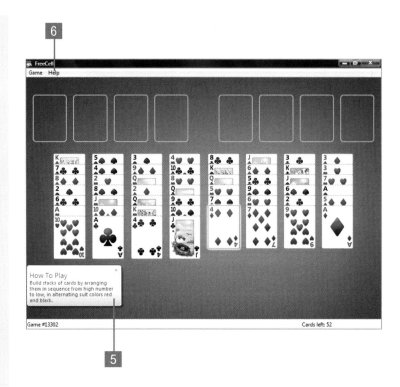

5 To close the How To Play box, click the x in the top right corner of the box.

6 To get more help regarding the game, click the Help button and choose View Help.

7 Have fun playing the game!

Using Vista applications: Part 2

Introduction

Windows Vista has even more applications. Although we don't have room in this book to introduce each and every one of them, there are some definitely worth noting. In this chapter you'll learn about two applications targeted specifically at keeping your computer running properly: Disk Cleanup and Disk Defragmenter. Both will help you keep your computer free of unwanted data and keep the data you have optimised on the hard drive. You'll also learn about Sync Center, a tool for syncing your computer with mobile phones or music players, and the Mobility Center, a tool you'll use when giving a presentation. If you're thinking that you don't give presentations any more, think outside the box. You can give a PowerPoint presentation at a family reunion or birthday party, and be the hit of your next party.

7

What you'll do

Use Disk Cleanup

Use Disk Defragmenter

Disk Cleanup

Disk Cleanup is a safe and effective way to reduce unnecessary data on your PC. With unnecessary data deleted, your PC will run faster and have more available disk space for saving files and installing programs. With Disk Cleanup you can remove temporary files, empty the Recycle Bin, remove setup log files and downloaded program files (among other things), all in a single process.

Disk Cleanup has changed just a little from the version included with Windows XP. The only thing that will stand out initially is that you can choose to clean up only your files or all users' files on the PC. Additionally, there is a More Options tab, where you can free additional disk space by deleting programs you don't need, and you can now remove all but the most recent System Restore points and shadow copies if desired. Disk Cleanup also lets you clean all of your drive's partitions, to enable you to optimise the entire PC.

Did you know? ?

If you run Disk Cleanup to clean your files only, you won't see the More Options tab.

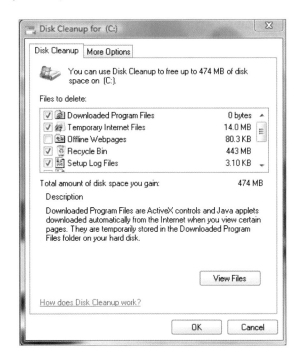

Disk Cleanup lets you safely remove the following (and you get to pick and choose which):

- Downloaded Program Files – these are files that download automatically when you view certain webpages. They are stored temporarily in a folder on your hard disk, and accessed when and if needed.

- Temporary Internet Files – these files contain copies of webpages you've visited, so that you can view the pages more quickly when visiting the page again.

- Offline Webpages – these are webpages that you've chosen to store on your computer so you can view them without being connected to the Internet. Upon connection, the data are synchronised.

- Recycle Bin – this contains files you've deleted. Files are not permanently deleted until you empty the Recycle Bin.

- Setup Log Files – these are files created by Windows during setup processes.

- Temporary Files – these are files created and stored by programs for use by the program. Most of these temporary files are deleted when you exit the program, but some do remain.

- Thumbnails – these are small icons of your pictures, videos and documents. Thumbnails will be recreated as needed, even if you delete them here.

- Per user archived Windows Error Reporting – files used for error reporting and solution checking.

- System archived Windows Error Reporting – files used for error reporting and solution checking.

Note that there's also a More Options tab. Take a look at the options here. You will see that you can view installed programs and remove them if desired, delete old backups and more.

Disk Cleanup (cont.)

7

Important

As with other programs that make system-wide changes, you'll be prompted to input the proper administrator's credentials before accessing Disk Cleanup. When prompted, click Continue or type the proper credentials.

Disk Cleanup (cont.)

Using Disk Cleanup

1 Click Start.

2 In the Start Search dialogue box, type Disk Cleanup.

3 In the results, under Programs, click Disk Cleanup. (As always click Continue or input administrator's credentials when prompted.)

4 Choose My files only to clean your files and nothing else. Choose Files from all users on this computer if you want to clean additional users' files or if you want access to the More Options tab, where you can delete unwanted programs and unnecessary backups and System Restore points.

5 If prompted, choose the drive or partition to clean up. If only one drive exists, you won't see the prompt shown here. Choose the letter of the drive that contains the operating system, which is almost always C. Click OK.

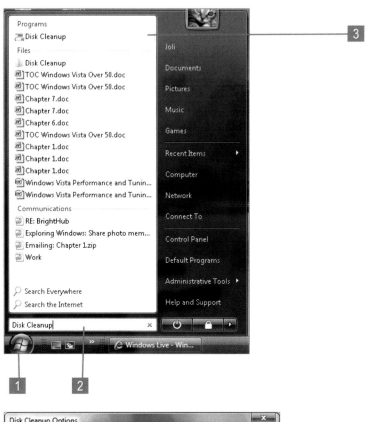

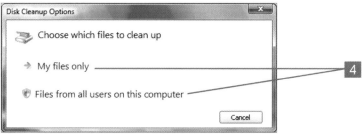

Disk Cleanup (cont.)

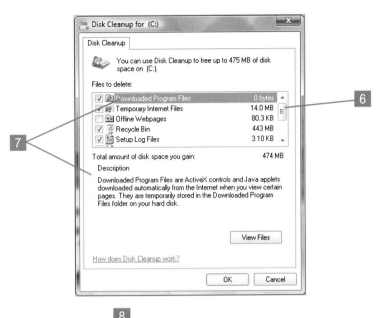

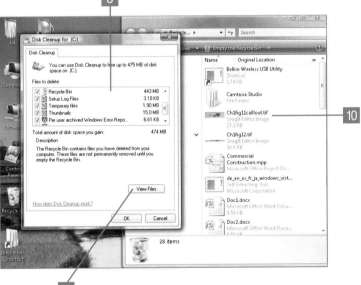

6 Wait while Disk Cleanup performs the required calculations. In the Disk Cleanup window, use the scroll bar to select or deselect the items to clean.

7 Select any item to see a description of it.

8 If you choose to empty the Recycle Bin, click Recycle Bin in the Files to delete list.

9 Click View Files.

10 Verify there is nothing in the Recycle Bin you want to keep.

11 If you see something in the Recycle Bin you want to keep, click it one time to select it.

12 From the Toolbar, click Restore this item.

Disk Cleanup (cont.)

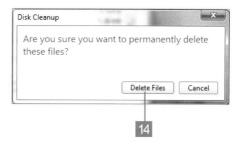

13 Click OK to start the cleaning process.

14 Click Delete Files to start.

15 If you opted to clean the files of all users on the computer in Step 4, you'll have access to the More Options tab. Click it.

16 Under Programs and Features, click Clean up.

17 Look through the programs listed. If you see a program you know you don't use and will never need, double-click it.

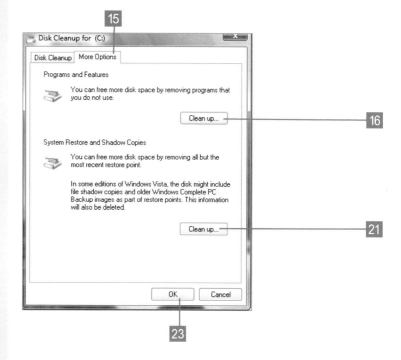

Important

Don't uninstall anything unless you are positive what it is! It's better to leave a program installed than delete it and realise you need it later, or to delete something that will cause subsequent errors to appear.

Did you know?

Did you know?

You can also click a program name once to select it, and then choose Uninstall from the available tabs.

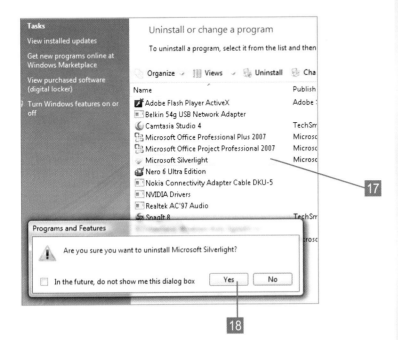

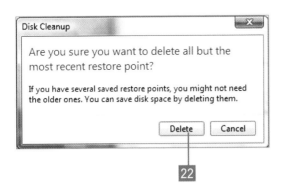

18 Click Yes to uninstall the program or No to cancel.

19 Work through the program's uninstall process; each process is different.

20 If necessary, click the x at the top of the window to close it.

21 Back at the Disk Cleanup dialogue box, under System Restore and Shadow Copies, click Clean up.

22 Click Delete.

23 If the Disk Cleanup dialogue box does not close automatically, click OK to apply changes or Cancel to close Disk Cleanup.

Important

System Restore points don't take up a lot of space and can be useful in an emergency. We do not suggest clicking Delete in Step 22.

Disk Defragmenter

A hard drive stores the files and data on your computer. When you want to access a file, the hard drive spins and data are accessed from the drive. When the data required for the file you need are all in one place, the data are accessed more quickly than if scattered across the hard drive in different areas. When data are scattered, the set is fragmented.

Disk Defragmenter analyses the data stored on your hard drive and consolidates files that are not stored together. This enhances performance by making data on your hard drive work faster by making data easier to access. Disk Defragmenter runs automatically once a week, in the middle of the night.

You won't ever need to *use* Disk Defragmenter, provided a schedule is set. You'll want to verify Disk Defragmenter is set to run on a schedule though and, if not, create one. Additionally, you can alter when Disk Defragmenter runs. If you do most of your computing in the middle of the night then you don't want Disk Defragmenter slowing down your PC while you're trying to work.

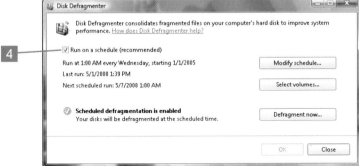

Disk Defragmenter (cont.)

Using Disk Defragmenter

1 Click Start.

2 In the Start Search dialogue box, type Defrag.

3 Under Programs, select Disk Defragmenter.

4 Verify that Disk Defragmenter is configured to run on a schedule. There should be a tick in the box, as shown here. If there is no tick, click inside the box to create one.

Disk Defragmenter (cont.)

5 If you want to change when Disk Defragmenter runs, click Modify schedule.

6 Select a choice for How often, What day, and What time, using the drop-down lists.

7 Click OK to close the scheduling dialogue box.

8 If you want to run Disk Defragmenter now, click Defragment now. There's generally no need to do this.

9 Click OK.

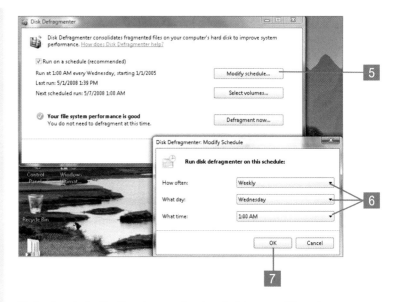

Note: by default all volumes (or hard-drive partitions) are selected, so there's no need to click Select volumes to make changes.

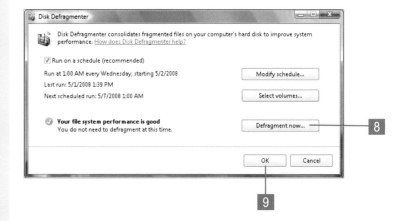

Managing files

You're going to have data to save. That data may come in the form of letters you type on the computer, pictures you take using your digital camera, music you copy (rip) from your own CD collection, music and media you purchase online, address books, videos from a DV camera, holiday card and gift lists, and more. Each time you click the Save or Save As button under a file menu (which is what you do to save data to your PC most of the time), you'll be prompted to tell Vista *where* you want to save the data. For the most part, Vista will *tell you* where it thinks you should save the data during this process. Documents go in the Documents folder, music in the Music folder, pictures in the Pictures folder, and so on.

While it's ultimately best to save data using the defaults, especially as you're getting used to the PC and how it works, as time passes, you'll need to tweak the folder structure a little. You might need to add your own folders, or folders inside folders (subfolders). You might want to copy data, move data or delete it. Eventually you'll have to search for data you can't find, share data and, at some point, restore data from the Recycle Bin. Restoring is a simple process that allows you to recover data you deleted accidentally. (At least until you empty the Recycle Bin!)

Browse Vista's built-in folder structure

Create your own folders and subfolders

Copy a file (or files)

Move a file (or files)

Delete a file (or files)

Move and copy with Cut, Copy and Paste

Create a Search folder and save it

Reopen a search folder

Restore folders (and files) from the Recycle Bin

Understanding Vista's built-in folder structure

Microsoft understands what types of data you want to save to your computer and built Vista's folder structure based on that information. Look at the Start menu. You'll see your name at the top. My name is Joli. It's at the top right of the Start menu.

Clicking your name on the Start menu opens your personal folder.

Your personal folder contains the following folders, which in turn contain data you've saved:

■ Contacts – this folder contains your information about your contacts – e-mail addresses, pictures, phone numbers, home and business addresses, and more. Each contact has a contact card, shown here. Note the tabs, which can hold additional information.

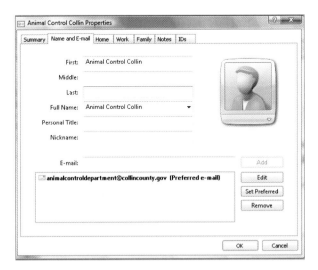

■ Desktop – this folder contains links to items for data you created on your desktop. As you can see here, Computer, Network, and Recycle Bin aren't listed, but shortcuts to folders I created are.

Understanding Vista's built-in folder structure (cont.)

■ Documents – this folder contains documents you've saved, subfolders you created and folders created by Vista including Fax, My Received Files, Remote Assistance Logs and Scanned Documents.

■ Downloads – this folder does not contain anything by default. It does offer a place to save items you download from the Internet, like drivers and third-party programs.

■ Favorites – this folder contains the items in Internet Explorer's Favorites list. It may also include folders created by the computer manufacturer or Microsoft, including Links, Microsoft Websites and MSN Websites.

■ Links – this folder contains shortcuts to the Documents, Music, Pictures, Public, Recently Changed, and Searches folders.

■ Music – this folder contains sample music and music you save to the PC.

■ Pictures – this folder contains sample pictures and pictures you save to the PC.

■ Saved Games – this folder contains games that ship with Windows Vista and offers a place to save games you acquire on your own.

■ Searches – this folder contains preconfigured Search folders including Recent Documents, Recent E-Mail, Recent Music, Recent Pictures and Videos, Recently Changed, and Shared By Me. If you need to find something recently accessed or changed and don't know where to look, you can probably locate it here. These folders get updated each time you open them.

■ Videos – this folder contains sample videos and videos you save to the PC.

When you're ready to save data, you're going to want to save it to the folder that most closely matches the data you're saving. Documents belong in the Documents folder and pictures belong in the Picture folder. You get the idea. Because it's important you understand where these folders are and how to access them, work through the steps here.

Understanding Vista's built-in folder structure (cont.)

8

Understanding Vista's built-in folder structure (cont.)

Browsing Vista's folder structure

1. Click Start.

2. Click your personal folder. It's the one with your name on it.

3. Drag the divider bars so that your personal folder shows all of the Favorite Links, most of the Folders list and your personal subfolders, as shown here.

Did you know?

I have a subfolder here called Backups that I created to hold backups of my data. You'll learn how to create subfolders like these shortly.

Favorite links

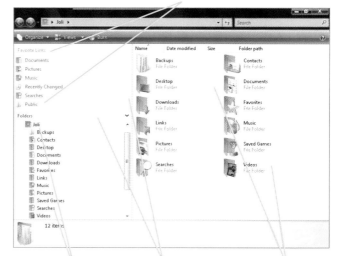

Folders

3 Drag here and here to resize panes

Folders inside your subfolders

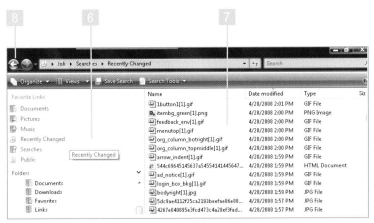

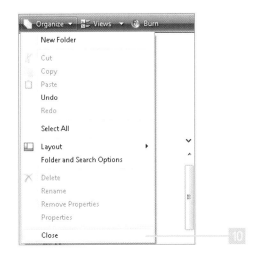

Understanding Vista's built-in folder structure (cont.)

Under Favorite Links, click Music.

Notice the Sample Music folder. This is contained inside the Music folder.

Click Recently Changed.

Note the list that is populated automatically. These are items you have recently altered. Among other things, you can see the name of the file and the date it was modified.

Click the Back button to return to the Music folder, and click Back again to return to your personal folder.

Continue experimenting navigating folders by clicking in other panes, for instance, click the Music folder in the Folders pane, or the Music folder in the thumbnail pane.

Click File, and click Close to close the window.

Create your own folders and subfolders

While Vista's default folders will suit your needs for a while, it won't last. Soon you'll need to create subfolders inside those folders to manage your data and keep it organised. For instance, inside the Documents folder, you may need to create a subfolder called Tax Information to hold scanned receipts, tax records and account information. Inside the Pictures folder you might create folders named 2008, 2009, 2010, or Weddings, Vacations, Grandkids, and so on. And in the Saved Games folder you might create subfolders named My Games, My Grandkids' Games or Downloaded Games. Creating subfolders in the existing folders often works just fine. Sometimes though, you may have specific hobbies or interests that require you to create your own folder structure. In this case, you'd extend what's there by adding your own folders to the mix.

The idea behind extending Vista's folder structure is to personalise it to meet your needs. If you travel a lot, you might want to create an entirely new folder called Travel, and put subfolders in that named for the cities or countries you visit. You could keep everything related to that city or country in it, including maps, documents, pictures and videos, and ignore all of Vista's existing folders altogether. Other folders you might consider creating include:

- Graduations
- Genealogy
- Places to Visit
- Quilting Patterns
- Bike Trails
- Lakes and Campgrounds
- Letters to Family
- Pets
- Doctor and Hospital Information
- Recipes
- Home Improvements
- Scanned Receipts.

And there's more; you need to decide what you need and make a list, then, inside each folder, create subfolders to organise your data. Once you know what folders you'd like to create, follow the directions next to create them.

Now, before we get started, consider this. Your personal folder, the one with your name on it that you can access from the Start menu, holds Vista's default folders like Documents and Pictures. If you're going to create new folders and subfolders, this is the place to create them. This will make them easy to find, but will also make them easy to back up. When you use Vista's Backup and Restore program, it'll automatically back up everything there. If you have folders scattered about the hard drive, you'll have to manually tell the program where they are and that you want to back them up. That said, in the following step-by-step, you'll create folders and subfolders in your personal folder, noting that you can create folders anywhere else on the hard drive, even the desktop.

Did you know?

You can create a new folder just about anywhere: on the desktop, in an existing folder or in a folder you create yourself. If you have an external hard drive or networked computer, you can create a folder called Backup in any of the Public folders and store backup data there.

8

Create your own folders and subfolders (cont.)

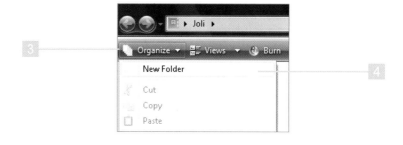

Creating folders and subfolders

1. Click Start.

2. Click your personal folder. That's the one with your name on it.

3. Click Organize.

4. Click New Folder.

5. Type a name for the new folder. (If the folder name is not highlighted like this, left-click once, wait a second, and left-click again. If you double-click quickly, the folder will open.)

6. Click Enter (or Return) on the keyboard.

7. The new folder will appear alphabetically in the list, by default.

Did you know?

You can change how the folder icons look from the View menu. In this section we're using Tiles. You can choose any of the options. Check out this image, where the icon size is set between Large Icons and Extra Large Icons.

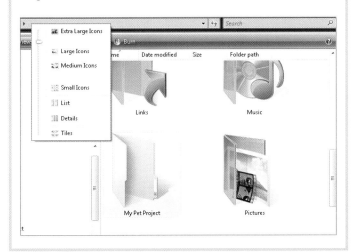

8 Double-click your new folder to open it. The folder will be empty. Now you will create subfolders (or folders inside the new folder). Note that you can create subfolders inside any folder at all, not just folders you create.

9 You could click Organize and click New Folder to create a subfolder, like you did in steps 3 and 4, but there's another way. Right-click in the empty folder and click New.

10 Look at all of the 'New' things you can create, including Shortcut, Contact, Text Document and more. Click Folder.

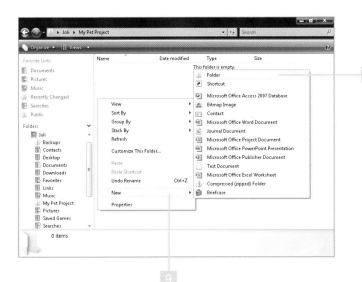

Create your own folders and subfolders (cont.)

11 Type a name for the new folder. (If the folder name is not highlighted like this, left-click once, wait a second, and left-click again. If you double-click quickly, the folder will open.)

12 Click Enter (or Return) on the keyboard.

13 The new folder will appear alphabetically in the list, by default, if more than one folder exists.

14 Click the Back button to return to the previous window, which is the main folder.

For your information

When you right-click inside a folder, you will see more than New, as noted in Step 10. One thing you will see is Sort By. The default sorting option is Ascending, but you can sort data in other ways too, including Name, Date Modified, Size, Folder Path, Descending, and more. Feel free to experiment with these settings. You can't hurt anything!

Did you know?

When a folder or subfolder is empty, its icon indicates this by showing an empty folder. When data are added to the folder, this is noted in the icon image. Compare an empty folder to one with data in it.

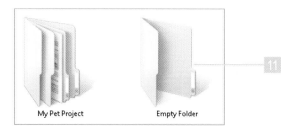

My Pet Project   Empty Folder

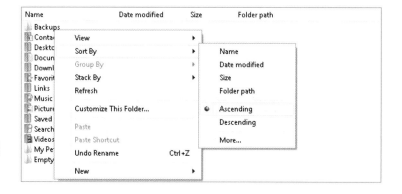

It might be helpful to think of folders and subfolders in a more physical way, as folders and subfolders in a filing cabinet. For instance, you could allot an entire physical file cabinet drawer to documents, name the drawer Documents, and then create subfolders to organise, sort and manage the printed documents you have. You can do the same thing on your computer, except on a computer the data are all digital, not physical. Thus, the next logical step after creating folders and subfolders is to put data in those folders. This will help you keep the data organised and easily available, just as you would in a filing cabinet.

You may want to start with your pictures. Often, Vista's Pictures folder becomes filled with unorganised pictures from your digital camera, the Web, e-mails or other sources. (In my case it becomes unorganised with screen shots for books!) To organise the data inside the folder, you create subfolders inside the Pictures folder and then move pictures into them to arrange and manage them. That's what we'll do in the next exercise.

Before we start moving data around though, it's important to understand the difference between copying and moving. When you copy something, an exact duplicate is made. The original data remain where they are and a copy is placed somewhere else. For the most part, this is not what you want to do when organising data: you want to move the data. If a picture of a graduation needs to be put in the Graduation Pictures folder, you need to move it, not copy it.

Copy, move and delete files

8

Did you know?

You might want to copy data instead of moving them if the data are linked to a PowerPoint or Excel presentation that looks for the data in a specific place, because if you move data, the application won't be able to find them; but I do believe we are getting ahead of ourselves here.

Copy, move and delete files (cont.)

When you back up data you want to copy it. This is about the only time you will want to copy data. And, you'll want to copy the data to a source you'll keep away from your PC. You can copy data to a CD or DVD drive, to an external hard drive or to a network drive. Copying allows you to create a backup of the data in one place, like your kids' houses or a safe deposit box, while keeping a local copy available for immediate use.

To move and copy data, you have quite a few choices. The first is to drag and drop with the mouse. You can left-click and drag and drop the data using a mouse, or you can right-click and drag and drop the data with the mouse. Left-clicking is easier, but there are rules to remember. When you right-click, there are no rules to remember. Let's look at the rules first, and then I'll suggest you always right-click when you drag and drop data.

When you drag and drop data using a left-click, certain things happen by default. If you drag and drop data from a folder to the desktop, the data is always moved. That means the data (or picture) is no longer in the folder, it's now on the desktop. If you drag and drop from one folder to another, again the file is moved out of the original folder and into the new one. If you drag and drop from one folder on one hard drive to a folder on another, the data are copied. Vista assumes in this case that you are backing up data to a secondary source, and don't want to move data. There are more rules, but let's cut our losses. If you right-click and drag and drop data, *you* get to choose what to do with the data. You can copy, move, create a shortcut or even cancel.

Copy Here

Move Here

Create Shortcuts Here

Cancel

Copying a file (or files)

1. Click Start.

2. Click Pictures.

3. Take a look at the data inside your Pictures folder. You may see pictures that are unorganised, not in subfolders or perhaps not even pictures at all. If you only see the Sample Pictures folder, open it.

4. Click the Restore button or otherwise change the size of the window you can see as part of the desktop. (For more information about resizing windows, see Chapter 3.)

Copy, move and delete files (cont.)

5 Right-click any picture, either from the Sample Pictures folder or any of your personal pictures.

6 Drag and drop the image to the desktop. (Don't worry that it says Move to Desktop, since you right-clicked, you get to decide if it's moved or copied.)

7 Let go of the mouse, and select Copy Here.

8 Notice the picture now appears on the desktop and also in the folder. It's been copied.

Copy, move and delete files (cont.)

Moving a file (or files)

1 (The Pictures folder may already be open and sized properly. If so, skip to Step 5.) Click Start.

2 Click Pictures.

3 Take a look at the data inside your Pictures folder. You may see pictures that are unorganised, not in subfolders or perhaps not even pictures at all. If you only see the Sample Pictures folder, open it.

4 Click the Restore button or otherwise change the size of the window you can see as part of the desktop. (For more information about resizing windows, see Chapter 3.)

8

Copy, move and delete files (cont.)

5 Right-click any picture, either from the Sample Pictures folder or any of your personal pictures.

6 Drag and drop the image to the desktop. (Don't worry that it says Move to Desktop, since you right-clicked, you get to decide if it's moved or copied.)

7 Let go of the mouse, and select Move Here.

8 Notice the picture now appears on the desktop and also in the folder. It's been copied.

Note: To select multiple files to copy or move, hold down the Ctrl key while selecting each. With the Ctrl key you can select multiple non-contiguous files. To select contiguous files, hold down the Shift key while selecting.

Deleting files and folders is as simple as right-clicking and selecting Delete. When you delete an item or a folder the deleted data go to the Recycle Bin. If you delete something by mistake, you can get it back if need be, by opening the Recycle Bin, locating the data and clicking Restore. Note that once you empty the Recycle Bin, those data are no longer available for restoring.

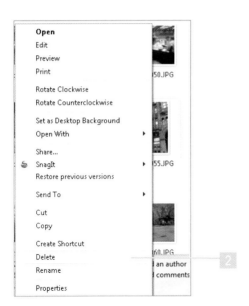

Deleting a file (or files)

1 Right-click any file or folder you want to delete.

2 Click Delete.

As noted, you can also move and copy data using the commands Cut, Copy and Paste. You access these commands from the window's Organize or Edit menu or by right-clicking.

- Cut – copies the data to Vista's clipboard (a virtual, temporary, holding area). The data will be deleted from the original location as soon as you 'paste' them somewhere else. Pasting Cut data moves the data.

- Copy – copies the data to Vista's clipboard. The data will be not deleted from the original location even when you 'paste' them somewhere else. Pasting Copy data will copy the data, not move them.

- Paste – copies or moves the data to the new location. If the data were Cut, they will be moved. If the data were Copied, they will be copied.

Copy, move and delete files (cont.)

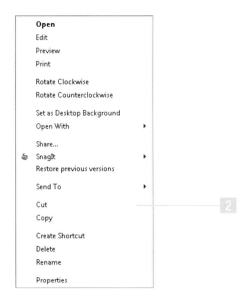

Moving and copying with Cut, Copy and Paste

1 Right-click any data you want to move or copy.

2 To move the data, click Cut. To copy the data, click Copy.

3 Browse to the location to copy or move the file. This may require you to click Start, select your personal folder and then double-click a subfolder inside it.

4 Right-click and select Paste.

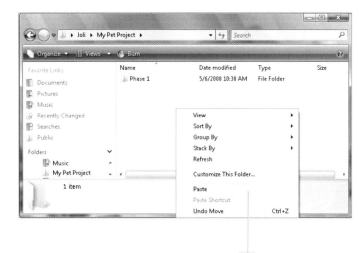

Vista lets you search from the Start Search menu, as you know. Just click Start, and in the Start Search dialogue box, type a few letters of what you're looking for, and results will appear in a list. Here, I've typed Jennifer, and the results are shown.

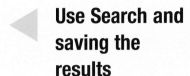

In these results, there are folders, pictures and contact information, all relating somehow to the word Jennifer. However, I know there are more results. There are videos, e-mail, documents, and more, that contain the word Jennifer or that I've 'tagged' manually to include Jennifer. (Tagging is the process of editing the properties for a file, photo, document, and the like; in this case, adding the word Jennifer to it, so that the data tagged appear in search results.)

In order to locate everything on the computer that has to do with Jennifer, a more thorough search must be performed. That is easily done by clicking Search Everywhere in the results pane.

Use Search and saving the results (cont.)

After clicking Search Everywhere, the results will appear in a new window. Although the results aren't necessarily organised, they do appear.

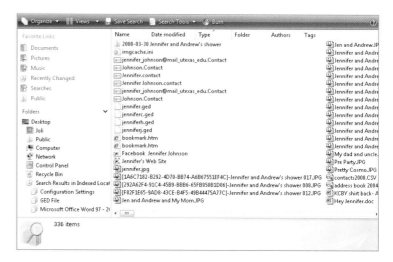

Organise search results

If you're looking for something in particular, you'll probably want to organise the results in a way that promotes actually finding what you want. You can do that by right-clicking an empty area in the folder results window, selecting Stack By and then selecting an option. Stacking organises the data by name, date modified, type, folder, authors or tags, and offers more options.

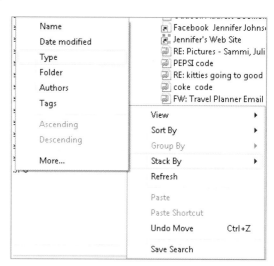

To keep from getting bogged down in options, consider choosing from these three:

- Name – organises the data in stacks by the data's name. If you know the name of the file, picture or folder you want, this is a good option.

- Date Modified – organises the data in stacks including Last week, Earlier this year, or A long time ago. If you have an idea regarding when the data were last modified, meaning uploaded, edited, e-mailed, or opened, select this option.

- Type – organises the data by the type of data they are, such as an image, document, shortcut, etc. This is a good option if you know you're looking for a photo, document and the like.

Here the results for Jennifer are stacked by Type. Notice there are contact files, folders, Internet shortcuts, JPG files (pictures), text documents and e-mail messages.

Once stacked, you can double-click any stack to see its contents. Here are the results from the JPG folder.

Use Search and saving the results (cont.)

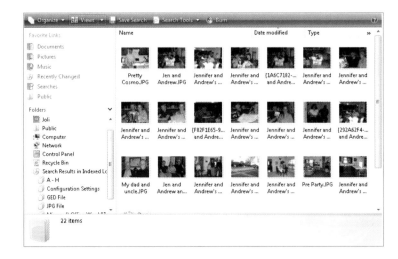

Important

There are other search features. For instance, you can click Advanced Search to search by location, date received, date modified, date created, size, date taken (for pictures) and more.

As you may have noticed in the previous figure, search results windows offer their own ways to sort through the search results. As you can see here, you can show all of the results or only results that pertain to e-mail, documents, pictures, music and other types (data that do not fit into these categories). To sort the results, click any category. Here, I've selected E-mail, so only results that are e-mails are shown. Note you can also preview the e-mail in the Preview pane.

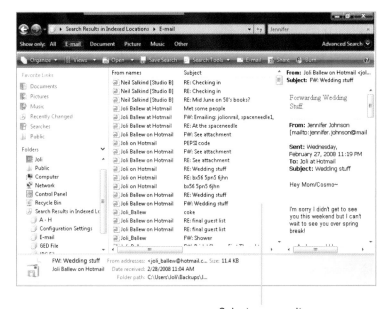

Select any result to preview it

Creating a search folder

Once you perform a search, and the search results appear in a window, and even after sorting through the results, you can save the results in a search folder. Once saved, you can access the results any time you like, simply by opening the folder. Search folders are 'smart' too; each time you open the folder after saving it, it performs a new search, and adds any new data it finds that match the search folder's criteria. There are all sorts of uses for search folders, so let your imagination run wild. You can create a search folder for anything you can type into the Start Search dialogue box.

If you choose to perform an advanced search, you'll save those results just as you would any other search. We don't think you're going to need to perform advanced searches any time soon though, and basic searches with sorting options will probably be just fine.

Did you know?

A search folder only offers a place to access data that match the search criteria; it does not move the data there or create copies of data.

8

Use Search and saving the results (cont.)

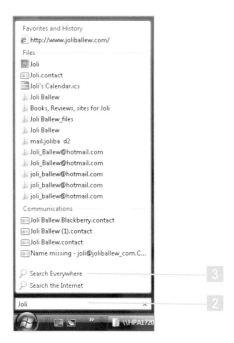

Creating a search folder and saving it

1. Click Start.

2. In the Start Search dialogue box, type something you'd like to search for. To practise, type in your first name.

3. Click Search Everywhere.

4. If you see the following warning: There are more results than will fit in this view. Narrow your results with the Search box or click to see all results, go ahead and click to see all of the results.

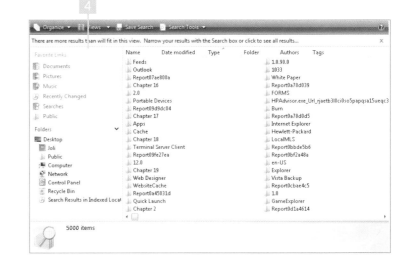

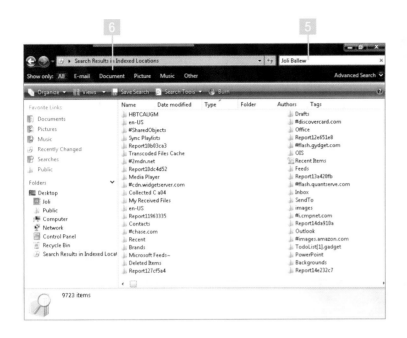

5 In the Search window, note that your first name is listed. Type your last name behind it. Watch the results change.

6 In Show Only, click Document. Again, notice the results change. Only documents show in the results.

7 In Show Only, choose Picture.

8 Click Save Search.

9 Name the search descriptively.

10 Click Save.

11 Close the window by clicking the x in the top right corner.

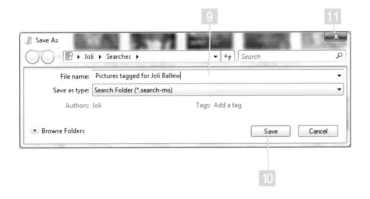

Important

The search folder will be stored in the Search Folder. You'll learn how to open that folder and the saved search folders next.

Use Search and saving the results (cont.)

Reopening a search folder

Once a search folder is saved, you can access it and its contents just like any other folder on your hard drive. By default, search folders are saved in your personal folder, in the Searches folder as a subfolder.

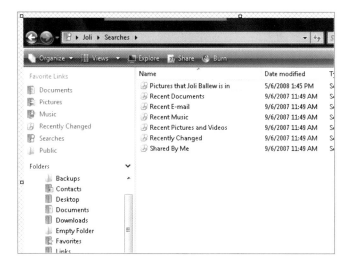

Every time you access the folder, a new search is performed, to make sure the folder's contents are up-to-date. That means if you add data to the PC that match the criteria for the search folder, the next time you open the folder, those data will be included.

You may see results in a folder that do not seem to belong. That's because an item always gets tagged with information as it's copied or saved to the PC. That tag will include the date it was put on the PC, the owner of the data, or even what type of camera was used to obtain the picture. So, although you may not be in a picture that appears in a folder from results obtained by searching for your own name, the picture may be in that folder because you are the 'author' or 'owner' of that picture: because you put it on the computer. So don't be surprised if search folders contain odd-looking data; it's normal.

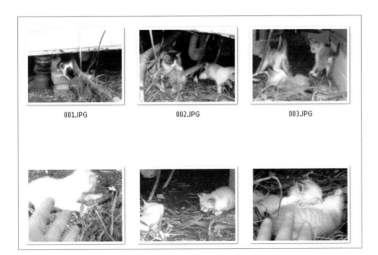

001.JPG   002.JPG   003.JPG

Although I am not in any of the pictures in the saved search folder that contains pictures for Joli, I did upload the picture, which the computer knows, and thus it appears in this search folder.

8

Use Search and saving the results (cont.)

Reopening a search folder

1 Click Start, and click your personal folder.

2 Double-click the Searches folder to open it.

3 Locate the new search folder. Double-click to open it.

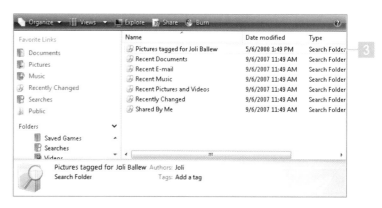

Since you learned to delete files and folders in this chapter it's only fair to tell you how to recover them if you deleted them accidentally. Every file or folder you delete is sent to the Recycle Bin. Until the Recycle Bin is emptied, which you must do manually or using Disk Cleanup, you can 'restore' the file, which means you will put it back where it was before you deleted it.

The Recycle Bin sits on the desktop. Double-click it to open it.

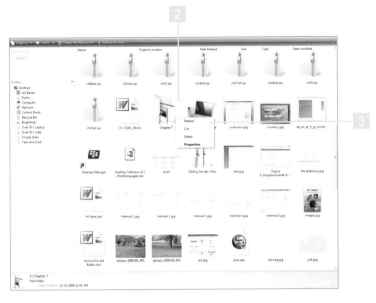

If you find a file you want to restore (recover), right-click it and choose Restore. The file will reappear in the same location it was in prior to deleting.

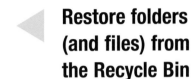

Restore folders (and files) from the Recycle Bin

Restoring folders (and files) from the Recycle Bin

1 Double-click the Recycle Bin, it's on the desktop.

2 Browse through the files, folders, shortcuts, pictures and other data. If you find something you did not mean to delete, right-click it.

3 Choose Restore from the drop-down list.

8

Jargon buster

Icon – a visual representation of a file or folder that you can click to open.

Windows Mail

Introduction

Windows Mail runs with Microsoft Windows Vista, and is the only thing you need to send and receive e-mail, manage your contacts, manage sent, saved and incoming e-mail, and read *newsgroups* (that don't have anything to do with news at all), which we'll talk about later. Within Windows Mail you can also print e-mail, create folders for storing e-mail you want to keep, manage unwanted e-mail, open attachments, send pictures inside an e-mail and more.

To use Windows Mail, you need an e-mail address and two e-mail server addresses, all of which you can get from your ISP. With this information in hand, you'll work through the New Connection wizard, inputting the required information when prompted, to set up the program. Once Mail is set up, you're ready to send and receive mail. Don't worry, it's easy!

What you'll do

Set up an e-mail address

View an e-mail

Open an attachment and view an attachment

Print an e-mail

Send an e-mail

Reply to and forward e-mail

Attach a picture or file using the insert menu

Attach a picture or file by right-clicking

Add a contact

Create a group

Deal with junk mail

Create a basic message rule

Create a new folder

Clean Windows Mail

Set up an e-mail address

As noted, to use Windows Mail you need to set up an e-mail address. This is first and foremost, and is done even before exploring the Mail interface. That's because the first time you use Windows Mail you'll be prompted to input the required information regarding your e-mail address and e-mail servers. When creating your first e-mail address (and any subsequent ones), you'll need to input the following information:

- Display name – this is the name that will appear in the From field when you compose an e-mail and in the sender's Inbox (under From in their e-mail list) when they receive e-mail from you. Don't put your e-mail address here; put your first and last name, and any additional information. I use Joli Ballew, MVP.

- E-mail address – here's where you type the e-mail address you chose when you signed up with your ISP. It often takes this form: *yourname@yourispname.com*.

- Mail servers – this is where you'll enter the information your ISP gave you about its mail servers. Most often this includes a POP3 incoming mail server and an SMTP outgoing mail server. Often the server names look something like *pop.yourispnamehere.com* and *smtp.yourispnamehere.com*.

- Logon name and password – this is where you'll enter the name and password you chose when setting up your online account with your ISP.

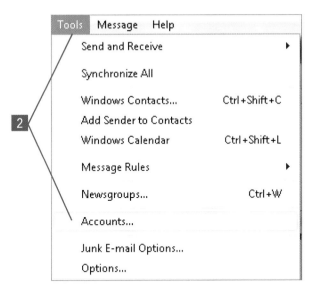

Setting up an e-mail address

1 Click Start, and in the Start menu, click Windows Mail.

2 You should be prompted to set up an e-mail account automatically; if you aren't, click Tools, and click Accounts. Then click Add. (You'll need to perform this step to create a secondary account, if you decide to do so.)

9

Set up an e-mail address (cont.)

3 Click E-mail Account to add an e-mail account.

4 Click Next.

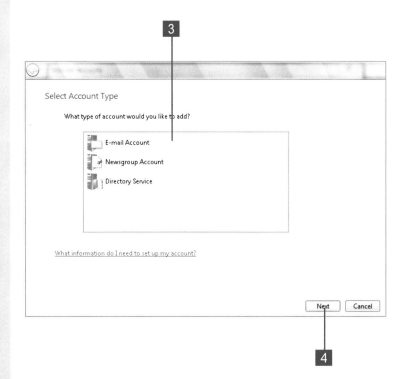

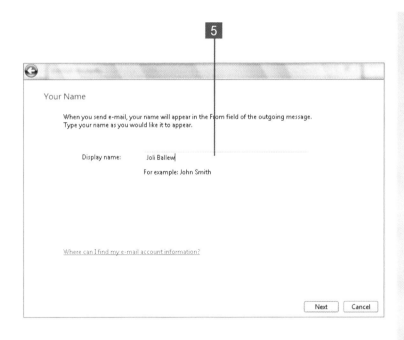

Set up an e-mail address (cont.)

5 Type your display name. Remember, this isn't your e-mail address, it's the name you want people to see when they get e-mail from you.

6 Type your e-mail address. E-mail addresses are not case sensitive.

7 Click Next.

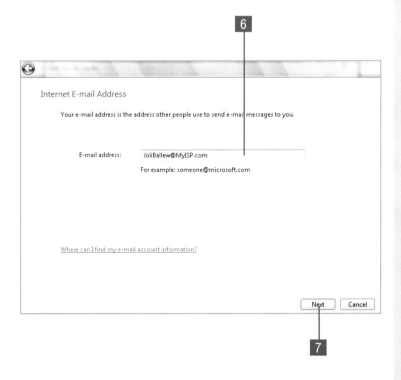

9

Set up an e-mail address (cont.)

8. Choose your Incoming e-mail server type. Most likely, it's POP3. If you aren't sure, call your ISP or visit its website.

9. Type the name of the incoming and outgoing mail servers. If you aren't sure, call your ISP or visit its website.

10. If your ISP told you your outgoing server requires authentication, tick the box. If you aren't sure, don't check it.

11. Click Next.

12. Type your e-mail username. This is often your e-mail address.

13. Type your password. Passwords are case sensitive.

14. If you want Windows Mail to remember your password, leave Remember password ticked.

15. Click Next.

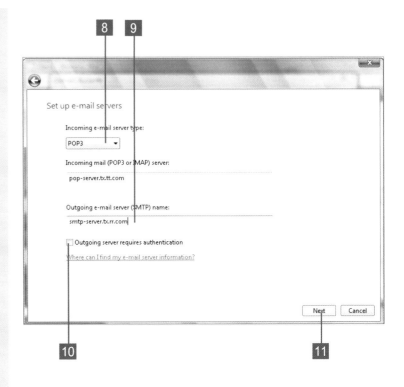

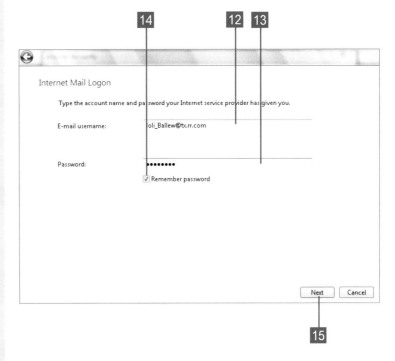

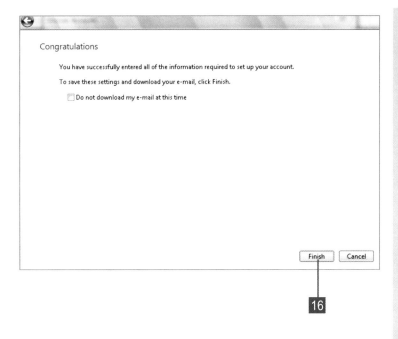

16 Click Finish to download any e-mail already sent to your account, which will include an e-mail from Microsoft, welcoming you to Windows Mail.

17 If you get an error, read it carefully. Note in this example that the host 'pop-server.tx.tt.com' could not be found. That's because of a typographical error during setup; it should have been pop-server.tx.rr.com. You may also receive an error stating that the outgoing server requires authentication. Whatever the case, click Hide. (This happens a lot, so don't worry!)

9

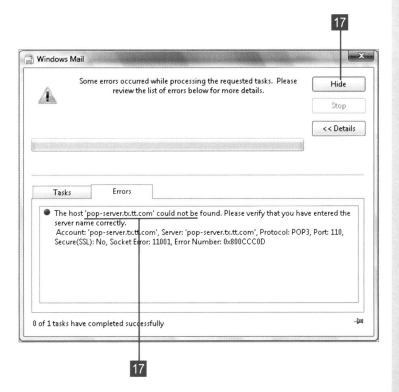

Set up an e-mail address (cont.)

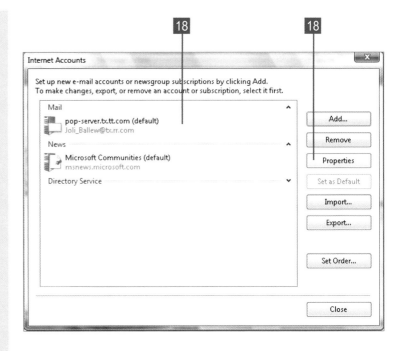

18 To resolve errors, in the Internet Accounts dialogue box, which will still be available, click the e-mail address to repair, and click Properties.

19 In the Properties dialogue box, browse through the tabs and repair the mistake. As you can see here, fixing the type for the Incoming mail server is achieved using the Servers tab. When in doubt, call your ISP. It is there to help.

20 Click OK.

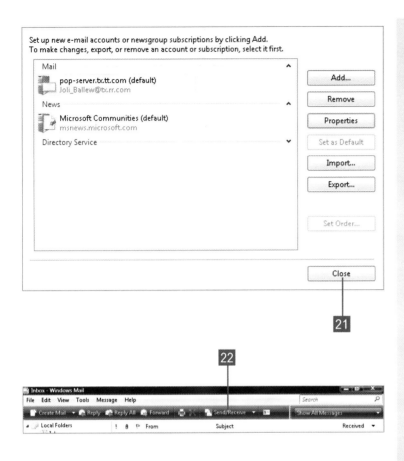

Set up new e-mail accounts or newsgroup subscriptions by clicking Add.
To make changes, export, or remove an account or subscription, select it first.

Mail
  pop-server.tx.tt.com (default)
  Joli_Ballew@tx.rr.com

News
  Microsoft Communities (default)
  msnews.microsoft.com

Directory Service

Add...
Remove
Properties
Set as Default
Import...
Export...
Set Order...
Close

21

22

Inbox - Windows Mail
File   Edit   View   Tools   Message   Help   Search
Create Mail ▾   Reply   Reply All   Forward   Send/Receive ▾   Show All Messages ▾
Local Folders   !   ⬤   ⚑   From   Subject   Received ▾

21 Click Close.

22 To view your first e-mail, a welcome message from Microsoft, click the Send/Receive button. Note you may get additional e-mails.

9

Get to know the Windows Mail interface

Now that you have at least one e-mail in your 'Inbox', you can explore how Windows Mail organises your e-mail in the Folder List pane on the left side of the interface. There are six default folders, but you can add your own if desired:

■ Inbox – this folder holds mail you've received.

■ Outbox – this folder holds mail you've written but have not yet sent.

■ Sent Items – this folder stores copies of messages you've sent.

■ Deleted Items – this folder holds mail you've deleted.

■ Drafts – this folder holds messages you've started, but not completed. Click File and click Save to put an e-mail in progress here.

■ Junk E-mail – this folder holds e-mail that Windows Mail thinks is spam. You should check this folder occasionally, since Mail may put e-mail in there that you want to read.

In addition, the Microsoft Communities folder offers access to available Microsoft newsgroups and communities. You'll learn more about this later in the chapter.

For your information

You can configure Windows Mail so that the Deleted Items folder empties every time you exit Windows Mail, but we don't suggest it. It's better to empty the Deleted Items folder manually because, like the Recycle Bin, once it's emptied, the data are irretrievable. If you must though, you can configure Mail to empty on exit, from the Tools menu. Choose Options, and select the Advanced tab. Click Maintenance, and tick Empty messages from the 'Deleted Items' folder on exit.

Here are the areas of Windows Mail available in the default configuration.

Folders Bar   Reading Pane   Message Pane   Views Bar

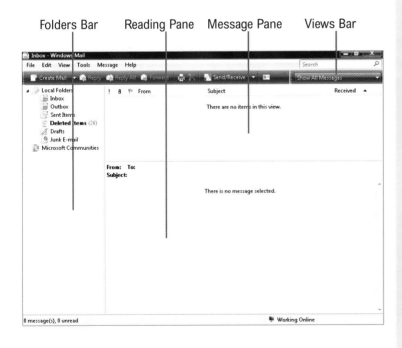

9

Get to know the Windows Mail interface (cont.)

You can customise the interface by clicking View, and selecting Layout. This opens the Layout window shown here. Notice you can hide panes, or show the Folder Bar not shown by default. You can also change the layout so the Reading pane is shown on the right instead of the bottom. For now, leave the defaults; later you can return here and personalise the interface.

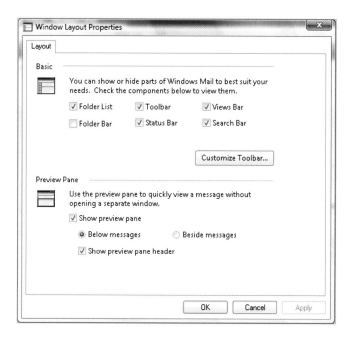

Each time you click the Send/Receive button, Windows Mail checks to see if you have any new mail on your ISP's mail server. By default, Windows Mail will check every 30 minutes. When you receive mail, there are two ways to read it. You can click the message one time and read it in the Preview pane, or double-click it to open it in its own window. Most people just click the e-mail one time, that way you don't have to close any windows after reading it (which is what you'd have to do if you double-clicked). You can also adjust the size of the panes by dragging the grey border between any of them up or down when using the Reading pane, which makes it even more convenient.

For your information

To have Windows Mail check for e-mail more often than every 30 minutes (or less often), click Tools, and click Options. From the General tab, change the number of minutes from 30 to something else.

Receive and view an e-mail

9

Receive and view an e-mail (cont.)

Viewing an e-mail and opening an attachment

1 In Windows Mail, click the Send/Receive button to check for mail.

2 When new mail arrives, click it one time to read it in the Preview pane.

3 You may see the message shown here: 'Some pictures have been blocked to help prevent the sender from identifying your computer. Click here to download pictures.' If you do, and if you know the sender, click the yellow bar to see the image. If you don't know the sender, it's probably junk e-mail, and you'll want to either delete it or mark it as Junk.

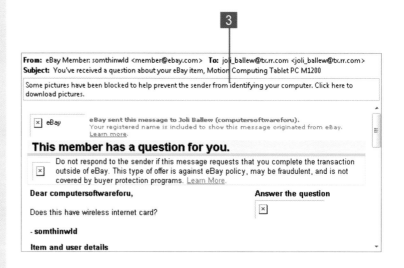

4 If the e-mail contains an
attachment, you'll see a
paperclip in both the Message
pane and the Preview pane. To
open the attachment, click the
paperclip icon in the Preview
pane, and click the
attachment's name.

9

Receive and view an e-mail (cont.)

5 When prompted, click Open. NEVER open an attachment from someone you do not know! It could be a virus!

6 If you have a program installed on your computer that can open the attachment, it will open. If not, you'll receive an error like this one. If you receive this error, refer to the troubleshooting section at the end of this book.

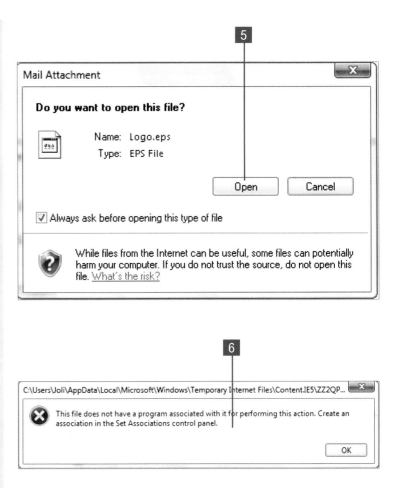

5

Mail Attachment

Do you want to open this file?

Name: Logo.eps
Type: EPS File

Open   Cancel

☑ Always ask before opening this type of file

While files from the Internet can be useful, some files can potentially harm your computer. If you do not trust the source, do not open this file. What's the risk?

6

C:\Users\Joli\AppData\Local\Microsoft\Windows\Temporary Internet Files\Content.IE5\ZZ2QP...

This file does not have a program associated with it for performing this action. Create an association in the Set Associations control panel.

OK

Did you know?

You can also save the attachment to your computer by clicking Save Attachments in Step 4. This will be necessary if you need to edit the attachment and resend it.

Sometimes you'll need to print an e-mail or its attachment. The e-mail could contain a receipt, a great joke you want to share with your friends who don't have or use e-mail, or test results from a doctor. Whatever the case, Windows Mail makes it easy to print. Just check out the printer icon on the toolbar; click it once to print. (An e-mail has to be selected to print it.) After clicking the Print icon, the Print dialogue box will appear, where you can select a printer, set print preferences, choose a page range and, well, print.

Print an e-mail

9

Print an e-mail (cont.)

Printing an e-mail

1 Select the e-mail to print by clicking it in the Message pane.

2 Click the Print icon.

3 In the Print dialogue box, select the printer to use, if more than one exist.

4 Click Print.

Print icon

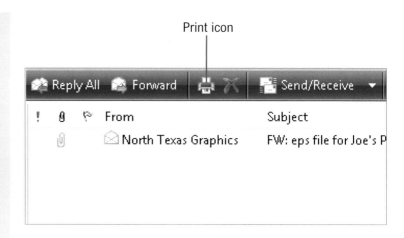

3

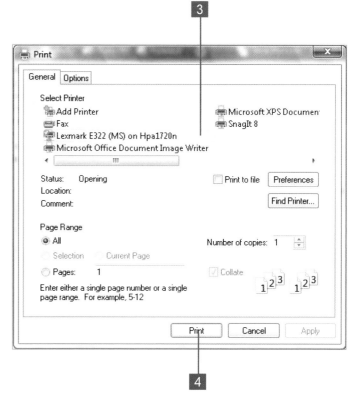

4

240

You compose an e-mail message by clicking Create Mail on the toolbar. This icon sits right above the Folder bar.

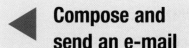
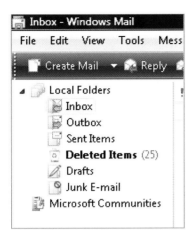

A new message is shown here. Notice that all of the available fields are empty. You will fill them in. Some of the New Message parts are labelled here.

Header

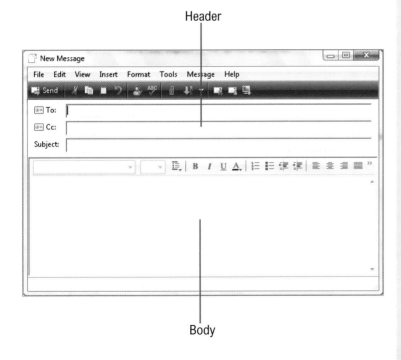

Body

9

Compose and send an e-mail (cont.)

The header is where you input who the e-mail should be sent to and the subject. The body is where you type the message. There's also a menu bar and a toolbar, which you can use to access other features including tools you're already familiar with like: Cut, Copy and Paste; spell check; font, font size, font colour and font style; and access to tools including Windows Calendar and Windows Contacts.

Here are some things to consider before and while you compose an e-mail:

- You'll need the e-mail address of the recipient; you'll type this into the 'To:' field. Alternatively, you can select Tools, and click Select Recipients to choose from your address book.

- To send the e-mail to more than one person, type their e-mail address and put a semicolon between each entry, like this: *joli@isp.com; bob@microsoft.com; kim@aol.com.* Alternatively, you can select Tools, and click Select Recipients to choose from your address book, and Mail will insert the semicolons automatically.

- If you want to send the e-mail to someone and you don't need them to respond, you can put them in the CC line. (CC stands for carbon copy.)

- If you want to send the e-mail to someone and you don't want other recipients to know you included them in the e-mail, add them to the BCC line. (You can show this by clicking View, and then clicking All Headers.) BCC stands for blind carbon copy and is a secret copy.

- Type the subject of the message in the 'Subject:' field. Make sure the subject adequately describes the body of your e-mail. Your recipients should be able to review the subject line later and be able to recall what the e-mail was regarding.

- Type the message in the body of the e-mail. Note that you can edit the data as you would in any word-processing program, you can Cut, Copy and Paste, change the font and more.

Beyond send a 'new' e-mail, you can reply to an e-mail or forward an e-mail. Replying lets you send a response to the sender (you can reply to everyone if there are multiple recipients in the e-mail). Forwarding lets you send the entire e-mail to another person, which is often used to send an e-mail to someone not included in the e-mail you received.

People spend a lot of time forwarding e-mails, and even though it's a common practice, beware. Most forwarded e-mails contain bad jokes, untrue information (hoaxes) or just plain unnecessary junk you don't want to read. Do your part by limiting what you forward; just because you think it's true or funny doesn't make it so.

Compose and send an e-mail (cont.)

9

Compose and send an e-mail (cont.)

Composing and sending an e-mail

1 Click Create Mail.

2 In the To: field, type the e-mail for the recipient. If you want to add additional names, separate each e-mail address by a semicolon.

3 Type a subject in the Subject: field.

4 Type the message in the body pane.

5 Format the text as desired using the formatting tools shown.

6 Click Send.

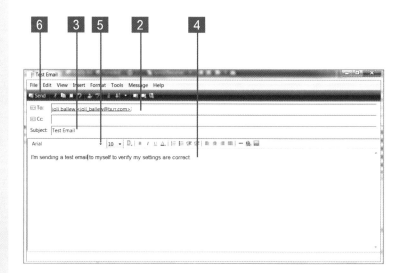

Did you know?

You can choose Tools, and click Select Recipients to choose multiple recipients from your Contact list. This way you can add multiple recipients quickly. There will be more on this later in the Create Groups section.

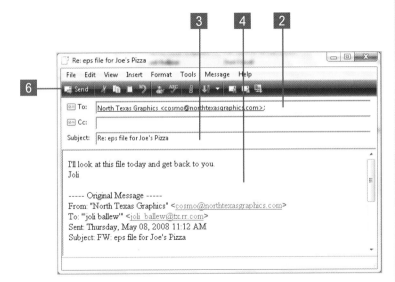

Replying to and forwarding an e-mail

1 Click Reply, Reply All or Forward.

2 In the To: field, type the e-mail for the recipient. If you want to add additional names, separate each e-mail address by a semicolon.

3 Type a subject in the Subject: field.

4 Type the message in the body pane.

5 Format the text as desired using the formatting tools shown.

6 Click Send.

9

Important

Be careful when you click Reply All. Doing so means your response will go to all of the recipients of the original message, including any CC recipients. (It won't go to BCC recipients.) You might mean to tell the sender something private, and end up telling everyone your business!

Attachments

Although e-mail that contains only a message serves its purpose quite a bit of the time, often you'll want to send a photograph, a short video, a sound recording, document or other data. When you want to add something to your message other than text, it's called adding an attachment. There are many ways to attach something to an e-mail.

You can use the Insert menu, and choose File Attachment. Then, you can browse to the location of the attachment, which will probably be in one of your personal folders. As with selecting and deleting multiple files in other scenarios, you can hold down the Ctrl key to select non-contiguous files, or the Shift key to select contiguous ones. The only problem with this method is that you have to be able to browse to the file you want to add. Sometimes, you won't be able to find it quickly or you won't know where it is. There are other ways to attach data.

If you can locate the file you want to attach (probably in your personal folder or its subfolders), you can drag the file to the e-mail in progress. It will attach itself automatically. (It won't be removed from your computer; instead, a copy will be created for the attachment.) The problem with this method is that both windows have to be open to drag from one to the other. Because dragging and dropping requires you to open two windows, Windows Mail and the window that contains the item to attach, and because you have to resize those windows to perform a drag and drop, this method is not suggested here.

You can also right-click the file's icon, select Send To: and select Mail Recipient. This method attaches the files to a new e-mail, which is fine if you want to create a new e-mail. The only problem with this is that it doesn't work if you'd rather send forwards or replies. This method only produces a new e-mail message. However, this method has a feature other methods don't. With it, you can resize any images you've selected before sending them. This is a great perk because many pictures are too large to send via e-mail, and resizing them helps manage an e-mail's size.

You can also e-mail from within applications, such as Microsoft Word or Excel. Generally, you'll find the desired option under the File menu, as a submenu of Send. Other than having to open the file in the appropriate application, there is no downfall to using this method.

9

Attachments (cont.)

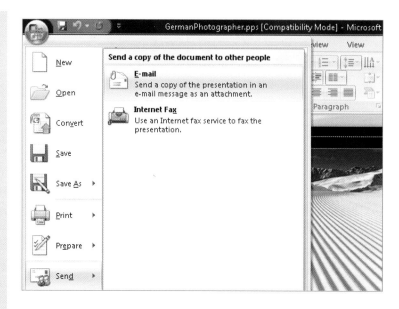

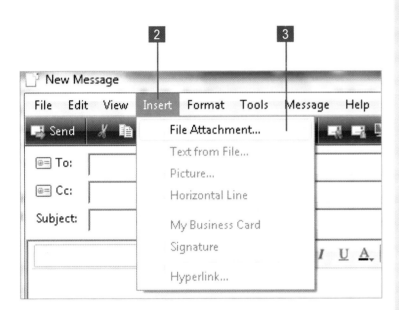

Attaching a picture or file using the Insert menu

1 With Windows Mail open, click Create Mail.

2 Click Insert.

3 Click File Attachment.

4 If the item you want to attach is saved in your Documents folder, skip to step 6.

9

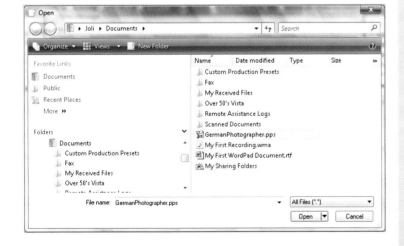

Attachments (cont.)

5 If the item you want to attach is not in the Documents folder, locate the folder's location in the Folders pane. Here, I've selected the Pictures folder and subfolder '2008-05-05 iPhone'.

6 Click the item to add and select Open.

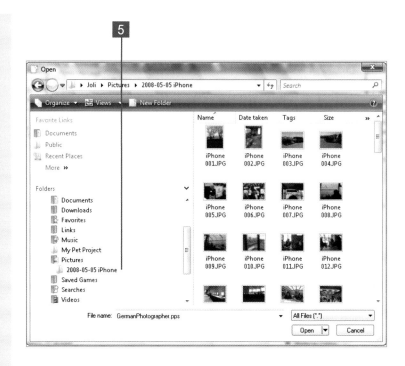

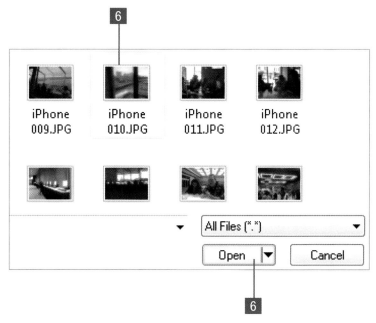

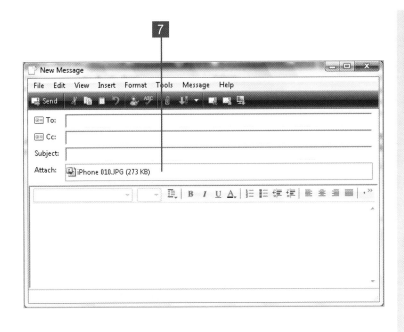

Attachments (cont.)

7 Notice the attachment in the new message.

9

Attachments (cont.)

Attaching a picture or file by right-clicking

1. Locate the picture or file to attach to a new e-mail message. You will probably have to open a folder, unless the file is stored on your desktop.

2. Right-click the file or picture.

3. Select Send To.

4. Click Mail Recipient.

5. Select the appropriate size. I prefer to receive e-mail at the Small size, 800 x 600. At this size they appear perfectly in Windows Mail.

6. Click Attach.

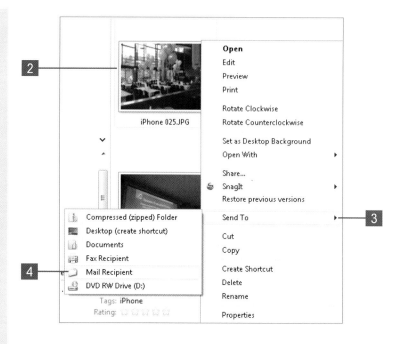

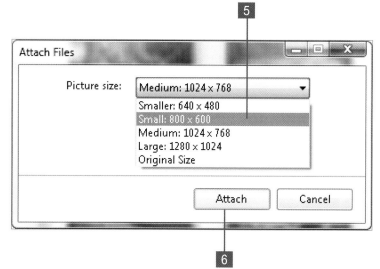

Here's how the image might appear in the recipient's Inbox. This image shows the e-mail in Microsoft Outlook, one of the applications in Microsoft Office 2007.

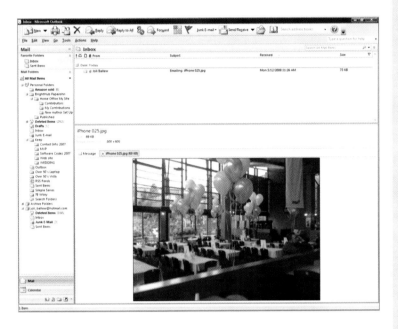

9

Manage contacts

A Windows Mail contact is a data file that holds the information you keep about a person. You can think of it like a digital Rolodex. The contact information looks like a 'contact card', and the information can include a picture, e-mail address, mailing address, first and last name and similar data. By default, Windows Mail creates a contact for each person you e-mail and the data include the e-mail address. You don't need to do anything to the contacts Windows Mail creates unless you want to add data to the contact. Here's a contact Properties page. Notice in this example, data are minimal, and include only a name and e-mail address.

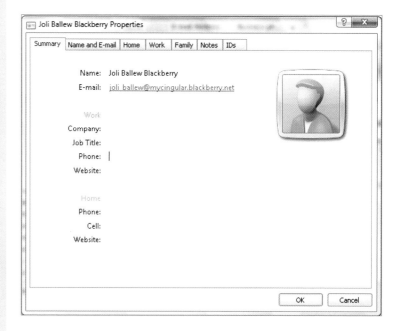

You can easily add data though, using the tabs offered. For instance, from the Home tab, you can add a street address, country or region, phone and other information. There's even a Family tab where you can input gender, birthdays, anniversaries and children's names.

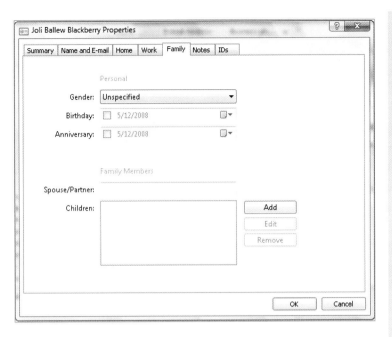

When someone gives you their e-mail address and other personal data, you can create a contact card for them. From the File menu, select New, and then select Contact.

Manage contacts (cont.)

You can see all of your contacts a number of ways, but note that your contacts' information is stored in your personal folder. This makes it easy to back up, because backing up your personal folders will automatically back up your contact data too. To locate your contact data just open your personal folder, and then the Contacts folder.

As you can see here, not all contacts will have an e-mail address; some will contain only phone numbers. You can edit any contact card by double-clicking it. If Animal Control ever gets an e-mail address, I'll be certain to add it here.

You can also access contact information inside Windows Mail in the following ways:

- Click Tools, and click Windows Contacts.
- Click the Contacts button on the toolbar. (It looks like a contact card.)
- Click Create Mail, and in the new mail message click Tools, and click Windows Contacts.
- Click Create Mail, and in the new mail message click Tools and click Select Recipients. Click Properties.

Manage contacts (cont.)

9

Manage contacts (cont.)

Adding a contact

1 From Windows Mail, click the Contacts icon on the toolbar.

2 Click New Contact.

3 Type all of the information you desire to add. Be sure to add information to each tab.

4 Click OK.

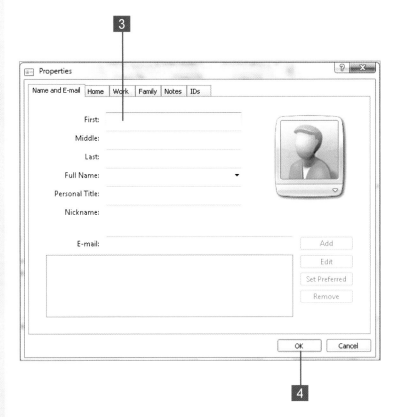

If you forward jokes you receive via e-mail to your kids, friends and/or colleagues, you know each time you forward something you have to manually type each of your recipient's e-mail address for each e-mail you send. Alternatively, you can click Tools, and click Select Recipients to add multiple users quickly. However, it's also possible to create a group of contacts, and when you want to send an e-mail to everyone in the group, you only need select the group; you no longer have to select each recipient individually. Let's look at both of these options for sending e-mail to multiple recipients, first by using the Select Recipients feature and then by creating a group to hold these recipients.

Create a group

Jargon buster

Group – a collection of e-mail addresses you create that are related in some way. You may create a group for people you send jokes to, a group for all your clients (e.g. to send a newsletter) or a group that contains only relatives (e.g. to send 'virtual' Christmas cards).

9

Create a group
(cont.)

Sending an e-mail to multiple recipients

1 In Windows Mail, click Create Mail.

2 Click Tools.

3 Click Select Recipients.

4 In the left pane, select a name from the list.

5 To add that name to the To line, click the To: button. To add the name to the CC line, click the CC: button. To add the name to the Blind CC line, click the BCC: button.

6 Click OK when finished.

Did you know?

You can type your own name in the To: field, and put everyone else in the BCC: field. That way, you'll get a copy of the message you send and others won't be able to see who else received the e-mail or their personal e-mail addresses.

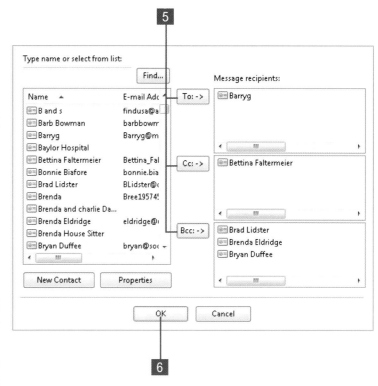

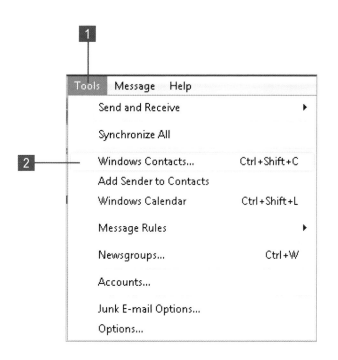

Creating a group

1 Click Tools.

2 Click Windows Contacts. (Alternatively, you could click the Contacts icon on the toolbar.)

3 Click New Contact Group.

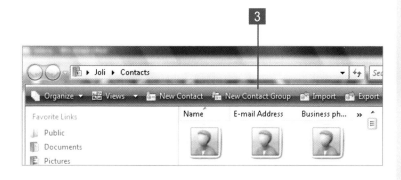

9

Create a group (cont.)

4 Type a name for the group.

5 Click Add to Contact Group.

6 Click the first contact to add. As with selecting and deleting multiple files in other scenarios, you can hold down the Ctrl key to select non-contiguous contacts, or the Shift key to select contiguous ones.

7 Click Add.

8 If you desire, click the Contact Group Details tab and add group information.

9 Click OK.

10 Click the x in the Contacts window, upper right, to close the Contact window.

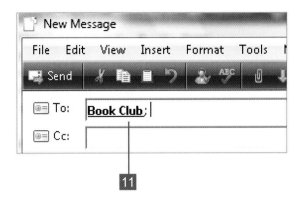

11

For your information

You can remove contacts from the group by selecting the contact and clicking Remove Selected Contacts.

11 Now when you create a new e-mail message, in the To: line, simply type the group name.

9

Unwanted e-mail

Just like you receive unwanted information via the phone and through the post you're going to get advertisements in e-mails. This is referred to as junk e-mail or spam. Unfortunately for you, there's no governing agency placing rules on what can and cannot be sent in an e-mail, as there is with television, radio and other transmission media. This means not only are most of the advertisements scams and rip-offs, they also often contain pornographic images. Even if you were to purchase something via a spam e-mail, it's not guaranteed that the item will arrive or that it will meet any legislation regarding quality. And you can be sure that someone is more interested in having your credit card numbers than sending you an actual product.

Before you read any further, take note: never, never buy anything in a junk e-mail, send money to a sick Nigerian, send money for your portion of a lottery ticket, order medication, reply with bank account numbers, social security numbers, or any other personal information, believe that Bill Gates himself will pay you for forwarding an e-mail to friends, believe you'll have good luck (or bad) if you don't forward a message to friends, or otherwise do anything but delete the e-mail. Do not attempt to unsubscribe from a mailing list, do not click Reply, and do not perpetuate hoaxes.

That said, if you purposefully ask for a legitimate company to send you e-mail, perhaps Amazon.com, it's often OK to click on the link in the e-mail to visit the site. However, always make sure to check the web address once connected. Just because you click on a link in an e-mail to visit www.amazon.com doesn't mean you're going to get there. You might get to a site named www.1234.amazon.com/validate your creditcardnumber, which would indeed be a scam. It's best to delete all spam. And that's all I have to say about that.

There are a lot of options for reducing the amount of junk e-mail, or spam, you receive. First, don't give your e-mail address to any website or company, or include it in any registration card, unless you're willing to receive junk e-mail from them and their partners. Understand that companies collect and sell e-mail addresses for profit. Don't get involved in that. Second, keep Mail's Junk E-mail Options configured as high as you can, and train it to filter unwanted e-mail automatically. Third, if Windows Mail doesn't catch certain spam, create a message rule that will do it for you. With vigilance, you can keep spam to a minimum.

Mail's Junk E-Mail Options

Windows Mail helps you avoid unwanted e-mail messages by catching evident junk e-mail and moving it to the Junk E-mail folder. You get to decide how strict Mail is, as you'll learn shortly. Additionally, you can block messages from specific e-mail addresses by adding them to the Blocked Senders list and prevent blocking of valid e-mail using the Safe Senders list.

There are four filtering options in Windows Mail:

- No Automatic Filtering – use this only if you do not want Windows Mail to block junk e-mail messages. Windows Mail will continue to block messages from e-mail addresses listed on the Blocked Senders list.

- Low – use this option if you receive very little junk e-mail. You can start here and increase the filter if it becomes necessary.

- High – use this option if you receive a lot of junk e-mail and want to block as much of it as possible. Use this option for children's e-mail accounts. Note that some valid e-mail will probably be blocked, so you'll have to review the Junk E-mail folder occasionally, to make sure you aren't missing any e-mail you want to keep.

- Safe List Only – use this option if you only want to receive messages from people or domain names on your Safe Senders list. This is a drastic step, and requires you to add every sender you want to receive mail from to the Safe Senders list. Use this as a last resort.

9

Unwanted e-mail (cont.)

Configuring Windows Mail Junk E-Mail Options

1 Click Tools.

2 Click Junk E-mail Options.

3 From the Options tab, make a selection. We suggest starting at Low and moving to High if necessary later.

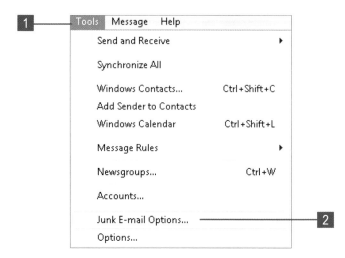

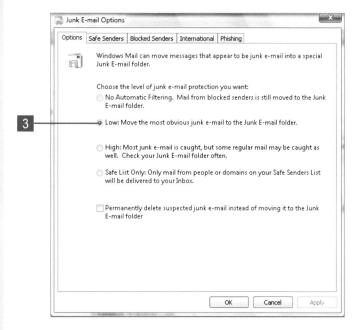

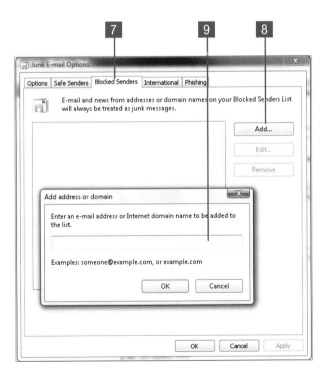

Unwanted e-mail (cont.)

4 Click the Safe Senders tab.

5 Click Add.

6 To add a person to the Safe Senders list, type their e-mail address. To a domain, type the domain name. (Domain names include Amazon.com, Facebook.com or GeneralMotors.com.)

7 Click the Blocked Senders tab.

8 Click Add.

9 To add a person to the Blocked Senders list, type their e-mail address. To a domain, type the domain name. (Domain names include porn.com, hate.com and the like.)

9

Unwanted e-mail (cont.)

10 Click the International tab. Read the information offered and decide if you want to block domains from different countries. By blocking these domains, you will reduce the amount of spam you receive from other countries, in languages you do not understand. To configure this, click Blocked Top-Level Domain List. Then, select the countries to block. Click OK.

11 Click the International tab. Read the information offered and decide if you want to block specific character sets. You can block e-mail from various countries with this method. By blocking these encodings, you will reduce the amount of spam you receive from other countries, in languages you do not understand. To configure this, click Blocked Encoding List. Then, select the countries to block. Click OK.

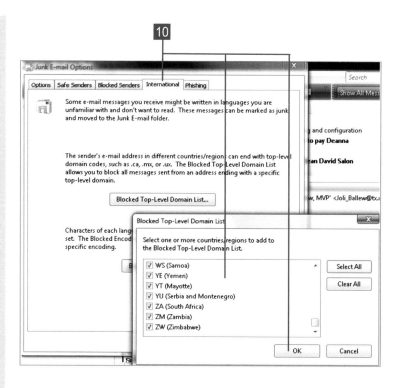

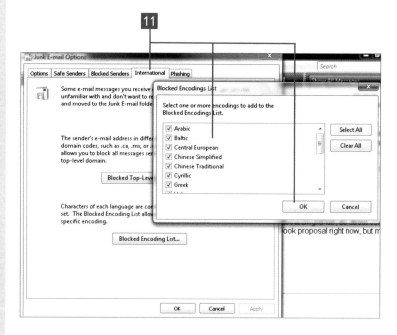

12 Click the Phishing tab.

13 Select Protect my Inbox from messages with potential Phishing links. Additionally, move phishing e-mail to the Junk E-mail folder.

14 Click OK.

9

Unwanted e-mail (cont.)

Getting started with message rules

If the Junk E-mail Options in Windows Mail don't work to get rid of the spam you receive you can supplement the feature by creating your own message rules. You can create rules to put your own specific filters in Mail. For instance, you can create a rule that will automatically delete messages that contain certain words, names of medications and similar data. You create a message rule by clicking the Tools menu, then Message Rules, and then Mail.

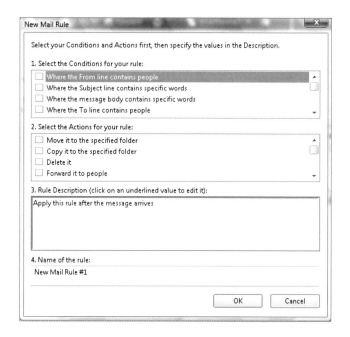

Jargon buster

Message rule – something you create for organising or managing e-mail. You might create a message rule that deletes any incoming e-mail containing the words 'refinance' or 'mortgage', for instance.

As you can see here, it's easy to get started. Just click a condition and a resulting action. For instance, a condition might be to scan incoming e-mail and look for the word Viagra in the body of the e-mail. The action would be to delete it. Now, each time an e-mail arrives with the word Viagra in it, possibly it will automatically be deleted. And yes, this includes e-mails from friends with the word in it, possibly in the form of a joke.

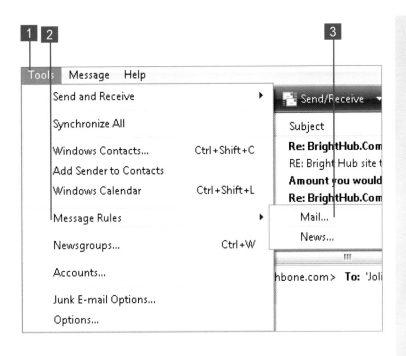

Creating a basic message rule

1 Click Tools.

2 Click Message Rules.

3 Click Mail.

4 Select a condition. For this example, click Where the message body contains specific words.

5 Select an action. For this example, click Delete it.

6 Click contains specific words.

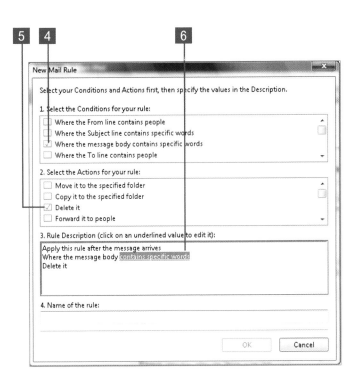

9

Unwanted e-mail (cont.)

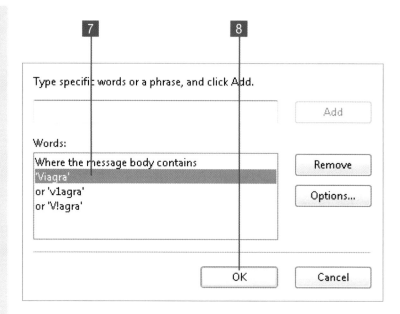

7 Type Viagra. Click Add. Type
v1agra. Click Add. Type
V!agra. Click Add. (As you'll
learn, spammers have learned
about message rules, and
create their own spelling to
get around them.) Feel free to
add other 'words' before
continuing.

8 Click OK.

9 Type Viagra for the name of
the rule.

10 Click OK.

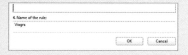

11 Click OK once more to close
all dialogue boxes.

It's important to perform some housekeeping chores once a month or so. If you don't, Windows Mail may become bogged down, perform slower than it should, hang up or shut itself off unexpectedly. Additionally, you may find it hard to manage the e-mail you want to keep and find e-mail when you need to access it again; if every e-mail you want to keep is still in your Inbox you probably have a long list to sift through.

That said, we'll end this chapter with three tasks: creating a new folder to hold e-mail you want to keep and moving mail into it, deleting items in the Sent Items and Deleted Items folders, and changing configuration options in the Options dialogue box.

Keep Windows Mail clean and tidy

9

Keep Windows Mail clean and tidy (cont.)

Creating a new folder

1 Right-click Local Folders.

2 Select New Folder.

3 Type a name for the new folder.

4 Select Local Folders.

5 Click OK.

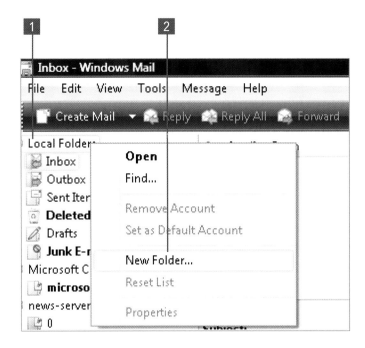

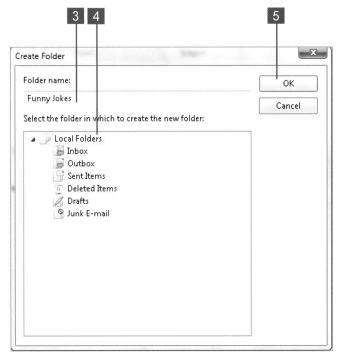

6 Note the new folder in the Local Folders list.

7 To move any e-mail message to the new folder, select it (you probably have to click Inbox first), and drag it to the new folder. Drop it to complete the move.

Did you know?

Using the same technique, you can create subfolders inside folders you create.

9

Keep Windows Mail clean and tidy (cont.)

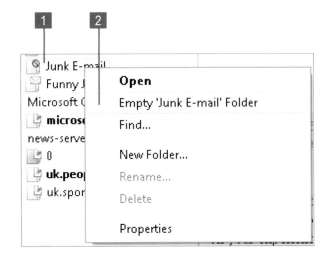

Cleaning Windows Mail

1 Right-click Junk E-mail.

2 Click Empty 'Junk E-mail' Folder.

3 Right-click Deleted Items.

4 Click Empty 'Deleted Items' Folder.

5 Select any e-mail in the Inbox no longer needed, and click the red x to delete it.

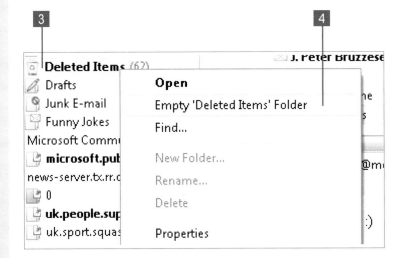

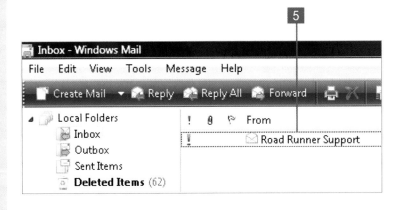

Internet Explorer

Windows Vista comes with Internet Explorer, an application you can use to surf the Internet. Internet Explorer is a 'web browser', and it has everything you need, including a pop-up blocker, zoom settings and accessibility options, as well as tools you can use to save your favourite webpages, set home pages and sign up for read RSS feeds. Internet Explorer has a feature called 'tabbed browsing' too, new to this version of the application. With tabs, you can have multiple webpages open at one time, without having multiple instances of Internet Explorer open and running.

! Important

Internet Explorer 8 is on its way; it's an improved version of what we'll introduce here. No worries though, the look is pretty much the same and you'll be able to find your way around it if and when you decide to install the update.

What you'll do

Open Internet Explorer

Explore tabbed browsing and surfing the Internet

Set up a home page

Mark a Favorite

Organise Favorites

Change the zoom level

View and clear History

Print an entire webpage

Print a selection on a webpage

Configure website fonts and colours

Override website font and colour settings

The Internet Explorer interface

Internet Explorer 7, from here on referred to as IE7, offers all of the tools you'll need to surf the Internet. As with other applications, it has toolbars and icons where you can access everything you need to perform Internet-related tasks. You can save links to your most often accessed websites, use tabs to open multiple websites at the same time, and type words into a Search window to help you locate anything at all on the Web. There's also RSS for subscribing to websites that offer an RSS feed (which allow you to download only current information for the site, which is often news headlines, new articles or new travel discounts), and better security than ever. (Don't worry, you'll learn about RSS later – it's all the rage these days.)

You can open Internet Explorer in a number of ways. If you've enabled Quick Launch on the taskbar, look for the big blue E. Click it once to open the program. You can also open Internet Explorer from the Start menu. It's at the top.

As you can see here, there are several parts to the Internet Explorer interface. These include but are not limited to:

■ Address bar – used to type in Internet addresses, also known as URLs (universal resource locators). Generally, an Internet address takes the form of *http://www.companyname.com*.

■ Command bar – used to access icons such as the Home and Print icons. See Table 11.1 for a list of icons and their uses.

■ Tabs – used to access websites when multiple sites are open.

■ Search window – used to search for anything on the Internet.

■ Status bar – used to find information about the current activity.

Address bar   Tabs   Command bar Search window

Status bar

The Internet Explorer interface (cont.)

Table 10.1 Command bar icons from left to right	
Command bar icon	**What it does**
Favorites Center	View Favorites you've added RSS feeds to, and browsing history.
Add to Favorites	Add the current page to your Favorites list.
Home	Access your home page (or home pages). This icon includes a drop-down menu too, which lets you change your home page(s) and add and remove home page(s).
Feeds	Provides a way to manage the RSS feeds you subscribe to.
Print	Lets you print a webpage (or part of one).
Page	Offers a drop-down menu that allows access to features such as zoom and text size. You can also send a copy of the page you're viewing as an e-mail attachment.
Tools	Offers a drop-down menu that lets you access security feature configuration, Internet Options, and personalisation options.
Help	Offers a drop-down menu that is similar to the Help menu item in the Classic Menu.

Note: throughout this chapter you'll learn how to use these and other features of Internet Explorer; all you need to learn from the above are the names of the interface features.

Locating a website

Your first order of business is to type in a URL and go to a website. URLs and website names (as far as we're concerned right now) start with http://www. I don't want to go into detail about why this is, but suffice it to say, in almost all instances you'll need to type this first. After the www., you'll type the website's name. Often this is the name of the company, like Amazon or Microsoft, and its ending, which is often .com, .edu, .gov, .org or .net.

?

Did you know?

.com is the most popular website ending, and it means the website is a company, business or personal website. .edu is used for educational institutions, .gov for government entities, .org for non-profit organisations (mostly), and .net for miscellaneous businesses and companies, or personal websites. There are others though, including .info, .biz, .tv and .uk.com.

Here are some examples of websites you can type into the address bar:

- http://www.microsoft.com/uk

- http://www.amazon.com

- http://www.greatbritain.com

?

Did you know?

When a website name starts with https://, it means it's secure. When purchasing items online, make sure the payment pages have this prefix.

Terms to know

There are a few words you're going to see often, including URL, link, website and others. To get the most out of this chapter, you need to know what these mean. Here are some terms you should know before continuing:

- Domain name – for our use here, a domain name is synonymous with a website name.

- Favorite – a webpage that you've chosen to maintain a shortcut for in the Favorites Center.

- Home page – the webpage that opens when you open IE7. You can set the home page and configure additional pages to open as well.

10

- Link – a shortcut to a webpage. Links are often offered in an e-mail, document or webpage to allow you to access a site without having to actually type in its name. In almost all instances, links are underlined and in a different colour than the page they are configured on.

- Load – a webpage must 'load' before you can access it. Some pages load instantly while others take a few seconds.

- Navigate – the process of moving from one webpage to another or viewing items on a single webpage. Often the term is used as follows: 'Click the link to navigate to the new webpage.'

- Search – a term used when you type a word or group of words into a Search window. Searching for data produces results.

- Scroll up and scroll down – a process of using the scroll bars on a webpage or the arrow keys on a keyboard to move up and down the pages of a website.

- Website – a group of webpages that contains related information. Microsoft's website contains information about Microsoft products, for instance.

- URL – the information you type to access a website, like http://www.microsoft.com.

Tips for using IE7

There are a few tips and tricks you can use when using IE7. The first one I want to mention applies to typing in a website using the address bar. You'll want to commit this key combination to memory: Ctrl + Enter. Here's how it works. Instead of typing, say, http://www.microsoft.com into the Address bar, just type Microsoft. Then, hold down the Ctrl key on the keyboard and press the Enter key. IE7 will automatically add the http://www to the beginning and .com to the end!

There are other key combinations and mouse movements you might want to use once you've navigated to a website. Mouse options are shown in Table 11.2. Keyboard shortcuts are shown in Table 11.3.

Table 10.2 Mouse action shortcuts

Mouse action	What it does
Click the middle mouse button once	Open a link for a webpage in a tab other than the one you're using.
Click the middle mouse button on the tab	Close the active tab.
Double-click an empty space to the right of the New Tab button	Open a new tab that does not contain a website.
Ctrl + mouse wheel up	Zoom page by 10 per cent.
Ctrl + mouse wheel down	Decrease page zoom by 10 per cent.

Table 10.3 Keyboard shortcuts

Keyboard shortcut	What it does
Alt+left arrow key	Go to the previous page visited in the current tab.
Alt+right arrow key	Go forward to a page visited in the current tab.
F11	Toggle between full-screen mode and 'regular' mode.
Esc	Stop the current page from loading.
Alt+Home	Go to your home page.
Ctrl+Enter	Automatically add www and .com to what you typed in the Address bar.
Alt+F4	Close the current tab.
Ctrl+D	Add the current page to your Favorites list.
Shift+mouse click	Open a link in a new window.
Ctrl+mouse click	Open a link in new background tab.
Ctrl+Shift+mouse click	Open a link in new foreground tab.
Ctrl+T	Open a new tab.
Ctrl+Tab	Switch between available tabs.
Ctrl+(+)	Zoom page by 10 per cent.
Ctrl+(-)	Decrease page zoom by 10 per cent.
Ctrl+0	Zoom to 100 per cent (normal view).

10

The Internet Explorer interface (cont.)

Opening Internet Explorer

1 Click Start.

2 Click Internet.

Timesaver tip

You can also click the IE7 icon in the Quick Launch area.

Jargon buster

Surfing – the act of moving from website to website and viewing webpages. Often surfing is called 'googling', 'searching' or 'browsing'.

Exploring tabbed browsing and surfing the Internet

1 With Internet Explorer open, drag your mouse over the address currently showing on the Address bar. Do this even if the Address bar shows about:blank. The contents of the Address bar should appear blue.

2 Type the following: http://www.microsoft.com/uk

3 Use the scroll bars to view the entire webpage.

4 Look for a link named Support. When you hover your mouse over the word Support, the mouse icon will change to a hand. (Webpages change often, so you might not see Support exactly where it's shown here. If you can't find Support, click any link.)

10

The Internet Explorer interface (cont.)

5 Notice your Support options. Click Help & Support Home. (Again, webpages change, so this may not be exactly what you see.)

6 Read and browse the page as desired.

7 Using your keyboard, hold down the Ctrl key and then press the letter T. A new tab will appear.

8 In the new tab's Address bar, type amazon.

9 Hold down the Ctrl key, and press Enter. Notice the http://www and .com are added automatically.

10 Click the blank tab at the end of the open tab.

11 Type London in the Address bar.

12 Click Enter on the keyboard.

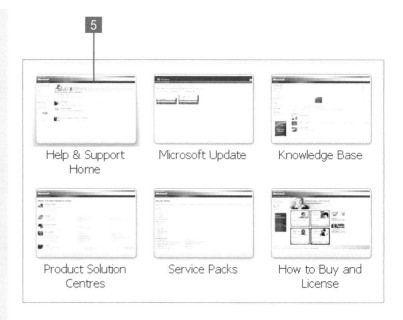

Help & Support Home   Microsoft Update   Knowledge Base

Product Solution Centres   Service Packs   How to Buy and License

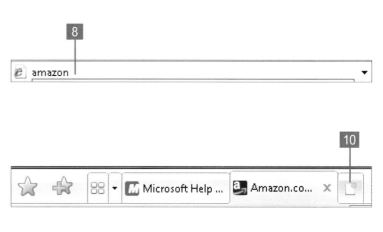

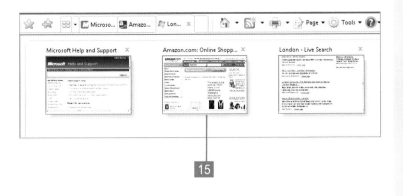

13 Try to locate a link to BBC – London – London Homepage. Since webpages and results change often, you may or may not see this. Whatever the case, click the link to navigate to that page. (Alternatively, you could type www.bbc.co.uk/London to access the page manually.)

14 Click the Quick Tabs button. It's located to the left of the first tab, and has four squares on it.

15 Notice all of your open pages are shown on a single page. Click any page to go to the webpage.

16 Click the Alt key once on your keyboard. Notice that a menu bar appears. You can use these menus as you would in any other application; click each menu title one time to see the options underneath. One thing you might be particularly interested in is Help, specifically, Internet Explorer Tour.

16 Click the x in the top right corner of IE7.

17 If you're prompted to close all open tabs, click Yes.

10

Personalise Internet Explorer

There are many more ways to personalise IE7 than we have room to detail here. However, there are a few things you will certainly want to know how to do, including adding a home page or multiple home pages, adding and organising Favorites and using the Zoom feature.

Designate home pages

You may recall that previous versions of Internet Explorer let you mark a webpage as your home page, and that page would be displayed each time you opened IE7. Starting with Internet Explorer 7, you can now assign multiple webpages as home pages. With multiple pages marked, when you start IE7, each website automatically loads in its own tab.

There are a number of ways to assign webpages as home pages, but you must always navigate to the pages first. Once you've opened a webpage you want to add as a home page, click the arrow next to the Home button and choose Add or Change Home Page. You can then choose from three options:

- Use this webpage as your only home page – select this option if you only want one page to serve as your home page.

- Add this webpage to your home pages tabs – select this option if you want this page to be one of several home pages.

- Use the current tab set as your home page – select this option if you've opened multiple tabs and you want all of them to be home pages.

Jargon buster

Home page – the web page that opens when you open Internet Explorer. The home page may be presented by your ISP but you can change it.

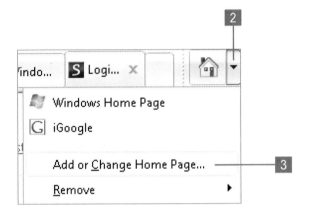

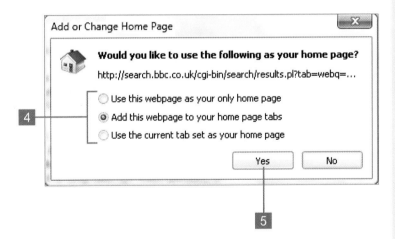

Setting a home page

1 In IE7, use the Address bar to locate a webpage you want to use as your home page.

2 Click the arrow next to the Home icon.

3 Click Add or Change Home Page.

4 Make a selection using the information provided regarding each option.

5 Click Yes.

6 Repeat these steps as necessary.

10

Save and organise Favorites

Favorites are websites you save links to for accessing more easily at a later time. They differ from home pages because, by default, they do not open when you start IE7. The Favorites you save appear in the Favorites Center, which you can access by clicking the large yellow star on the Command bar. You will see some Favorites listed, including Microsoft Websites and MSN

Personalise Internet Explorer (cont.)

Websites. You can use the Favorites Center to quickly access your Favorites, places you've recently visited and any RSS feeds you've subscribed to, and they're all accessible from one location. Every time you save a Favorite, it will appear here.

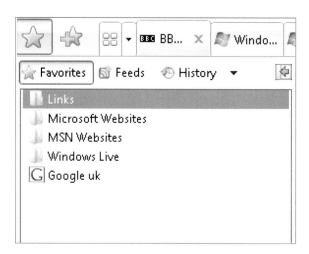

Did you know?

You can also access Favorites from the Favorites menu (which you can access by pressing Alt on the keyboard), if you're a fan of menus.

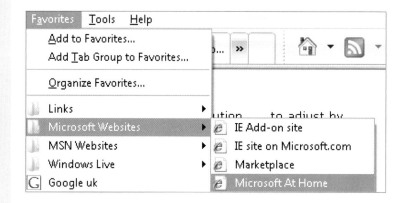

In addition to holding links to your favourite websites, the Favorites Center includes access to History and Feeds. Feeds contain links to RSS feeds to which you've subscribed. History lists the links to the webpages you visited recently. Take a look at the History list here.

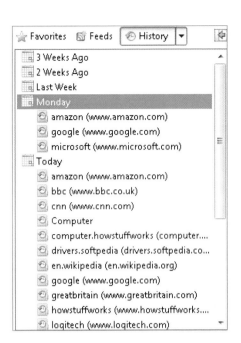

When adding favourites, you have two options. You can either add a single webpage as a Favorite or add a group of webpages to create a Tab Group of Favorites.

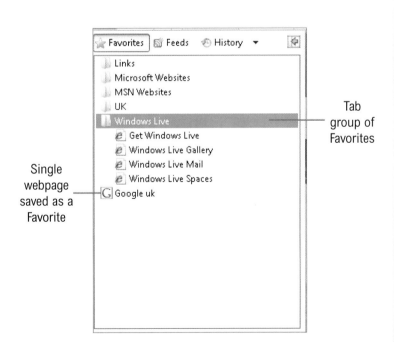

Single
webpage
saved as a
Favorite

Tab
group of
Favorites

10

Personalise Internet Explorer (cont.)

Making a Favorite

1 Go to the webpage (or webpages) you want to configure as a Favorite (or Group of Favorites).

2 Click the Add to Favorites icon.

3 To add a single webpage as a Favorite, click Add to Favorites. To add all open websites (every tab that's open) as a tab group, select Add Tab Group to Favorites.

4 Type a Name or a Tab Group Name when prompted.

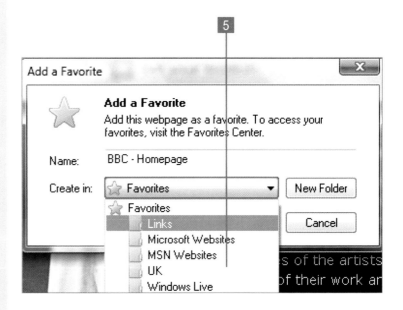

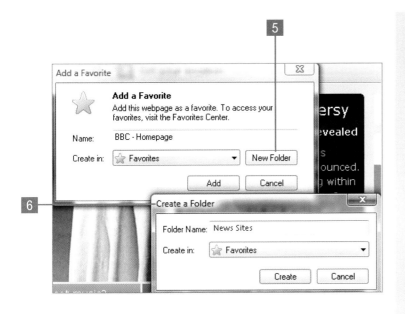

5 If you are saving a single webpage, in the Create in drop-down list, select a folder to save the Favorite to. If you don't see a folder you like, click New Folder instead.

6 If you selected New Folder, type a folder name and click Create.

7 Click Add.

8 If you are saving a Tab Group, type in a Tab Group Name.

9 Leave Create in set to Favorites. (This will create a new tab group in the Favorites folder that contains links to all of the pages in your group.)

10 Click Add.

There will probably come a time when your Favorites Center becomes unwieldy. Perhaps you haphazardly saved Favorites and now need to organise them, or maybe you have Favorites you want to delete. You may even have Favorites you want to move to another Tab Group. While you can do this inside the Favorites Center by right-clicking and dragging and dropping files, a better way is to open the Favorites folder inside your personal folder. That's because each time you make a change in the Favorites Center, it closes. This does not happen with the Favorites folder.

Personalise Internet Explorer (cont.)

Organising Favorites

1 Click Start.

2 Click your personal folder.

3 Double-click the Favorites folder to open it.

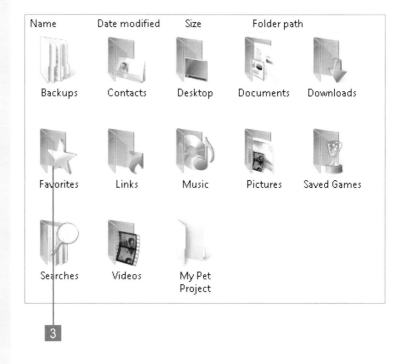

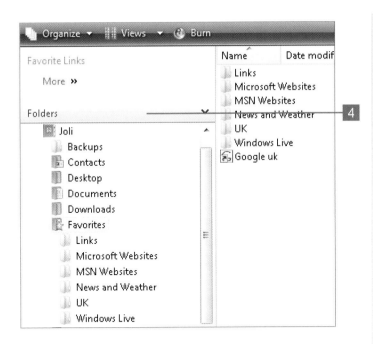

4 Drag the Folders pane so you can see the content of the Favorites folder.

5 Click any subfolder under Favorites to see its contents.

6 To delete an entire subfolder, right-click it and choose Delete. This will delete the subfolder and all of its contents.

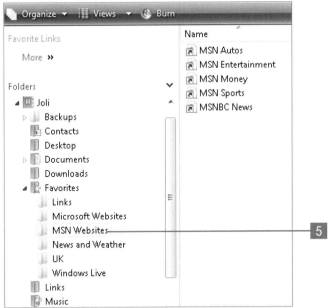

10

Personalise Internet Explorer (cont.)

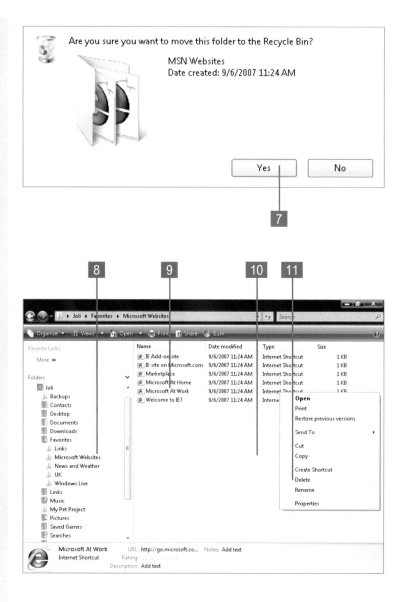

7 When prompted, click Yes.

8 In the Folders pane, under Favorites, select a subfolder that contains a Favorite link you'd like to delete.

9 Select the link.

10 Right-click the link.

11 Click Delete.

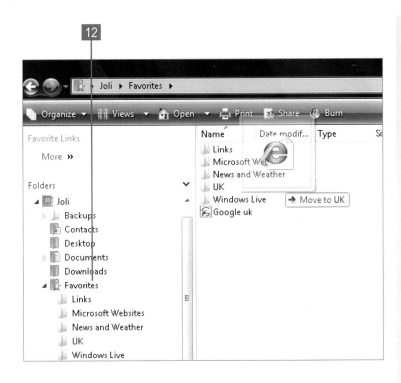

12 To move a Favorite link from one subfolder to another, or from the Favorites folder to a subfolder, select it and drag it to the desired folder.

13 Repeat these steps as necessary.

14 Click the x in the top right corner of the Favorites folder to close it.

10

Personalise Internet Explorer (cont.)

Using Text Size and Page Zoom

If you have trouble reading what's on a webpage because the text is too small, you can make it larger in two specific ways. First, you can access the Text Size options from the View menu, and choose from Largest, Larger, Medium (the default), Smaller and Smallest. Remember, this menu doesn't appear by default, so you'll have to tap the Alt key on the keyboard to make it visible. This option works okay, but often it changes the layout of the webpage because it causes the text to become so large that it runs over images or other text on the page. Here's an example.

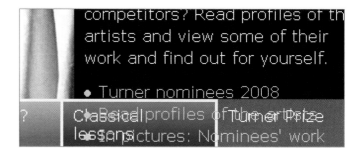

Another option is to use the new Page Zoom feature. Unlike the Text Size options, Page Zoom works by preserving the fundamental design of the webpage you're viewing. This means that Page Zoom intelligently zooms in on the entire page, which maintains the page's integrity, layout and look.

The Page Zoom options are located under the Page icon on the Command bar, under Zoom, but it's much easier to use the link at the bottom right of the browser window, on the Status bar. Just click it to show zoom options.

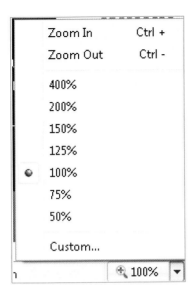

In the example, we'll stick with the zoom options on the Status bar.

10

Personalise Internet Explorer (cont.)

Changing the zoom level

1 Open Internet Explorer and browse to a webpage.

2 Click the arrow located at the bottom right of the Status bar to show the zoom options.

3 Click 150%.

4 Notice how the webpage text and images increase. Use the scroll bars to navigate the page.

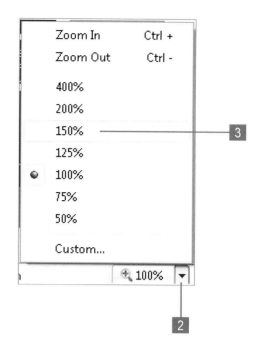

There's a lot going on behind the scenes in IE7 and a lot of it is security-related. There's a pop-up blocker to keep unwanted ads from appearing when you visit webpages configured with them, there's a phishing filter to block you from accessing websites that have been reported to Microsoft as suspicious, and there are preconfigured Security Zones and Privacy Settings to help protect against any other threats you may run across while surfing the Web. Since much of this is preconfigured, and because security is covered in Chapter 11, we won't go into the details here regarding those features.

However, there are a few things to discuss; specifically cleaning up IE7 by deleting files that can be used to trace where you've been on the Internet. If your grandchildren use your computer, and do not have their own user account, you'll want to do this before they start surfing the Web. You'll also want to print information from webpages and configure accessibility options.

Deleting your web footprint

If you don't want people to be able to snoop around on your computer and find out what sites you've been visiting, first, create a password-protected user account for yourself. If you're worried beyond that, or if you don't always log off when you've finished using the computer (or if you're doing something online you shouldn't be!) you'll want to use a new feature called Delete Browsing History. Delete Browsing History is located under the Tools menu.

Work with Internet Explorer

Jargon buster

Footprint – the trail you leave behind after you've finished surfing the Web.

Work with Internet Explorer (cont.)

Delete Browsing History lets you delete the following files:

- Temporary Internet Files – these are files that have been downloaded and saved in your Temporary Internet Files folder. A snooper could go through these files to see what you've been doing online.

- Cookies – these are small text files that include data that identify your preferences when you visit particular websites. Cookies are what allow you to visit, say, www.amazon.com and be greeted with Hello <your name>. We have recommendations for you! Cookies help a site offer you a personalised web experience.

- History – this is the list of websites you've visited and any web addresses you've typed. Anyone can look at your History list to see where you've been.

- Form data – information that's been saved using Internet Explorer's autocomplete form data functionality. If you don't want forms to be filled out automatically by you or someone else who has access to your PC and user account, delete this.

- Passwords – passwords that were saved using Internet Explorer autocomplete password prompts.

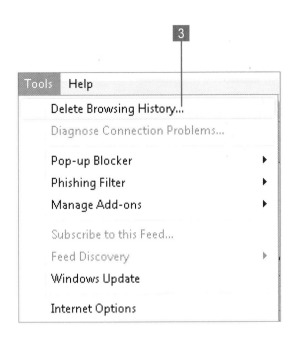

Viewing and clearing History

1 In IE7, click the Alt key.

2 Click Tools.

3 Click Delete Browsing History.

4 To delete any or all of the listed items, click the Delete button.

5 Click Close when finished.

10

Work with Internet Explorer (cont.)

Printing

Printing features are accessed, of all places, from the Print icon on the Command bar. Clicking the Print icon one time will print the page to the PC's default printer. You won't be able to set options (although it's somewhat likely the same options you configured last time will still apply). Clicking the arrow next to the Print icon offers the menu shown here; clicking the Print icon will take you directly to the Print dialogue box.

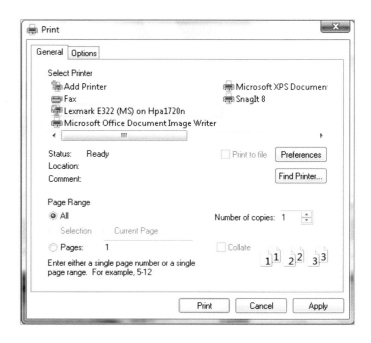

There are three menu options under the Print icon:

- Print – clicking Print opens the Print dialogue box where you can configure the page range, select a printer, change page orientation, change print order and choose a paper type. Additional options include print quality, output bins and more. Of course, the choices offered depend on what your printer offers. If your printer can only print at 300 x 300 dots per inch, you can't configure it to print at a higher quality.

- Print Preview – clicking Print Preview opens a window where you can see before you print what the printout will actually look like. You can switch between portrait and landscape views, access the Page Setup dialogue box and more.

- Page Setup – clicking Page Setup opens the Page Setup dialogue box. Here you can select a paper size, source, and create headers and footers. You can also change orientation and margins, all of which is dependent on what features your printer supports.

You'll use these options as desired to print webpages.

Work with Internet Explorer (cont.)

10

Work with
Internet Explorer
(cont.)

Printing an entire webpage

1. Locate a page on the Internet you'd like to print.

2. To print the page without configuring any print options or preferences, click the Print icon.

3. To see how the page will look after it's printed, click the down-arrow next to the Print icon and choose Print Preview.

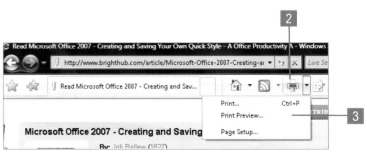

4. If you are happy with the way it looks, click the Print icon in the top left corner of the window and the page will print. If you do not like the way it appears, click the x in the top right corner to close the window and skip to Step 5.

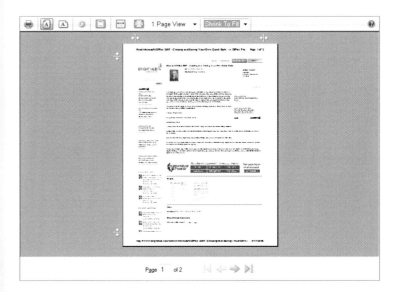

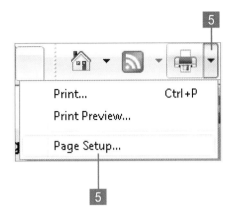

5 Click the arrow next to the Print icon and click Page Setup.

6 In the Page Setup dialogue box, click the down-arrows to apply a paper size, source and other options.

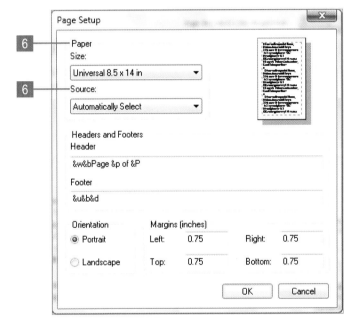

Work with Internet Explorer (cont.)

7 In the Page Setup dialogue box, click the desired orientation.

8 Click OK.

9 Click the arrow next to the Print icon and choose Print.

10 What happens next depends on how many printers you have installed. If you have more than one, you'll need to select a printer and, depending on the printer make and model, you may be able to configure preferences for the printer, including what paper tray to use, how much ink to apply, etc.

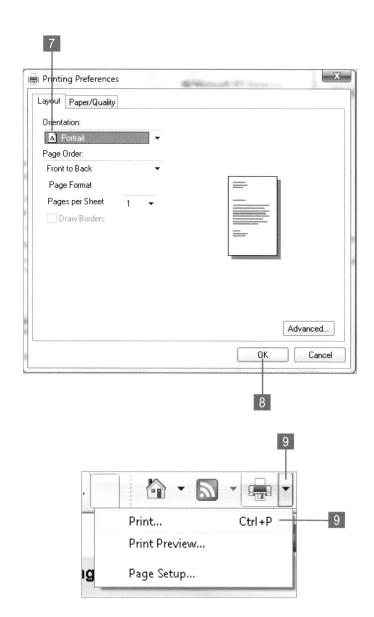

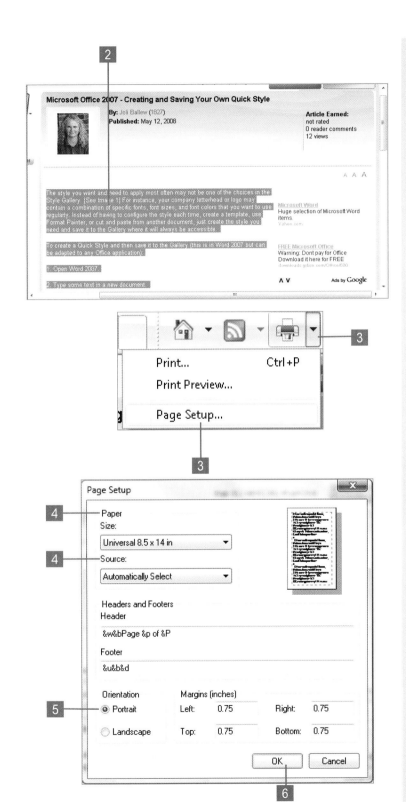

Printing a selection on a webpage

1 Locate a page on the Internet you'd like to print.

2 If you do not want to print the entire webpage, which often includes advertisements and unnecessary data, use your mouse to highlight what you want to print.

3 Click the arrow next to the Print icon and click Page Setup.

4 In the Page Setup dialogue box, click the down-arrows to apply a paper size, source, and other options.

5 In the Page Setup dialogue box, click the desired orientation.

6 Click OK.

10

Work with Internet Explorer (cont.)

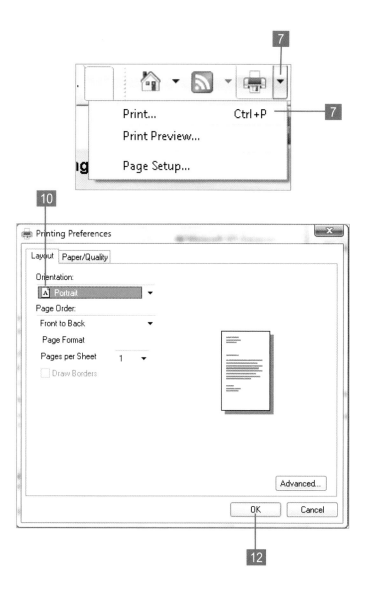

7 Click the arrow next to the Print icon and choose Print.

8 Select a printer.

9 Click Preferences.

10 Configure preferences as desired.

11 Under Page Range, choose Selection.

12 Click OK.

13 Click Print.

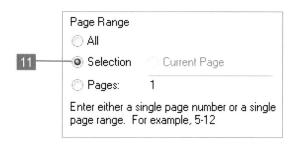

Accessibility options

If Zoom doesn't allow you to view webpages effectively, because other issues exist (colour blindness, visual impairment or other disability), you can completely change the appearance of webpages by configuring the accessibility options in IE7. For the most part this involves selecting your own fonts and colours, and overriding the fonts and colours set by the web designer. You can also specify the colour used for links in webpages to make those links stand out. These customisations are useful if you have impaired vision, but also if you simply want to view larger fonts or need high-contrast colours. Accessibility options are located in Internet Options, which you will open from the Tools menu.

Work with Internet Explorer (cont.)

10

Work with Internet Explorer (cont.)

Configuring website fonts and colours

1 Open Internet Explorer.

2 Click Tools.

3 Click Internet Options.

4 Click the General tab if it is not already selected.

5 Click Fonts.

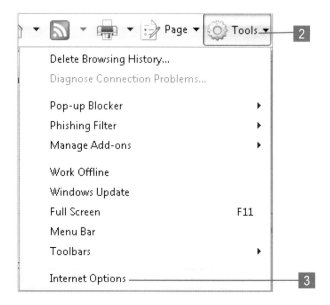

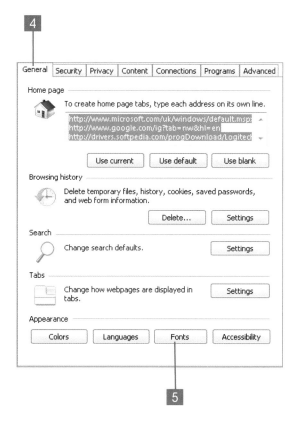

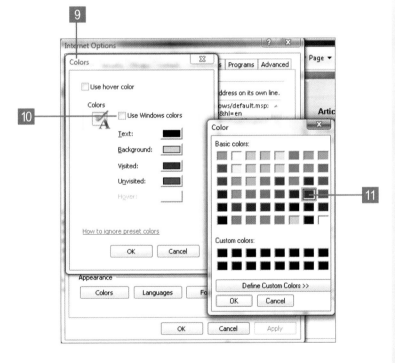

6 Select the webpage font to use by selecting it in the list.

7 Select the plain text font to use by selecting it from the list.

8 Click OK

9 Click Colors. (Back at the General tab.)

10 Clear the Use Windows colors tick box.

11 Click any colour box.

12 Select a colour and click OK.

13 Continue selecting colours until you are finished.

14 Click OK.

15 Click OK.

10

Work with Internet Explorer (cont.)

Overriding website font and colour settings

1. Open Internet Explorer.
2. Click Tools.
3. Click Internet Options.
4. Click Accessibility.
5. Tick the boxes for: Ignore colors specified on webpages; Ignore font styles specified on webpages; and Ignore font sizes specified on webpages.
6. Click OK.
7. Click OK.

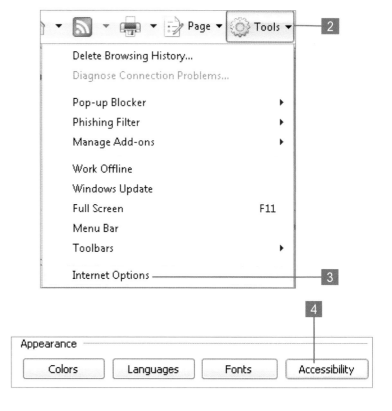

Staying secure

Introduction

Windows Vista comes with a lot of built-in features to keep you and your data safe from Internet ills, nosy children and download-happy grandchildren. Vista also offers help in avoiding e-mail and web criminals whose only purpose in life is to steal your data, get your bank account or credit card numbers, or steal your identity. Mail even informs you if it thinks an e-mail is 'phishing' for information you shouldn't give out.

Now, your reaction to these statements may be that you feel I've exaggerated the actual computer threats you may encounter, or it may make you not want to share your computer, go online or read e-mail ever again. Whatever the case, it's important to understand there are threats out there, and Vista does its best to offer you protection. If you take advantage of the available safeguards, you'll be protected in almost all cases. You just need to be aware of the dangers, heed warnings when they are given and use all of the available features in Vista to protect yourself and your PC.

Your PC was not shipped to you with all of the available safety measures in place. While many measures are enabled by default, which you'll learn about later, some require intervention from you.

Here's an example. If you have grandchildren who use your computer, they can probably access or delete your personal data, download harmful content, install applications or change settings that will affect the entire computer, all very easily. You can solve all of these problems by creating a computer

What you'll do

Add a new user account

Require passwords

Enable System Restore

Configure Windows Update

Use Windows Firewall

Use Windows Defender

Resolve Security Center Warnings

Set up Parental Controls

Create your first backup

account just for them. In conjunction, every account you create should be password-protected, especially yours. It wouldn't do much good to create accounts and not assign passwords!

Beyond creating user accounts, here are some other ways to protect your PC, which we'll discuss in depth in this chapter:

- System Restore – if enabled, Vista stores 'restore points' on your PC's hard drive. If something goes wrong you can run System Restore, choose one of these points and revert to a pre-problem date. Since System Restore only deals with 'system data', none of your personal data will be affected (not even your last e-mail).

- Windows Update – if enabled and configured properly, when you are online, Vista will check for security updates automatically and install them. You don't have to do anything, and your PC is always updated with the latest security patches and features.

- Windows Firewall – if enabled and configured properly, the firewall will help prevent hackers (people whose job it is to get into your computer and do harm to it) from accessing your PC and data. The firewall blocks most programs from communicating outside the network (or outside your PC). If you want to allow a program to communicate outside your safety zone you can 'allow' a program by adding it to an 'exceptions' list. This is all very easy to do.

- Windows Defender – you don't have to do much to Windows Defender except understand that it offers protection against Internet threats. It's enabled by default and it runs in the background. However, if you ever think your computer has been attacked by an Internet threat (virus, worm, malware, etc.) you can run a manual scan here.

- Security Center warnings – the Security Center is a talkative application. You can be sure you'll see a pop-up if your anti-virus software is out of date (or not installed), if you don't have the proper security settings configured, or if Windows Update or the Firewall is disabled. You'll also get a user account control prompt each time you want to install a program or make system-wide changes. You'll learn about warnings and what to do about them in this chapter.

- Parental Controls – if you have grandchildren, children or even a forgetful or scatterbrained partner who needs imposed computer limitations, you can apply them using Parental Controls. With these controls you are in charge of the hours a user can access the computer, which games they can play and what programs they can run (among other things).

- Backup and Restore Center – this feature lets you perform backups and, in the case of a computer failure, restore them (put them back). However, there are other backup options too, including copying files to a CD or DVD, copying pictures and media to an external hard drive, USB drive or memory card, or storing them on an Internet server.

User accounts and passwords

If every person who accesses your PC has their own standard user account and password, and if every person logs on using that account and then logs off the PC each time they're finished using it, you'd never have to worry about anyone accessing anyone else's personal data. That's because when a user logs on with his own user account, he can only access his data (and any data other users have specifically elected to share).

Additionally, every user with his or her own user account is provided with a 'user profile' that tells Vista what desktop background to use, what screen saver, and preferences for mouse settings, sounds and more. Each user also has their own Favorites in Internet Explorer 7, and their own e-mail settings, address books and personal folders. User accounts help everyone who accesses the computer keep their personal data, well, personal.

Also, by creating standard accounts for users (yes, even yourself) instead of administrator accounts, you can keep the computer safe by requiring administrator credentials to make system-wide changes like installing applications, changing security settings and accessing every file on the PC. Even if you are the only person who accesses your PC, you should still create a standard account for yourself and use it. If someone does break into your home or come by unexpectedly, they won't be able to use your PC without your standard account password. And, if they try to do something that may harm the PC, they'll also have to know your administrator credentials and administrator password. That being the case, hackers won't be able to get in as easily either.

Adding a new user account for a child, grandchild or partner

1 Click Start.

2 Click Control Panel.

3 Click Add or remove user accounts.

4 Click Create a new account.

Important

If your administrator account is not password-protected, or if you see any other accounts that are not password-protected, work through the instructions on page 326 to apply them.

User accounts and passwords (cont.)

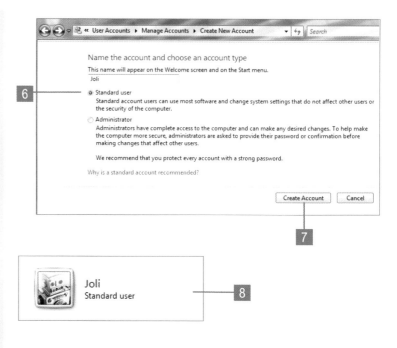

5 Type a new account name. This should be the user's name. If you are creating a new standard account for yourself, stop. Read the section **The administrator account dilemma** before continuing. These steps are for creating an account for someone else, like a child, grandchild or partner.

6 Verify Standard user is selected.

7 Click Create Account.

8 Click the new account.

9 Click Create a password.

10 Type the new password, type it again to confirm it and type a password hint.

11 Click Create password.

12 Click the x in the top right corner to close the window.

For your information

You can also click Change the picture, Change the account name, Remove the password and other options to further personalise the account.

320

The administrator account dilemma

It's very likely you're logging on to your PC using an administrator account. That's because when you set up Vista, it made you create an administrator account! Nowhere did it tell you to create a standard account later or otherwise inform you of the importance of it. That said, all of your personal data, preferences, e-mail settings and other configurations are probably applied to an administrator account, which causes several problems with moving to a standard account.

As stated, you should be using a standard account exclusively. Unfortunately, if you simply create a new standard account for yourself, when you log on to the PC using your new account, it's like logging on to the PC for the first time. You have to reconfigure your desktop background, screen saver, applications, e-mail, Internet Favorites, and find some way to move or copy your personal folders to the new account. Although it's not impossible, it is a royal pain. That being the case, if you really want to switch from an administrator account to a standard one, you'll have to work through the steps in Move from an administrator to a standard account.

Finding out account status

To find out if you're logging on using an Administrator account:

1 Click Start.

2 Click Control Panel.

3 Click Add or remove user accounts.

4 If the account you log on with says Administrator, as shown here, you're using an Administrator account.

Joli Ballew
Administrator
Password protected

4

User accounts and passwords (cont.)

Moving from an administrator to a standard account

1 Click Start.

2 Click Control Panel.

3 Click Add or remove user accounts.

4 Click Create a new account.

Important

Only work through these steps if you've read The Administrator Account Dilemma and are positive you currently log on using an administrator account.

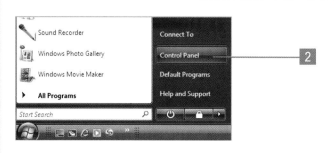

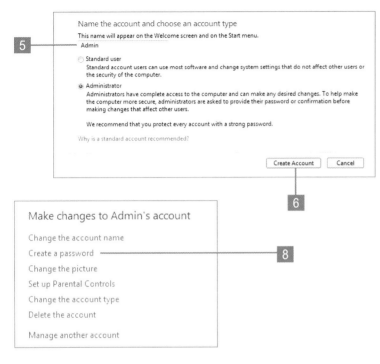

Name the account and choose an account type

This name will appear on the Welcome screen and on the Start menu.

Admin

○ Standard user
Standard account users can use most software and change system settings that do not affect other users or the security of the computer.

◉ Administrator
Administrators have complete access to the computer and can make any desired changes. To help make the computer more secure, administrators are asked to provide their password or confirmation before making changes that affect other users.

We recommend that you protect every account with a strong password.

Why is a standard account recommended?

Create Account   Cancel

Make changes to Admin's account

Change the account name
Create a password
Change the picture
Set up Parental Controls
Change the account type
Delete the account

Manage another account

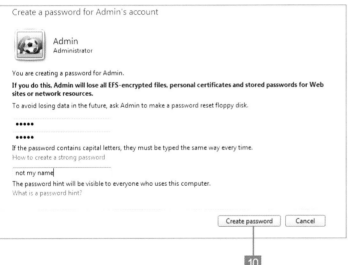

Create a password for Admin's account

Admin
Administrator

You are creating a password for Admin.

If you do this, Admin will lose all EFS-encrypted files, personal certificates and stored passwords for Web sites or network resources.

To avoid losing data in the future, ask Admin to make a password reset floppy disk.

•••••

•••••

If the password contains capital letters, they must be typed the same way every time.
How to create a strong password

not my name

The password hint will be visible to everyone who uses this computer.
What is a password hint?

Create password   Cancel

5 Type Admin for the account name. Select Administrator.

6 Click Create Account.

Admin
Administrator

7 Click the new Admin account.

8 Click Create a password.

9 Type the new password, type it again to confirm it and type a password hint. It's best to create a password that contains upper- and lower-case letters and a few numbers. Write the password down and keep it somewhere out of sight and safe. Each time you need to make a system-wide change, you'll need to input Admin and the password to obtain access.

10 Click Create password.

User accounts and passwords (cont.)

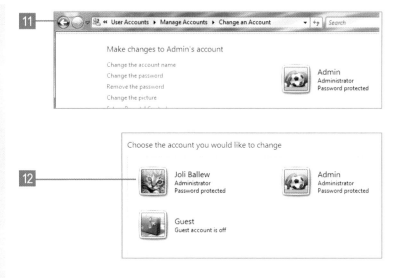

11 Click the back arrow to return to the previous screen.

12 Click your old administrator account, not the new Admin account.

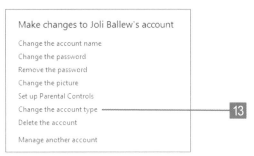

13 Click Change the account type.

14 Click Standard user.

15 Click Change Account Type.

Important

Write down your user name and password and keep it in a safe place.

For your information

When logged on as a standard user, and when you need to make a change to the system that affects everyone, you will either be prompted to insert the Admin password or simply be told you are not allowed to make this change. If prompted that you simply don't have access, you'll have to log off and log back on as an Admin to complete the change. It's much more likely you'll be prompted to input the Admin password. What you see depends on how other security features are configured. Whatever happens though, the security enhancement you get by using a standard account far outweighs the nuisance of the occasional security message.

16 Click Start.

17 Click the right-arrow.

18 Click Log Off.

19 Log back in using your new standard account (which is your old user name and credentials).

User accounts and passwords (cont.)

Requiring passwords

1 Click Start.

2 Click Control Panel.

3 Click Add or remove user accounts.

4 If you're logged on as an administrator, you'll be prompted to type the Admin's password. Type it. Otherwise, click Continue.

5 Click the user account to apply a password to.

6 Click Create password.

7 Type the new password, type it again to confirm it, and type a password hint. It's best to create a password that contains upper- and lower-case letters and a few numbers. Write the password down and keep it somewhere out of sight and safe. Each time you need to make a system-wide change, you'll need to input Admin and the password to obtain access.

8 Click Create password.

9 Click the x in the top right of the window to close it.

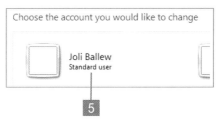

Choose the account you would like to change

Joli Ballew
Standard user

5

Create a password for Admin's account

Admin
Administrator

You are creating a password for Admin.

If you do this, Admin will lose all EFS-encrypted files, personal certificates and stored passwords for Web sites or network resources.

To avoid losing data in the future, ask Admin to make a password reset floppy disk.

•••••

•••••

If the password contains capital letters, they must be typed the same way every time.
How to create a strong password

not my name

The password hint will be visible to everyone who uses this computer.
What is a password hint?

Create password   Cancel

6

You learned a little about System Restore, Windows Update, Windows Firewall and Windows Defender in the introduction, and now it's time to take a look at each of these more closely, and to verify they are set up properly and running as they should be.

System Restore

System Restore lets you restore your computer to an earlier time without affecting your personal files, including documents, spreadsheets, e-mail and photos. You'll only use System Restore if and when you install a program or driver that ultimately produces error messages or causes problems for the computer and uninstalling the problematic application or driver doesn't resolve the issue.

System Restore, by default, regularly creates and saves restore points that contain information about registry settings and deep-down system information that Windows uses to work properly. Because System Restore works only with its own system files, it can't recover a lost personal file, e-mail, or picture. In the same vein, it will not affect these data either. It's important to verify that System Restore is enabled and configured properly.

For your information

System Restore can't be enabled unless the computer has at least 300 MB of free space on the hard disk or if the disk is smaller than 1 GB.

Protect your PC (cont.)

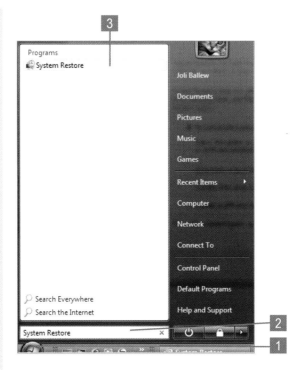

Enabling System Restore

1. Click Start.

2. In the Start Search box, type System Restore.

3. Click System Restore under the Programs results.

4. Click Open System Protection.

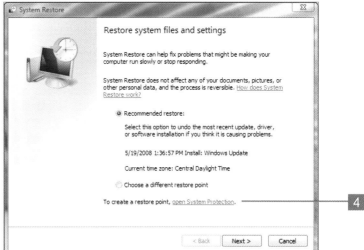

5 Verify that the C: drive, or the System drive, is selected. If it is not, select it.

6 Click OK.

7 In the System Restore window, click Cancel.

Did you know?

You can create a restore point manually by clicking Create.

Note: to run System Restore, open it as noted in Steps 1–4, and click Next to start the wizard.

Protect your PC (cont.)

Windows Update

It's very important to configure Windows Update to get and install updates automatically. This is the easiest way to ensure your computer is as up-to-date as possible, at least as far as patching security flaws Microsoft uncovers, having access to the latest features and obtaining updates to the operating system itself. I suggest you verify that the recommended settings are enabled as detailed here and occasionally check for optional updates manually.

When Windows Update is configured as recommended in the instructions here, updates will be downloaded automatically when you are online (on the Internet), installed and, if necessary, your computer will be rebooted automatically. You can configure the time of day you want this to happen. Once updates are installed, you'll see a pop-up as shown here.

For your information

The Windows Help and Support Center offers pages upon pages of information regarding Windows Update, including how to remove updates or select updates when more than one is available. I think the above paragraphs state all you need to know as an average 50+ computer user, and that you need not worry about anything else regarding Windows Update.

Security ————— 3
Check for updates
Check this computer's security status
Allow a program through Windows
Firewall

4
Windows Update
Turn automatic updating on or off | Check for updates | View installed updates

5

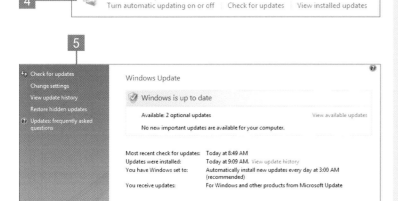

Check for updates
Change settings
View update history
Restore hidden updates
Updates: frequently asked questions

Windows Update

Windows is up to date

Available: 2 optional updates   View available updates

No new important updates are available for your computer.

Most recent check for updates: Today at 8:49 AM
Updates were installed: Today at 9:09 AM. View update history
You have Windows set to: Automatically install new updates every day at 3:00 AM (recommended)
You receive updates: For Windows and other products from Microsoft Update

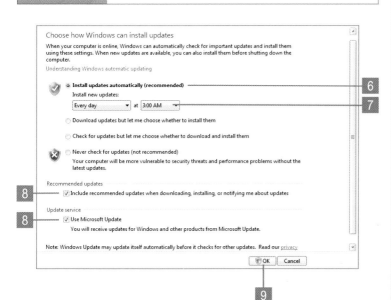

Choose how Windows can install updates

When your computer is online, Windows can automatically check for important updates and install them using these settings. When new updates are available, you can also install them before shutting down the computer.

Understanding Windows automatic updating

○ **Install updates automatically (recommended)** ————— 6
   Install new updates:
   [Every day ▼] at [3:00 AM ▼] ————— 7

○ Download updates but let me choose whether to install them

○ Check for updates but let me choose whether to download and install them

○ Never check for updates (not recommended)
   Your computer will be more vulnerable to security threats and performance problems without the latest updates.

Recommended updates
8 ——— ☑ Include recommended updates when downloading, installing, or notifying me about updates

Update service
8 ——— ☑ Use Microsoft Update
   You will receive updates for Windows and other products from Microsoft Update.

Note: Windows Update may update itself automatically before it checks for other updates. Read our privacy

[OK] [Cancel]

9

Configuring Windows Update

1 Click Start.

2 Click Control Panel.

3 Click Security.

4 Click Windows Update.

5 You may see here that Windows is up-to-date, or you may see that there are available updates. Anything else means that Windows Update is not configured using recommended settings. Whatever the case, click Change settings.

6 Verify the settings are configured to Install updates automatically (recommended) as shown here. (If you desire, you can choose another setting, but I don't recommend it.)

7 Notice the default time of 3:00 AM. Change this to a time when your PC is connected to the Internet but is not being used. This is not necessary, actually; if the computer is not online at 3:00 AM, it will check for updates the next time it is.

Protect your PC
(cont.)

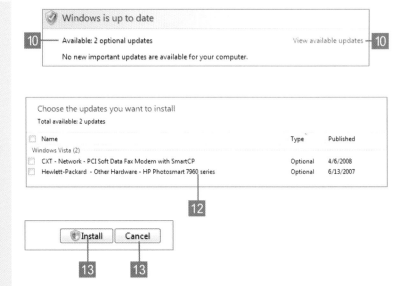

Windows is up to date

10 — Available: 2 optional updates   View available updates — 10

No new important updates are available for your computer.

Choose the updates you want to install

Total available: 2 updates

Name	Type	Published
Windows Vista (2)		
CXT - Network - PCI Soft Data Fax Modem with SmartCP	Optional	4/6/2008
Hewlett-Packard - Other Hardware - HP Photosmart 7960 series	Optional	6/13/2007

12

Install   Cancel

13   13

8 Verify the items checked here are checked on your PC: Include recommended updates when downloading, installing, or notifying me about updates; and Use Microsoft Update.

9 Make changes if needed, and click OK.

10 Back at the Windows Update window, if you see that optional components are available (or any other updates for that matter), click View available updates.

11 Install any required updates, critical updates, or security updates. To do this check the update and click Install.

12 Read the optional updates descriptions and, if desired, check and install those. Optional updates may not be necessary: for instance, I no longer own the HP Photosmart 7960 series printer, so there is no reason to install the update.

13 Click Install or Cancel.

14 Click the x in the top right corner to close the window.

Windows security features

There are two more security features to explore: Windows Firewall and Windows Defender. There isn't much you need to do with these features except to make sure they are both enabled and are protecting your PC. By default, both are enabled.

Windows Firewall is a software program that checks the data that come in from the Internet (or a local network) and then decides whether they are good data or bad. If it deems the data harmless, it will allow data to come though the firewall; if not, data are blocked. You have to have a firewall to keep hackers from getting access to your PC, and to help prevent your computer from sending out malicious code if it is ever attacked by a virus or worm.

Sometimes the firewall will block programs you want to use, including but not limited to:

■ Windows Live Messenger

■ Microsoft Office Outlook

■ Remote Assistance

■ Windows Media Player

■ Wireless Portable Devices.

These and others are blocked by default and the first time you try to use them you'll be prompted to unblock them. There is reasoning behind this and it has to do with protecting you from Internet ills. A hacker may try to come through the Internet to your PC using an application you don't normally use, like Remote Assistance. It can't come through unless you 'allow' it to. (When unblocking a program you can ask that you not be prompted again regarding that particular application.)

Windows Defender protects your PC against malicious and unwanted software. Generally this is a type of data called spyware, malware or adware. Spyware can install itself on your PC without your knowledge and can wreak havoc by causing these types of problems:

■ adding toolbars to Internet Explorer

■ changing Internet Explorer's home page

■ taking you to websites you do not want to visit

■ showing pop-up advertisements

■ causing the computer to perform slowly.

Windows Defender helps protect these types of data from getting onto your PC and thus limits infection on PCs.

It's up to you to make sure that the Firewall and Windows Defender are running and configured properly. That's what you'll do in the next two exercises. Additionally, you'll have the option of changing a few of the parameters, such as when scans are completed and what happens when potentially dangerous data are detected.

Important !

If you work through the steps for using Windows Firewall and it is turned off, it may be turned off because you have a third-party firewall installed. If you aren't sure, go ahead and enable Windows Firewall. If you know you have a third-party firewall, don't enable it. Running two firewalls can cause problems for the PC.

Protect your PC (cont.)

Using Windows Firewall

1 Click Start.

2 Click Control Panel.

3 Click Security.

4 Under Windows Firewall, click Turn Windows Firewall on or off.

5 Verify the firewall is On. If not, select On.

6 Click the Exceptions tab. Notice the exceptions already enabled. You can manually enable exceptions here or simply wait until you're prompted when trying to use the application.

7 Click OK.

Using Windows Defender

1 Click Start.

2 Click Control Panel.

3 Click Security.

4 Click Windows Defender.

5 Hopefully, you'll see that no unwanted or harmful software has been detected. If not, you'll be prompted regarding what to do next. (This is highly unlikely.) Click Tools.

6 Click Options.

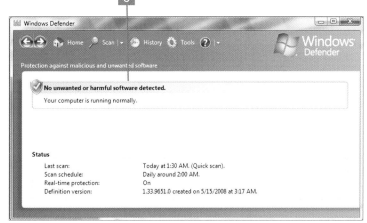

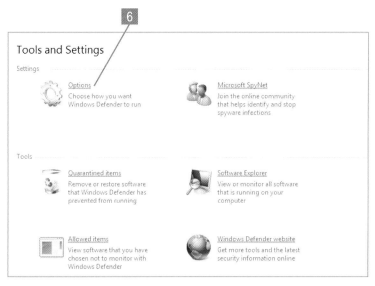

Protect your PC (cont.)

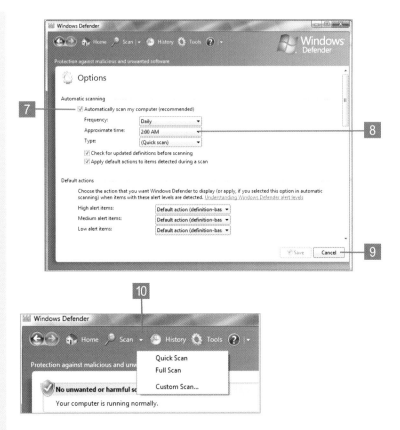

7 Verify that Automatic scanning is enabled.

8 If desired, change the approximate time of the scan. It's best to leave the other defaults as is.

9 Click Save if you've made changes, or Cancel if not.

10 Click the arrow next to Scan (not the Scan icon). Note that you can manually perform a Quick Scan or a Full Scan. Do this if you think the computer has been infected.

11 Click the x in the top right corner to close the Windows Defender window.

Resolving Security Center warnings

Last but not least, you need to occasionally visit the Security Center to see if any warnings exist. If you see anything in red or yellow, the problem needs to be resolved. In this example two problems exist. First, there's no virus protection and second, the firewall is disabled. In order to be protected, these items must be taken care of.

Protect your PC (cont.)

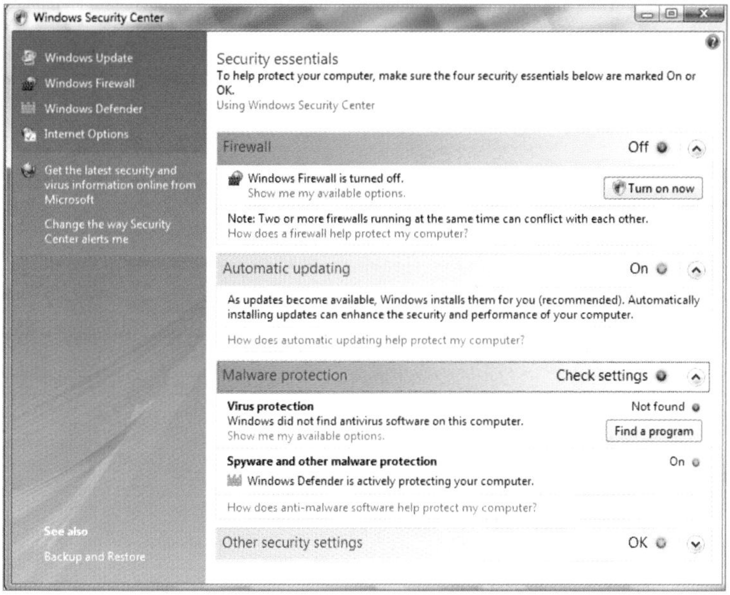

Protect your PC (cont.)

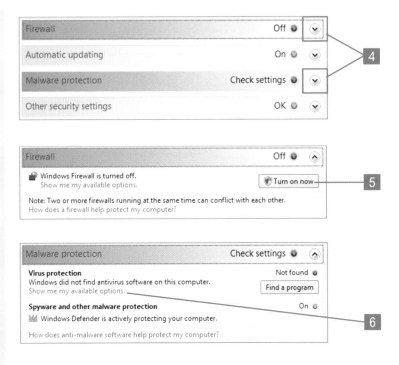

Resolving Security Center warnings

1 Click Start.

2 Click Control Panel.

3 Click Security.

4 If there's anything in red or yellow, click the down-arrow (if necessary) to see the problem.

5 Note the resolution and perform the task. For Firewall, click Turn on now.

6 For Malware protection, click Show me my available options.

7 Select from the two choices shown here. Ideally, you should install an anti-virus program like Windows Live OneCare. (If you install Windows Live OneCare or any other anti-virus application, Vista will probably find it automatically after installation.)

8 Continue in this manner to resolve all Security Center related issues.

9 Click the x in the top right corner of the Security Center window to close it.

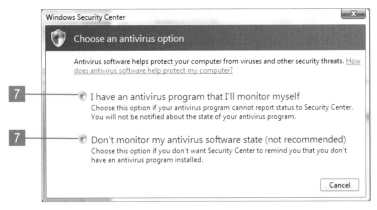

There are two other things you can do to protect your family and data. First, protect children or grandchildren with parental controls. Parental Controls isn't a cure-all, but it does help. You still have to find a way to protect your children from Internet bad guys when they're away from home, but at least while they're under your roof you can look after them. Second, learn how to create backups of your data and settings. Although it's unlikely something will happen in the immediate future that is so bad it would destroy your PC and all of your data, it could happen (and it does). It's best to be prepared.

Parental Controls

As noted in the introduction, Parental Controls can be applied to children, grandchildren, guests and even partners. You can configure Parental Controls to set limits on when a person can use the computer (and for how long), what games they can play, what websites they can visit and what programs they can run. Once you've configured Parental Controls, you can review 'activity reports' that let you see what that person has been doing with their computer time. You can also view what content has been blocked, which will allow you to see how far the user has been testing the limits of the controls you've set.

Protect your family and your data

11

Important

You can only apply Parental Controls to users with a Standard user account. All other user accounts should have passwords.

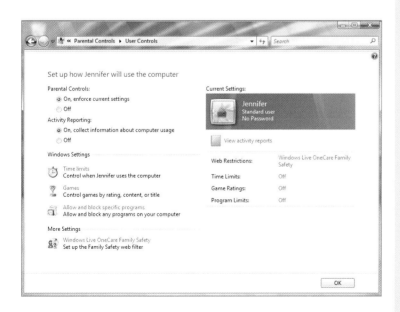

Protect your family and your data (cont.)

As you can see here, there are options to set time limits, games, access to programs and to set up the Windows Live OneCare Family Safety features (if you've signed up for Windows Live OneCare). There is also an option to view reports.

On an activity report you can view the following information:

- Top 10 Websites Visited
- Most Recent 10 Websites Blocked
- Web Overrides
- File Downloads
- File Downloads Blocked
- Logon Times
- Applications Run
- Application Overrides
- Games Played
- Email Events including Email Received, Email Sent, and Contact List Change
- Instant Messaging Events including Conversations, Web Cam, Audio, Game Play, File Exchange, Link Exchange, SMS Message, Contact List Change
- Media Events including Media Played.

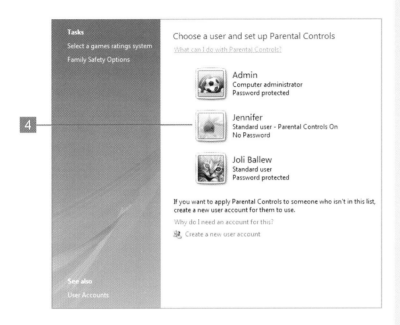

Setting up Parental Controls

1 Click Start.

2 Click Control Panel.

3 Under User Accounts and Family Safety, click Set up parental controls for any user.

4 Click the standard user account for which you want to set Parental Controls. It's OK if this is the only account without a password, but it is still suggested one is applied.

5 Under Parental Controls, click On.

6 Under Activity Reporting, click On.

7 Click Time limits.

8 Click and drag to set times to block and allow. Blue is blocked.

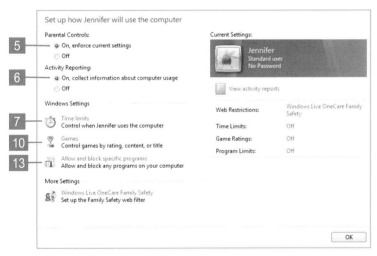

Protect your family and your data (cont.)

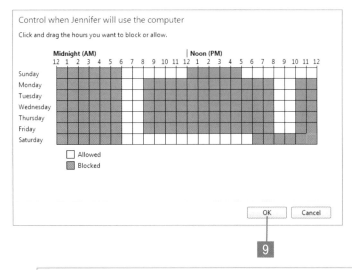

Control when Jennifer will use the computer

Click and drag the hours you want to block or allow.

Midnight (AM) | Noon (PM)

| | Allowed |
| | Blocked |

9. Click OK.

10. Click Games.

11. Click Yes to allow games to be played or No to disallow it. If you click Yes:

   a. Click Set game ratings and select an age group from the resulting list, and configure additional settings. Click OK.

   b. Click Block or Allow specific games and for each game listed, the configuration for each. By default, it's based on User Ratings. Click OK.

12. Click OK to close Game Controls.

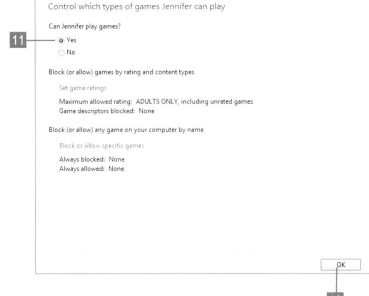

Control which types of games Jennifer can play

Can Jennifer play games?

○ Yes
○ No

Block (or allow) games by rating and content types

Set game ratings

Maximum allowed rating: ADULTS ONLY, including unrated games
Game descriptors blocked: None

Block (or allow) any game on your computer by name

Block or Allow specific games

Always blocked: None
Always allowed: None

13 Click Allow and block specific programs. If the user can access all programs, select <user name> can use all programs. Otherwise, choose <user name> can only use the programs I allow. For the latter, select and deselect programs the user can run. Click OK.

14 Notice in the Parental Controls window you can View activity reports. Come back here to view the activity reports created for this user or any other.

15 Click OK.

Protect your family and your data (cont.)

Creating your first backup

1 Click Start.

2 Click Control Panel.

3 Click Back up your computer.

4 Click Back Up Files.

5 Choose a place to save your backup. Since backups can be large, consider a USB drive, external hard drive or DVD. You can also choose a network location. For the first backup, if possible select a location that has at least 40 GB of space (like an external hard drive or network location), just to be safe.

6 Click Next. (If prompted for any other information, such as a hard drive partition, to insert a blank DVD or insert a USB drive, do so.)

? Did you know?

You can't create a backup on the hard disk of the computer you are backing up.

Backing up data

Windows Vista comes with a backup program you can use to back up your personal data. The backup program is located in the Backup and Restore Center.

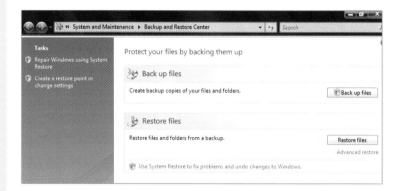

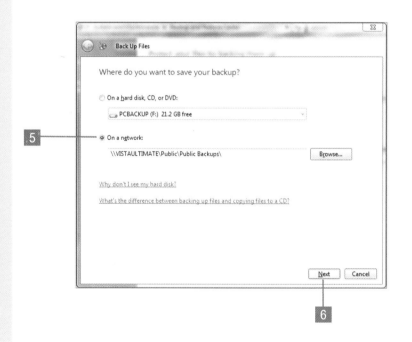

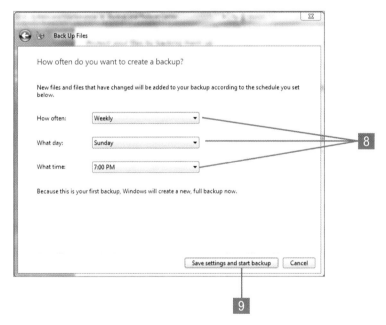

7 Select what to back up. First timers should select everything. Click Next.

8 Choose setting for how often, what day and what time future backups should occur.

9 Click Save settings and start backup.

Follow the same procedure to restore data from a backup if and when necessary.

Protect your family and your data (cont.)

Jargon buster

Adware – Internet advertisements (which are also applications) that often include additional code that can be used to track a user's personal information and pass it on to third parties, without the user's authorisation or knowledge.

Internet server – a computer that stores data off site. Gmail offers Internet servers to hold e-mail and data, so that you do not have to store them on your PC. Internet servers allow you to access information from any computer that can access the Internet.

Malware – stands for malicious software. Malware includes viruses, worms, spyware, etc.

Phishing – an attempt by an unscrupulous website or hacker to obtain personal data including, but not limited to, bank account numbers, social security numbers and e-mail addresses.

Virus – a self-replicating program that infects computers with intent to do harm. Viruses often come in the form of an attachment in an e-mail.

Worm – a self-replicating program that infects computers with intent to do harm. However, unlike a virus, it does not need to attach itself to a running program.

Using Windows Media Player

Introduction

Windows Media Player offers all you'll need to manage your music library, get music online and copy the CDs from your own music collection to your PC. You can also use it to burn music CDs that you can listen to in your car, share music using your local network and more.

Windows Media Player offers an interface that is different from most you've seen so far in this book. Yes, there are tabs, but they aren't necessarily familiar. Tabs include Now Playing, Library, Rip, Burn, Sync and Media Guide. By clicking a tab, you move through the interface and access features.

Windows Media Player stands apart from other applications because it's used to acquire, play, share and listen to music. You can also work with video and pictures, but for the most part, you'll use Media Player for music management. That said, if you've never used a music application on a PC or mobile device, there are a few things you'll need to know beforehand. So, before we get started, let's review some terms (see the **Jargon buster**) you'll see throughout this chapter.

If you've never used Windows Media Player 11, the first time you open it you'll have to work through a wizard to tell Windows Media Player how you want it to perform. You'll have two options, Express or Custom. If you're new to Media Player 11, it's OK to select Express and accept the defaults. You can always change any options you decide you don't like after you've worked with it for a while. However, if prompted (you'll only be prompted

Set up Windows Media Player

Explore Windows Media Player

Listen to sample music

Rip your CD collection

Burn a CD

Synch a music player

the first time you open Media Player), I suggest you choose Custom Settings, that way, you can configure the application the way you want it from the very start.

Jargon buster

Enhancements – these are features included in Media Player 11 that improve the quality of the music you listen to. There's a graphic equaliser (just like you used to have on your old stereo system), options for reducing the differences between loud and soft sounds in music and video (so you don't get blown out of your chair during DVD playback or when listening to music from different sources) and even an option to change how fast or slow a song plays (just in case you want to speed up or slow down a song to learn it or exercise to it).

Visualisations – these are graphical representations of the music you play. You can turn them off or on, and there are several to choose from. These visualisations move with the music and are computer generated.

Playlist – a group of songs that you can save and then listen to as a group, burn to a CD, copy to a portable music player and more.

Rip – a term used to describe the process of copying files from a physical CD to your hard drive and thus your music library.

Burn – a term used to describe the process of copying music from a computer to a CD or DVD. Generally music is burned to a CD, since CDs can be played in cars and generic CD players, and videos are burned to DVDs since they require much more space and can be played on DVD players.

Sync – the process of comparing data in one location to the data in another, and performing tasks to match them up. If data have been added or deleted from one device, for instance, synching can also add or delete them from the other. You might already be familiar with synching if you sync your mobile phone to your PC or if you've ever used offline files at work.

Media Guide – a tool for accessing an online music store, where you can purchase or lease music, videos and other media.

The first time you start Windows Media Player 11, you'll be prompted to set it up. If you have a few minutes to spare, click Custom. If you're in a hurry to get to where you're going, click Express. I'll suggest Custom and that's what we'll work through here. (If you choose Express, simply follow the prompts.) When you choose Custom, you'll be prompted to configure settings for privacy, playback and other options that would otherwise be configured automatically using Microsoft's default settings.

When working through the Custom setup, you'll have the ability to select or deselect the following options from the Privacy Options:

Set up Windows Media Player

12

- Display media information from the Internet – leave this option selected if you want Media Player to access the Internet to display information about the media you are watching or listening to. I see no reason to deselect this unless you have an extremely slow Internet connection or pay by how much bandwidth you use.

- Update my music files by retrieving media information from the Internet – deselect this option if you have an existing media library that you've added your own data to, like album art, artist names and other data. If this is the first time you've used Media Player, leave this option selected. Your media will be updated automatically.

- Download usage rights automatically when I play a file – leave this option selected; you don't want to worry about usage rights when Media Player can manage it for you.

- Send unique Player ID to content providers – leave this unselected. If you select it, media providers can uniquely identify your computer when you use their media servers. Although this can improve performance, in my opinion, it's an invasion of privacy.

- I want to help make Microsoft software and services even better by sending Player usage data to Microsoft – select this option to help Microsoft improve later editions of Media Player, otherwise, don't select it. No personally identifiable information will be sent to Microsoft either way.

Jargon buster

Bandwidth – generally this is used to represent how much data you send and receive on a paid connection, like a smart phone or Internet connection.

Set up Windows Media Player (cont.)

- Save file and URL history in the Player – leave this selected if you want to save your history in the Player. This allows the Player to display recently played files on the File menu and in the Open and Open URL dialogue box. It's simply a convenience. Deselect this if others have access to your account and you do not want them to see what you've been listening to or watching.

- Add a shortcut to the desktop – select this to add a shortcut to Windows Media Player to your desktop.

- Add a shortcut to the Quick Launch bar – select this to add a shortcut to Windows Media Player to the Quick Launch toolbar.

- Make Windows Media Player 11 the default music and video player – select this to configure Media Player to play all music types it supports. Of this choice and the next, I suggest this.

- Choose the file types that Windows Media Player will play – select this to choose the exact file types that it will play, only if you use another player often, like iTunes, Microsoft Zune or RealPlayer. I suggest you do not select this, as it's quite complicated and probably unnecessary.

If more than one person uses the PC, each person can configure their own settings. This means you can use Media Player and your grandchildren can use Microsoft Zune or iTunes.

- Media Guide – select this only if you know you want to purchase media online and you are aware of other options for obtaining media. I suggest you do not set up a store now.

- Don't set up a store now (you can set one up later in the Player) – select this to set up a music store later. There are several to choose from, not just Media Guide, so it's best to configure this later.

Set up Windows Media Player (cont.)

Setting up Windows Media Player

1. Click Start.

2. Type Media Player.

3. Under Programs, click Windows Media Player to open it.

4. When prompted, click Custom Settings.

5. Click Next.

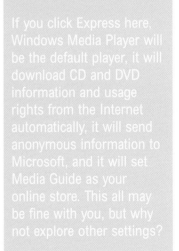

Important

If you click Express here, Windows Media Player will be the default player, it will download CD and DVD information and usage rights from the Internet automatically, it will send anonymous information to Microsoft, and it will set Media Guide as your online store. This all may be fine with you, but why not explore other settings?

Set up Windows Media Player (cont.)

6 Configure Privacy Options settings as desired.

7 Click Privacy Statement to view privacy information.

8 Click Next.

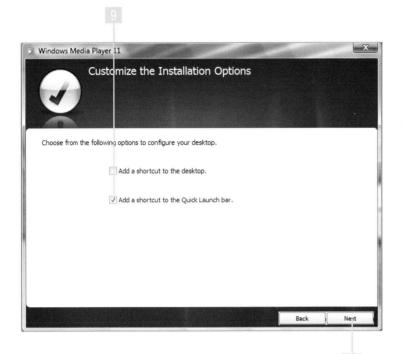

9 Select the desired shortcuts.

10 Click Next.

11 Select how to use Media Player. The settings I recommend are shown here.

12 Click Next.

Set up Windows Media Player (cont.)

13 Click Finish.

After completing setup, you'll probably see exactly what's shown here, including the sample music offered. You'll see familiar attributes, like the Back and Forward buttons, and tabs.

You'll also see tab titles: Now Playing, Library (the default view), Rip, Burn and Sync; plus Media Guide, Online Stores or something similar, depending on your preferences.

Notice also the left pane: there you can access playlists and everything in your music library. You can sort by artist, album, songs, genre, year and rating. Click the right-arrow by the notes icon and you can access media other than music, including Music (the default), Pictures, Video, Recorded TV and Other Media. To play any media, double-click it.

The Windows Media Player interface

The Windows Media Player interface (cont.)

As with other applications native to Vista, there are options for changing the layout and view, and a new Instant Search box. Let's look at a few of these options now.

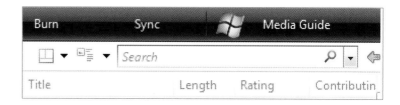

Choosing a category and the resulting view

So as not to get lost, we'll take this a step at a time. Here is the Category button. If you click this button, you can navigate to all of the media on your PC, including music, pictures, videos, recorded TV and other media.

The Music view is the default, because almost everyone will use Media Player for music and something else for other media. You'll probably prefer to work with photos in Photo Gallery, for instance, and television in Media Center.

When you make a selection from the Category button, what you see in the left pane will change. Here, Music is selected. Notice the pane contains playlists and options for sorting your music. By default, Songs is selected.

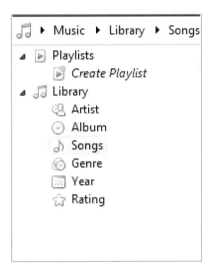

Here's what happens when you select Pictures from the Category button and Keywords under Library.

The Windows Media Player interface (cont.)

As you can imagine, selecting other categories offers similar results.

Layout Options

The Layout Options button lets you show or hide various parts of the interface. The Layout button is shown here.

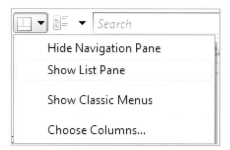

The Navigation pane, that's the pane on the left that you've already seen, lets you navigate through your media library easily. It's best to leave that enabled. The List pane can also be enabled, but it will appear automatically when needed. When it's not needed it's really just in the way.

Navigation Pane   List Pane

You can also enable the Classic menus, which are off by default, if you'd rather use the older menus in favour of the newer tabs. Here are the classic menus. As with Internet Explorer, you can click the Alt key to show the menus when you need them, thus leaving them off the rest of the time.

View Options

The View Options button offers three options: Icon, Tile or Expanded Tile, and Details. Here's the background on each:

- Icon – each item is displayed as an icon. This is the default for music. Albums, the default view, are icons of their album cover art. When you group the music differently, perhaps by year, artist or album, they look stacked.

- Tile/Expanded Tile – each item still appears as an icon, but additional information is offered, like the year, album name, etc.

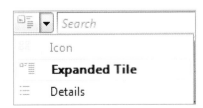

- Details – no icons are shown but additional information is, and you can configure what you want to show. Here you can see an example.

The Windows Media Player interface (cont.)

As with other views and layouts, simply click any song or video to play it.

Instant Search

As with other Vista applications, you can search for media using the Instant Search dialogue box. Just type in what you want to find. It searches 'live', so results show as you type and are culled down the more you type.

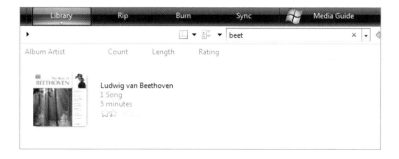

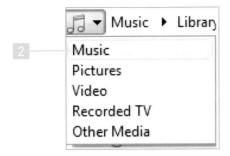

The Windows Media Player interface (cont.)

Exploring Windows Media Player

12

1. Open Windows Media Player.

2. If you are not in the Music library, click the Category button and select Music.

3. In the Navigation pane, select Artist, then Album, then Songs, then Genre, then Year, then Rating. (Return to Album when finished.)

4. From the Layout button, select and deselect each option. (Choosing Columns lets you choose what columns to show or hide.)

5. From the View button, select each option to view it. When finished, choose the Icon option.

6. In the Search window, type Posies. Note the results.

The Windows Media Player interface (cont.)

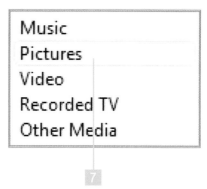

Music
Pictures
Video
Recorded TV
Other Media

7

7 From the Category button, select Pictures.

8 Repeat Step 3, this time working through the Pictures options in the Navigation pane.

9 Repeat Steps 4 and 5.

10 Continue experimenting as desired.

Now that you're somewhat familiar with the Media Player interface, let's play some media. To play any music track, view any picture, watch any video or view other media, simply navigate to it and double-click it. Windows Media Player may switch to the Now Playing tab.

Here I'm viewing a photo. Notice the controls at the bottom – by default, a slideshow of the images in that folder will play.

Play media (cont.)

You can also view DVDs, although if you have Windows Media Center you'll probably prefer watching them there. Since you'll likely be using Media Player for music though, we'll focus on that.

When completing the next exercise, explore other types of media. You can always return to the library by clicking the Library tab.

Listening to sample music

1. Open Media Player.

2. If necessary, click the Category button and choose Music.

3. Click Album. (Note you can also click Songs, Artist or any other category to locate a song.)

4. Double-click any album to play it.

5. Note the controls at the bottom of the interface. From left to right: Shuffle (to play songs in random order), Repeat, Stop, Previous, Play/Pause, Next, Mute and a volume slider. Use these controls to manage the song and to move from one song to the next.

6. Click the Now Playing tab. Note the album art. You'll learn more about this later. (Click Library to return to the Library.)

7. Continue experimenting with the controls until you are comfortable playing music.

To rip means to copy in media-speak. When you rip a CD, you copy the CD to your PC's hard drive. If you have a large CD collection, this could take some time, but it will ultimately be worth it. Once music is on your PC, you can listen to it in Media Player, burn compilations of music to other CDs, and even put the music on a portable music player, like a Zune.

To rip a CD, simply put the CD in the CD drive, close any pop-up boxes and, in Media Player, click the Rip button. During the copy process, you can watch the progress of the rip. By default, music will be saved in your Music folder.

Rip a CD

Ripping your CD collection

1. Insert the CD to copy into the CD drive.

2. If any pop-up boxes appear, click the x to close them. This step isn't actually necessary, as you can select Rip music from CD in Windows Media Player from the dialogue box shown here, but I'd like to introduce ripping from Media Player, not from a dialogue box, so that you can access all available options.

3. In Windows Media Player, click the Rip button.

12

Rip a CD (cont.)

4 Deselect any songs you do not want to copy to your PC.

5 Click Start Rip.

6 Watch as the CD is copied; you can view the rip status as shown here.

7 The ripped music will now appear in your music library under Recently Added, as well as Artist, Album, Songs, Genre and Year.

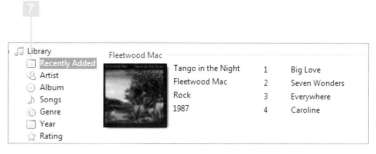

There are two ways to take music with you when you are on the road or on the go. You can copy the music to a portable device like a cell phone, Zune or other music player (and keep it synchronised using Media Player), or you can create your own CDs, choosing the songs to copy and placing them on the CD in the desired order. CDs you create can be played in car stereos and portable CD players, as well as lots of other CD devices. A typical CD can hold about 80 minutes of music, but don't worry, Media Player will keep track of the songs you select and will let you know when you're running out of space on the CD you're creating.

The Burn tab can assist you in creating a CD. Burn is media-speak for copying music from your PC to a CD. Clicking Burn brings up the List pane, where Media Player will tell you to insert a blank CD if one is not in the drive already, and allow you to drag and drop songs into the List pane to create a burn list. As music is added, the progress bar at the top of the List pane shows how much available space you've used.

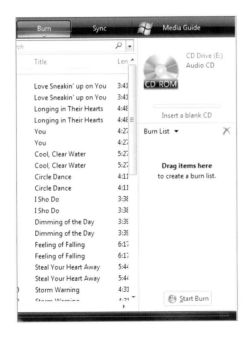

Once you've added music, the Start Burn button becomes active. Here, I'm dragging and dropping music to the List pane, something you'll learn to do in the next exercise.

Burn a CD (cont.)

Did you know?

You can right-click any song in the Burn list to access additional options, including the option to delete the song from the list (not the PC), or to move up or move down in the list order.

1 There is a CD in the CD drive.

2 There is still 46 minutes and 23 seconds remaining on the disk.

3 Songs have been added to the Burn List.

4 I Ka Barra (Your Work) is currently being dragged to the List pane to be added to the Burn List.

5 Start Burn is active and is ready to be clicked once all songs are added.

6 Songs is selected in the Library list, making dragging and dropping available songs simpler.

Notice what's going on in this image:

Did you know?

To listen to music in a car or portable CD player, you have to burn a CD, not a DVD.

Burn	Sync		Media Guide

Burn 'Quiet Songs' List to Drive E:

● Audio CD

Data CD or DVD

✓ Eject Disc After Burning

✓ Apply Volume Leveling Across Tracks on Audio CDs

More Options...

Help with Burning

4	Caroline	3:55	☆
5	Tango in the Night	4:02	☆
6	Mystfied	3:10	☆
7	Little Lies	3:41	☆
8	Family Man	4:07	★
9	Welcome to the Room......	3:42	☆
10	Isn't It Midnight	4:13	☆

Habib Koite & Bamada

Muso Ko   1   I Kα Bαrrα (Vαιιr Wαrk)   5:00

Burning a CD

1. Open Media Player.

2. Click the arrow under the Burn tab.

3. Verify Audio CD has a dot by it. If it does not, click it once.

4. Verify that Apply Volume Leveling Across Tracks on Audio CDs has a tick by it. This will make sure all songs on the CD are the same volume and that some tracks are not louder (or softer) than others.

5. Click outside the drop-down list to close it.

6. Insert a blank CD in the CD drive. (Close any pop-up dialogue boxes.)

7. Under Library, click Songs.

8. Click any song title to add and drag it to the List pane.

12

Burn a CD (cont.)

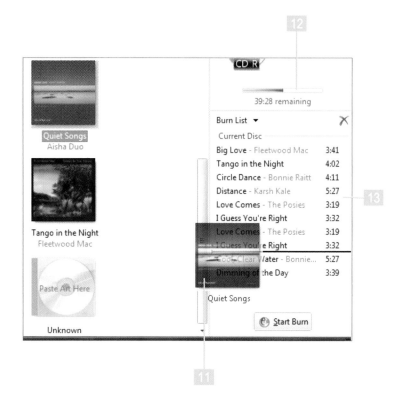

9   Drop the song in the List pane to add it to the Burn List.

10 Click Album.

11 Drag any album to the List pane to add the entire album.

12 Look at the slider in the List pane to verify there is room left on the CD.

13 Right-click any entry to access additional options including Remove from List, Move Up, Move Down.

14 When you've added the songs you want, click Start Burn.

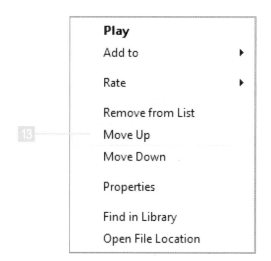

You can get all kinds of media online, from movies, to music, to radio, to games. From inside Windows Media Player, you do that from Media Guide. By clicking the arrow underneath Media Guide, you can browse all online stores to find one you like. Depending on the service you choose, and how you sign up for services, you may also be able to copy what you obtain from these services to a portable device, like a Zune or other portable music player. Understand what you want to do before you commit long term to a service (most offer a free trial period anyway).

Online stores

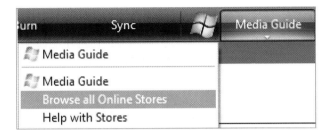

Here's what you see when you select Browse All Stores under the Media Guide tab. Notice there are a lot of online stores available. Some offer audiobooks, some movies, some music, some radio stations and others a combination of these. Additionally, some rent or lease media, while some sell it. Some offer both services.

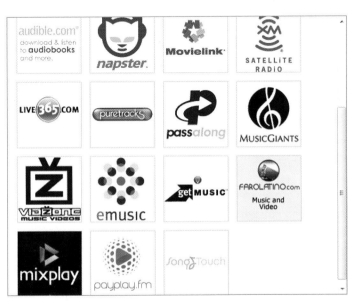

Online music and portable music players (cont.)

Because there are so many stores to choose from, and because rates, pricing, availability and other features change often, there's no way to offer the 'best' option for you. However, if you have already subscribed to a service you see here, you can input your information and use that service. For instance, because I currently subscribe to XM Radio for use in my car, I can also listen to XM Radio on my PC. Notice how the last tab of the Windows Media Player interface no longer says Media Guide, but XM Radio Online after selecting and configuring the service.

You may need more than one service. While XM Radio is great for listening to music, you can't download or purchase songs: it's simply radio. If you want access to music, DVD downloads, videos or books, you'll have to add another service. Services you add may come attached with a monthly fee or you can choose to pay as you go. Make sure you understand the options before choosing.

In order to get started then, browse through the stores that are available and see which one(s) offer what you need. I think Movielink is a great source for movies, and eMusic is a good choice if you want to experiment with online music. At the time this book was written, eMusic offered 25 free downloads and

Movielink offered no subscription fees and no late fees (you pay to rent or purchase only). Once you've decided on a service, click it and complete the sign-up process. Here's Movielink. Click Register to get started.

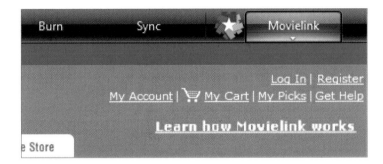

Once you've registered and created an account, you can start using the service. Each service responds differently, but all seem equally easy to use. Here I've browsed to the movie Ice Age in Movielink. All I have to do now is click Add to Cart, wait for the download to complete (this only takes a few minutes) and watch the movie. In this particular case, I'll be renting the movie.

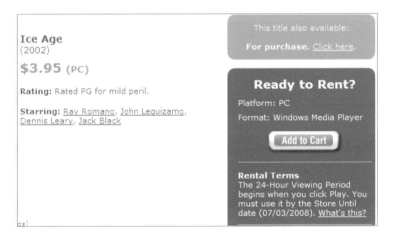

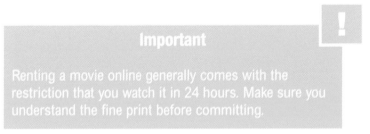

Important

Renting a movie online generally comes with the restriction that you watch it in 24 hours. Make sure you understand the fine print before committing.

Online music and portable music players (cont.)

Using portable players

If you choose an online service that lets you sync music to a portable device, you can perform that sync in Media Player, thus copying the newly added songs to the player you prefer. Additionally, you can sync a portable player with music you rip from your own CD collection. As you might suspect, you manage the syncing process through the Sync tab. As you can see, you'll be prompted to connect a device if one is not already connected.

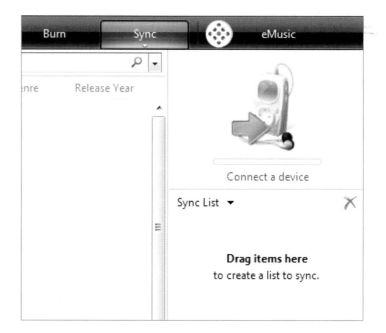

The first time you sync a new device, you'll be prompted to add songs to the Sync List. As with creating a burn list, you'll drag and drop songs to the Sync List. The next time you sync the device, it will sync automatically.

To get started, let's sync a new device to Windows Media Player.

Online music and portable music players (cont.)

Synching a music player

1. Open Windows Media Player.

2. Click the Sync tab.

3. Connect a portable media device. If you connect a device that's already been synced with another music library (on another PC), you'll be prompted regarding this. You'll need to choose to sync for this session only or to sync to this library permanently. Make the appropriate choice.

Online music and portable music players (cont.)

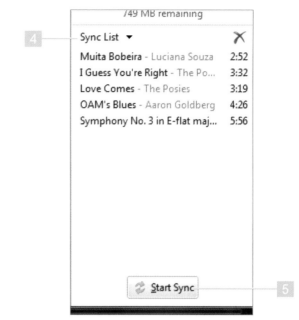

4. Drag and drop songs or albums (or other media) to the Sync List. As with creating a burn list, watch the slider to see how full the device is getting.

5. After adding the desired songs, click Start Sync.

The next time you plug in the device after the initial sync, you won't have to do anything. Windows Media Player will automatically perform the sync.

Flash Disk
ChipsBnk
999 MB

753 MB remaining

Windows Photo Gallery

Introduction

Windows Photo Gallery may be all you need to manage, manipulate, view and share your digital photos. Before you install additional software, including software that was included on the CD that was despatched with your digital camera, try this program. It's included in all editions of Windows Vista, and requires no additional hardware (like Media Center does). Note that you can also manage videos here, but Windows Media Center is better for that, if you have it and the required hardware.

Windows Photo Gallery offers many features, including but not limited to:

- importing pictures from a digital camera
- viewing and previewing pictures and videos
- easily setting a picture as your desktop background
- rotating pictures
- fixing flaws in pictures with tools like Auto Adjust, Adjust Exposure, Adjust Color, Crop Picture and Fix Red Eye
- 'tagging' pictures with descriptive names for sorting, organising and managing
- sorting pictures and videos based on their date, rating, folder name or 'tag'
- grouping and 'stacking' photos for organising them.

What you'll do

Explore the Photo Gallery Interface

Add a folder to Windows Photo Gallery

Personalise Photo Gallery

Import pictures from a digital camera, media card or USB drive

Fix pictures

Add picture information (tagging)

E-mail pictures

The Photo Gallery interface

Windows Photo Gallery has two default panes and each offers specific functionality. When you open Windows Photo Gallery, the pane to the left is the View pane, where you'll select the folder or subfolder that contains the pictures you want to view, manage, edit or share. The Thumbnail pane is on the right and this is where you preview the pictures in the folder selected in the View pane.

You can also work with pictures in the Thumbnail pane by selecting them. When you double-click a picture in the Thumbnail pane, it opens where you can then edit, share, add tags and perform other image-related tasks. Note that when you double-click an image, the View pane disappears and a new pane appears on the right. From that new pane, called the Info pane, you can rate the image, add a caption and add tags easily.

For your information

Your digital pictures are stored in the Pictures folder on your hard drive, not 'in' or 'by' Photo Gallery. Pictures may also be stored in the Public Pictures folder, or any folder or subfolder you create. Photo Gallery offers a place to work with images and has nothing to do with how they are stored on the PC.

Underneath all of this are the navigational controls. Here you can see the Zoom tool in action. Zooming is a great way to get to an area of an image that needs fixing, such as the red eye shown here.

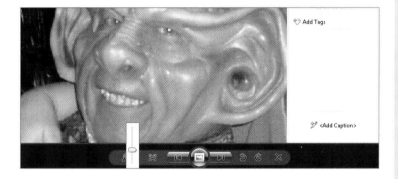

The next navigational options include, to the right of Zoom, a toggle switch to move from the image's actual size to fit to screen. Following that are arrows for Previous (to move to the previous picture in the folder), Play Slide Show (to play a slide show of the folder's pictures), Next (to move to the next picture in the folder), Rotate Counterclockwise, Rotate Clockwise and Delete.

13

The Photo Gallery interface (cont.)

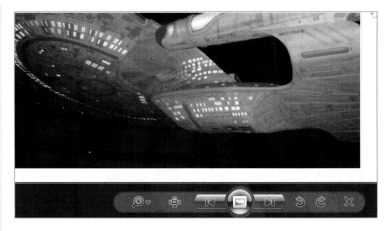

Another pane appears when you click Fix. Windows Photo Gallery displays the Edit pane as shown here.

And last but not least, there's the Menu bar. It appears at the top of the interface and contains menus you'll find in other programs, like File, Print and Burn. You'll use these menus to manage, edit, print, share and use your photos in movies (which will add the selected images to a Movie Maker project). It also contains Back and Forward buttons, which you'll use to navigate through folders and images.

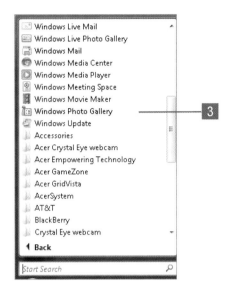

Exploring the Photo Gallery interface

1 Click Start.

2 Click All Programs.

3 Click Windows Photo Gallery.

4 Locate the Menu bar.

5 Locate the View pane.

6 Locate the Navigational Controls.

13

The Photo Gallery interface (cont.)

7 Click the triangle next to Folders.

8 Click the arrow next to Public Pictures to expand it, if necessary.

9 Click Sample Pictures.

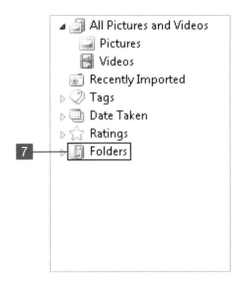

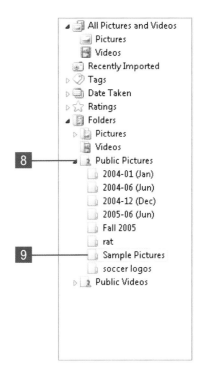

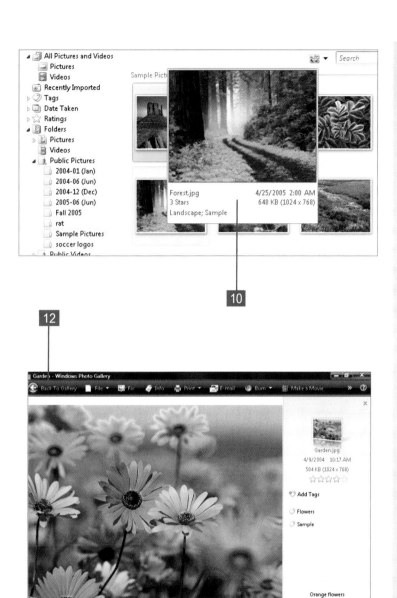

The Photo Gallery interface (cont.)

10 Hover the mouse over any picture in the Thumbnail pane. Note the large thumbnail that appears.

11 Double-click any picture in the Sample Pictures folder.

12 Notice how the interface changes. The View pane has gone and the Info pane now appears on the right. Also notice a Back To Gallery option appears in the Menu bar.

13 Click the Next option in the navigational tools. It's the right-arrow. Repeat to view all of the pictures.

13

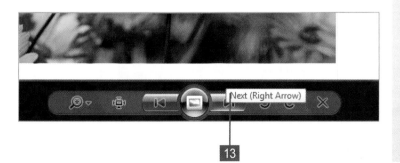

The Photo Gallery interface (cont.)

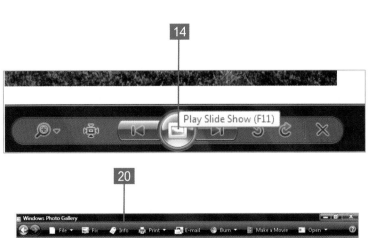

14. Click the Play Slide Show button. Wait at least three seconds.

15. When the slide show starts to play, move the mouse.

16. Note the navigational controls that appear at the bottom of the screen. Click the Pause button to pause the show, and click the Play button to restart it.

17. Click Exit to return to Windows Photo Gallery.

18. Click Back To Gallery.

19. Click any image.

20. Click Info. Note the new Info pane.

21. Click Fix. Note the Edit pane.

22. Click Back To Gallery.

23. If desired, click File, and click Exit to close Photo Gallery or simply leave it open for the next exercise.

Adding folders to Windows Photo Gallery

Vista takes care of storing your digital files and offers four folders for doing so: Pictures, Public Pictures, Videos and Public Videos. In addition Windows Photo Gallery lets you easily manage the data you put inside these folders in a single interface. However, Windows Photo Gallery only looks in *these four folders* for media. That means if you create a folder on your desktop called Digital Photos from my 2009 Trip to Italy, if you store pictures on a networked computer or external drive, or if you store photos in your Documents folder, the photos and videos in those folders won't appear in Photo Gallery by default. So, if you've stored pictures and videos in folders other than Pictures, Videos, Public Pictures and Public Videos, you have two options. You can either move the photos to those folders or tell Windows Photo Gallery you want it to watch those folders for media.

Timesaver tip

Remember, when moving data, right-click while dragging from one folder to another, and then select Move when you're ready to drop the data. Alternatively, you can select the data to move, right-click, choose Cut, and then right-click and choose Paste to move the data to the correct folder.

13

The Photo Gallery interface (cont.)

Adding a folder to Windows Photo Gallery

1 If you don't want to move pictures and videos from folders you've created outside of the default Pictures, Public Pictures, Videos or Public Videos folders, you'll need to perform the steps here to tell Windows Photo Gallery where they are. To start, open Windows Photo Gallery.

2 Click File.

3 Click Add Folder to Gallery.

4 Expand the 'trees' to locate the folder to add. To do this, click the down-arrow by the desired option. (Note that you can resize this window by dragging from the bottom right corner.)

5 Click OK.

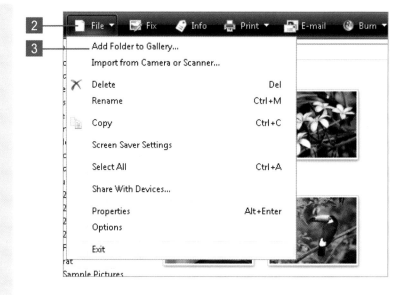

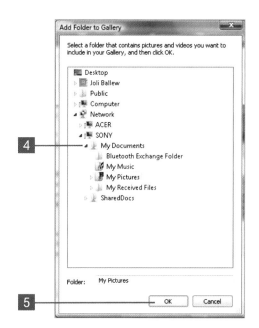

Here I've browsed to a folder located on my computer network, to a computer named Sony, to a folder called My Pictures. The computer Sony runs Windows XP, which explains why the folder is called My Pictures instead of the newer Pictures, used in Vista.

Add Folder to Gallery

This folder has been added to your Gallery.

It might take some time to add the files in this folder, and Photo Gallery might run slower while these files are being processed. When it's complete, you can view all the pictures and videos stored in this folder in your Gallery.

☐ Don't show this message again   OK

How do I control which folders appear in the Gallery?

6 Click OK again after reading the information in the dialogue box shown here.

6

13

Filter pictures with Windows Photo Gallery

Windows Photo Gallery lets you filter the photos and videos you've stored on your PC in a number of ways. You can view all pictures and videos together or filter them by Recently Imported, Tags, Date Taken, Ratings and Folders. Each of these larger options has sub-options, as you can see here under Tags. (There's a folder called Not Tagged for those photos that do not have tags.)

The Photo Gallery interface (cont.)

It's easy to add tags to a photo, all you have to do is right-click and choose Add Tags. You'll learn more about this later, but for now it's only important to understand that tagging photos can help you sort them.

7 Once added, a new folder will appear in the View pane.

7

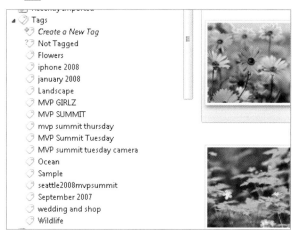

Change the Photo Gallery view

Next to the Search window (which works like other Search options in Vista), there's a thumbnail view button. Clicking it offers a menu that lets you choose how to view data in thumbnail view.

You can choose:

- Thumbnails – the default style. This option shows thumbnails you can resize using the Zoom tool, but the names of the pictures are not displayed.

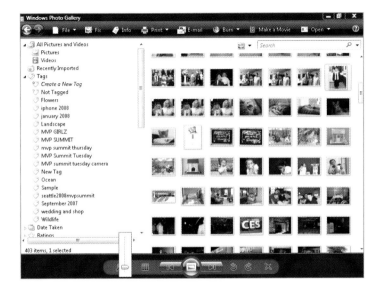

- Thumbnails with Text – this view is very similar to Thumbnails and what you see in that line of text depends on how other settings in Photo Gallery are configured.

13

The Photo Gallery interface (cont.)

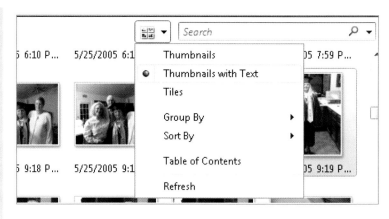

- Tiles – this view offers the most information. This view shows a picture's name, date modified, size, dimensions (resolution), rating and caption next to each image thumbnail.

For this 'tile', you can see the picture name (MVP Summit 2008 Sightseeing), the date the picture was taken, the time it was taken, the size of the picture, and the resolution used to take the picture (1600 × 1200). You can also see it's been rated (four out of five stars), and has a caption (Downtown Seattle). You can easily edit these data by double-clicking the thumbnail.

Sort and group

Under the Thumbnails button – after Thumbnails, Thumbnails with Text and Tiles – are a few other options. The two we'll cover here are Group By and Sort By.

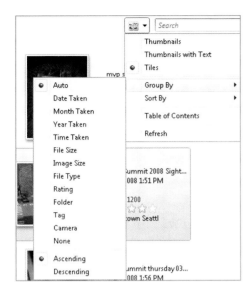

As you can see here, you can group pictures stored in a single folder in any number of ways. You may want to experiment with are Date Taken, Month Taken, Year Taken and Image Size, because this information is included with every digital picture you import with your digital camera. Other options, like Rating and Tag, are things you have to manually add yourself.

The Sort By option offers similar choices, including Date Taken, Date Modified, File Size, Image Size, Rating, Caption and File Name, and, as with Group By options, you can sort in ascending or descending order.

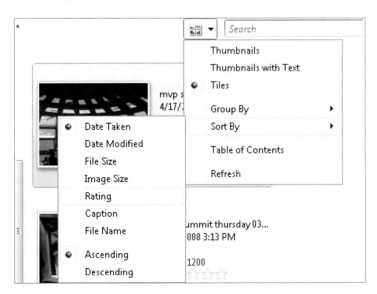

The Photo Gallery interface (cont.)

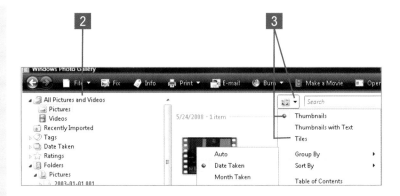

Personalising Photo Gallery

1. Open Windows Photo Gallery.

2. From the View pane, select All Pictures and Videos.

3. Click the Thumbnails button and select Tiles. (Note you can also select Thumbnails or Thumbnails with Text, but for this exercise, select Tiles.)

4. Click the Thumbnails button again.

5. Click Group By.

6. Click Date Taken. (Note how the images are now grouped by date.)

7. Click the Thumbnails button again.

8. Click Group By.

9. Click None.

10. Click the Thumbnails button again.

11. Click Sort By.

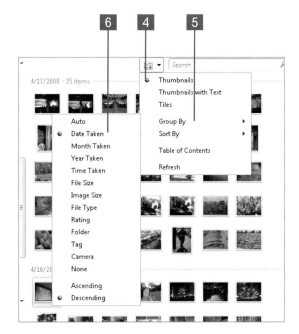

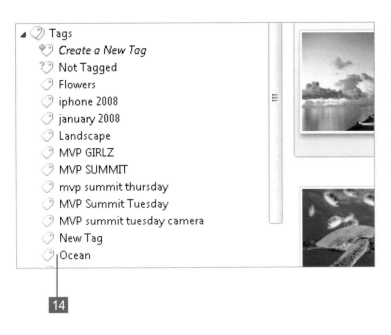

14

15

The Photo Gallery interface (cont.)

12 Click Image Size. (Note the images are sorted by size.)

13 In the View pane, expand Tags.

14 Click Ocean.

15 Use the Zoom button to enlarge the thumbnails.

16 Continue experimenting as desired.

13

Import pictures

There are lots of different hardware options for taking digital pictures, including mobile phones, smart phones, digital cameras, webcams and video cameras. And there are even more ways to store and carry pictures with you, including USB drives, music players and iPods and iPhones. Finally, there are multiple ways to get pictures onto a PC, including using digital cameras, media cards and even scanners. In this section we'll talk about the latter – importing pictures from a device to the PC. Remember, the device doesn't necessarily have to be something that takes the pictures; it can be a scanner, USB drive, media card or music player.

When you connect a digital camera, media card or other device that contains pictures, you'll be prompted to select a way to import them. You may see multiple options, as shown here, or only three or four. Whatever the case, choose Import pictures. This will walk you though the Import Pictures and Videos wizard, outlined in the next exercise.

Important

If nothing happens when you connect your camera, media card or other hardware, refer to the troubleshooting section at the end of this book, or click File and click Import from Camera or Scanner.

3

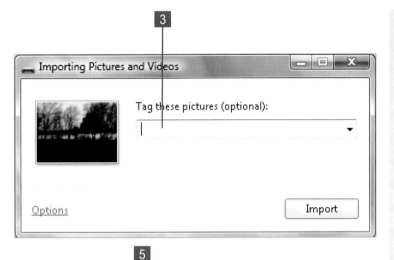

5

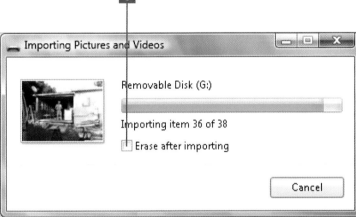

7

13

Importing pictures from a digital camera, media card or USB drive (and even an iPhone)

1 Connect the device. If applicable, turn it on.

2 When prompted, choose Import pictures using Windows.

3 Type a descriptive name for the group of pictures you're importing. (For now, we'll accept the default Options settings which include the date imported, so type a name only.)

4 Click Import.

5 If desired, tick Erase after importing. This will cause Vista to erase the images from the device after the import is complete.

6 Open Windows Photo Gallery.

7 Click Recently Imported. You'll see the imported images there.

Import pictures (cont.)

Windows won't recognise all devices, but it does a pretty good job. In fact, it will import pictures from many kinds of mobile phones, including the iPhone. However, on the slim chance your device isn't immediately recognised, you can click File, and click Import from Camera or Scanner, and you'll be given access to additional devices attached to your PC, even scanners.

With pictures now on your PC and available in Windows Photo Gallery, you will probably want to perform some editing. As noted earlier, Photo Gallery offers some editing options, including the ability to correct brightness and contrast, colour temperature, tint and saturation, as well as crop images and fix red eye. You may find after some time with Photo Gallery though, that you need more editing options. If that turns out to be the case, consider Photoshop Elements. It's a great program for beginners and offers all you'll probably ever need.

To begin editing a picture, first double-click it. From the Edit pane that appears you can choose from and apply the following:

- Auto Adjust – this tool automatically assesses the image and alters it, which most of the time results in a better image. However, there's always the Undo button and you'll probably use it on occasion.

- Adjust Exposure – this tool offers slider controls for Brightness and Contrast. You move these sliders to the left and right to adjust as desired.

- Adjust Color – this tool offers slider controls to adjust the temperature, tint and saturation of the photo. Temperature runs from blue to yellow, allowing you to change the 'atmosphere' of the image. Tint runs from green to red, and saturation moves from black and white to colour.

- Crop Picture – this tool remove parts of a picture you don't want.

- Fix Red Eye – this lets you draw a rectangle around any eye that has a red dot in it, and the red dot is automatically removed.

 Edit photos

13

Edit photos (cont.)

Fixing pictures

1 Open Photo Gallery.

2 In the View pane, select Pictures.

3 Position the Zoom slider so you can see several images at once.

4 Double-click a picture to edit. (Don't use the Sample Pictures.)

5 Click Fix.

6 Click Auto Adjust.

7 If you like the result, skip to Step 8. If not, click Undo.

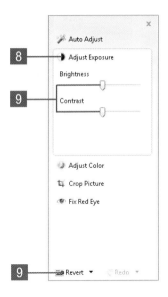

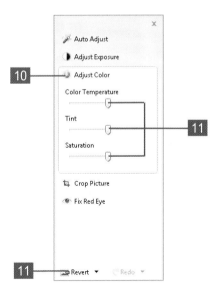

8 Click Adjust Exposure.

9 Move the sliders for Brightness and Contrast. Click Revert to return to the original image settings.

10 Click Adjust Color.

11 Move the sliders for Color Temperature Tint, and Saturation. Click Revert to return to the original image settings.

13

Edit photos (cont.)

12 Click Crop Picture.

13 Drag the corners of the box to resize it, and drag the entire box to move it around in the picture.

14 If desired, under Proportion, select any option. (Note you can also rotate the frame.)

15 Click Apply or Revert.

16 Click Fix Red Eye.

17 Drag the mouse over the red part of the eye. When you let go, the red eye in the picture will be removed.

18 Click Undo if desired.

19 To save the changes to the original file, i.e. write over the existing file, click Return to Gallery.

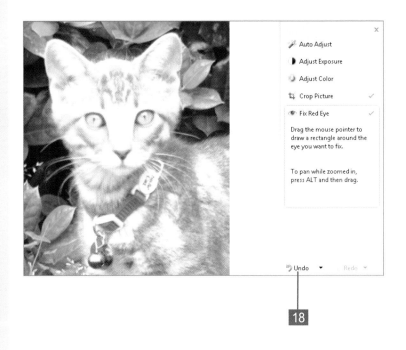

20 To revert to the original picture, click File, and click Revert to Original.

13

Tags

We've talked a little about tags throughout this chapter. That's because tags can be extremely useful when it comes to organising your photos. You have to apply tags to your photos though, which can be time consuming, but, once added, tags can be used to group pictures in useful ways. Some tags are applied automatically when you import pictures from a digital camera, including the date they were uploaded, along with any name you applied to the imported group. While the date is important, tagging a photo (or a group of photos) with a label like wedding, cat, Italy trip or similar name is a great addition.

Although there are several ways to add tags to photos, the easiest, in my opinion, is to create the tag in the View pane, and then select a photo or a group of photos, and drag those photos to the new tag name. The tag will be applied to those photos. Alternatively, you can select a photo and in the Info pane click Add Tags, or right-click any photo or group of photos and select Add Tags.

Pictures can have multiple tags too. You might tag a photo as Vacation, but also apply tags that name the people in the picture, the city or the country. To remove a tag, select the picture or pictures that have the tag and, in the Info pane, right-click the tag and select Remove Tag.

?

Did you know?

Another type of tag is a rating. You can rate pictures from one to five stars, and then filter the pictures as desired. You can add captions too. All of this can be done from the Info pane, among other places.

Edit photos (cont.)

Adding picture information (tagging)

1 Open Windows Photo Gallery.

2 Double-click any picture.

3 Click Add Tags.

4 Type a tag name.

5 Press Enter on the keyboard.

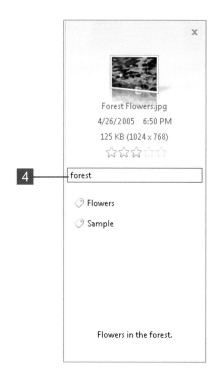

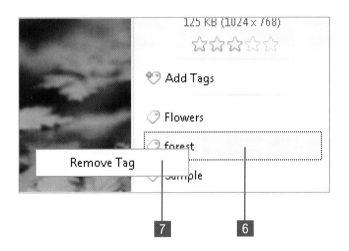

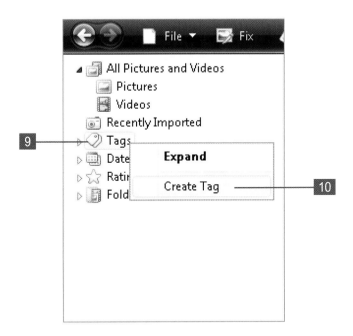

Edit photos (cont.)

6 To remove the tag (or any other tag), right-click the tag.

7 Click Remove Tag.

8 Click Back To Gallery.

9 Right-click Tags.

10 Click Create Tag.

13

Edit photos
(cont.)

11 Type a tag name. (To rename a tag, right-click the tag and choose Rename.)

12 Locate an image to apply the tag to. Select multiple images if desired.

13 Drag the selected image(s) to the new tag in the Tags list.

Timesaver tip

Hold down the Shift key to select contiguous images, and hold down the Ctrl key to select non-contiguous ones.

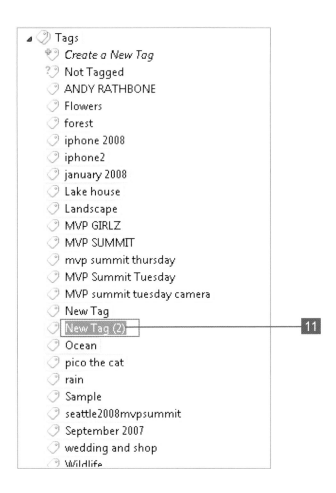

14 Click the tag name under Tags, to see the images.

15 To apply a rating, double-click any picture or select a group of pictures. In the Info pane, click the rating.

16 Repeat step 21 to add a caption. (Click Add Caption.)

13

Share photos

There are a number of ways to share your photos. You can view them on your PC, e-mail them to others and burn them to CDs and DVDs, just to name a few. You know (if you've worked through this book from the beginning) how to do most of this already. Here are a few ideas for sharing photos:

- Use your favourite photo as a desktop background – in Photo Gallery, right-click any photo and choose Set as Desktop Background.

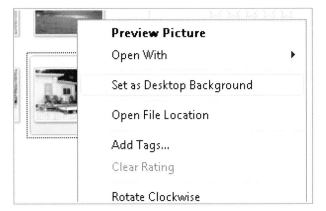

- Use a slide show of your photos as a screen saver – open Appearance and Personalization, and choose Screen Saver. (See Chapter 4.) For Screen Saver, select Photos. Click Settings to choose the folder to use.

- Print pictures using a photo printer – click Print in Windows Photo Gallery. Note you can also order prints online.

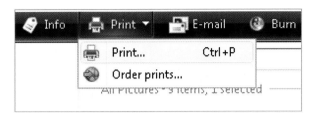

- Add pictures to a Movie Maker project – from Photo Gallery, click Make a Movie. Alternatively, you can browse for pictures from an existing Movie Maker project.

- Burn a DVD of pictures with Windows DVD Maker – from Photo Gallery, click Burn, and Video DVD. (For more information on Windows DVD Maker, see Chapter 14.)

- E-mail photos – in Photo Gallery, select the files to e-mail, click e-mail and, when prompted, choose either Small or Medium (for best results). Click Attach. (For more information on how to e-mail, see Chapter 9.)

Share photos
(cont.)

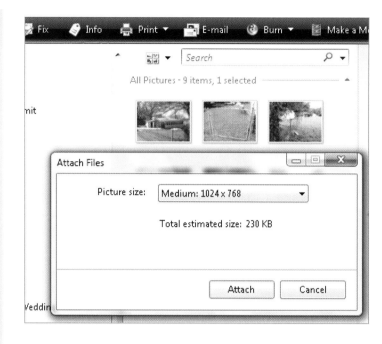

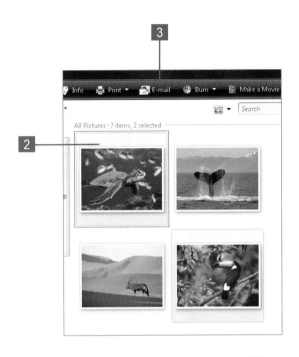

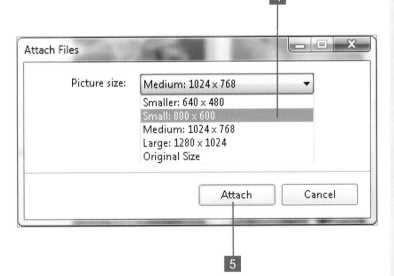

Share photos (cont.)

E-mailing pictures

1 Open Windows Photo Gallery.

2 Select pictures to e-mail.

3 Click E-mail.

4 Select a picture size. For e-mail, generally 800 x 600 is best. It's small enough to be sent and received quickly, even on dial-up, and it fits nicely in the recipient's inbox. The larger the image, the longer it will take to send and receive.

5 Click Attach.

13

Share photos
(cont.)

6 Type the recipient's name(s).

7 Consider rewriting the
   subject.

8 Consider deleting the text and
   writing your own in the body
   of the e-mail.

9 Click Send.

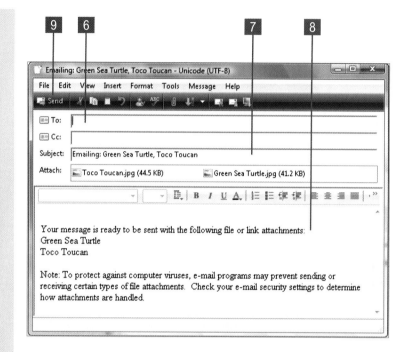

DVDs, videos and movies

Introduction

Windows Vista comes with two ways to view any DVDs you purchase or rent, or videos you produce using your own video camera: Windows Media Player and Windows Media Center. Windows Vista also allows you to create your own professional-looking DVDs using Windows DVD Maker or burn simple data DVDs with built-in drag and drop functionality. DVDs created with DVD Maker can contain pictures, videos and music, as well as menus, titles and backgrounds, just like the DVDs that you purchase. When you burn a DVD with Windows DVD Maker others can watch it on their televisions (using a DVD player). Finally, you can use Vista's Movie Maker to turn your own digital camera footage into a movie (and you can burn that to a DVD as well).

You may not have all of the tools and applications detailed in this chapter, because they don't all come with every Vista edition. Here's a summary:

■ Windows Media Player is included with every Windows Vista edition. You will watch DVDs and videos here if you have Windows Vista Basic or Vista Business. If you have Home Premium or Ultimate, you'll probably opt to watch DVDs in Media Center, because it's a more comprehensive media application.

■ Windows Movie Maker is included with every Windows Vista edition. You will create movies from footage you take with your digital video camera here no matter what edition of Vista you have. However, if you have Home Premium or Ultimate, you'll also have HD support.

What you'll do

Watch a DVD in Media Player

Watch a DVD in Media Center

Burn a simple data DVD

Create a professional DVD with Windows DVD Maker

■ Windows DVD Maker is included with Home Premium and Ultimate. If you have Basic, you'll have to use a third-party program to create professional-looking DVDs. It's likely though that if you have Basic, the DVD player included with the PC is not writeable anyway.

■ Windows Media Center is included with Home Premium and Ultimate. Windows Media Center is a fully-fledged application for watching television, getting movies online, organising media and more. Although you may have Media Center you still may not have the hardware required to use all of its features. For instance, you can't watch television without a television tuner installed, which you very well may not have.

You can watch a DVD on your computer just as you would on your home entertainment centre. In fact, some people are now getting rid of their home theatre systems in favour of a 'media center PC' that they connect to their large flat-screen TVs. New PCs built as media computers have television, DVRs, DVD players, music players, speakers, surround sound and more, installed and ready to use. And the best part is that it's often a more compact option than a combination of television, DVD player, cable box, DVR, stereo system, speakers and stacks of DVDs and CDs. That said, it's certainly possible to watch a DVD on your PC; it's one of the most basic entertainment options.

The first time you insert a DVD into the DVD drive, you'll be given at least one of the options shown here (and possibly more): Play DVD movie using Windows Media Player or Play DVD movie using Windows Media Center. You'll see other options if you have third-party software installed on the PC that can also play DVDs. Here you can see a third option, Play Movie using Play Movie (that's a third-party program that came preinstalled on this PC, and has nothing to do with Vista).

To watch a DVD, simply make a choice. Once the movie has started, you'll have access to controls, including fast forward, pause, rewind, stop, resume, volume and more. Here you can see an exercise video that's just about to start in Windows Media Player. Windows Media Player was covered in depth in Chapter 12.

14

Watch DVDs (cont.)

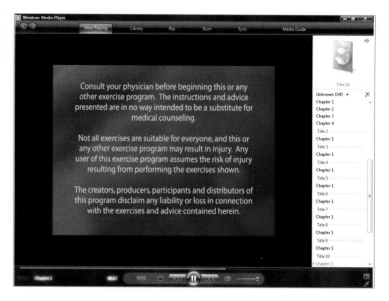

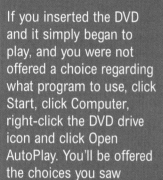

Important

If you inserted the DVD and it simply began to play, and you were not offered a choice regarding what program to use, click Start, click Computer, right-click the DVD drive icon and click Open AutoPlay. You'll be offered the choices you saw earlier. (There's a step-by-step on this later.)

Here's the same movie in Windows Media Center. The controls are very similar to Media Player's controls, except there are options for changing the channel, and a few more fast-forward and rewind controls, which let you move more effectively backward and forward.

If you have Home Premium or Ultimate, I'll suggest you start out with Windows Media Center the first time you watch a DVD. If not, Windows Media Player will do just fine.

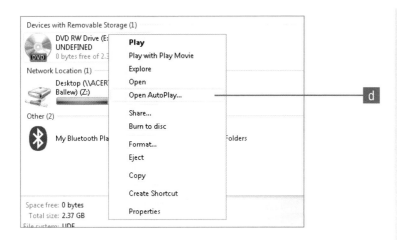

Devices with Removable Storage (1)

DVD RW Drive (E:
UNDEFINED
0 bytes free of 2.3

Network Location (1)

Desktop (\\ACER
Ballew) (Z:)

Other (2)

My Bluetooth Pla

Space free: 0 bytes
Total size: 2.37 GB
File system: UDF

| **Play** |
| Play with Play Movie |
| Explore |
| Open |
| Open AutoPlay... |
| Share... |
| Burn to disc |
| Format... |
| Eject |
| Copy |
| Create Shortcut |
| Properties |

Folders

d

Watch DVDs (cont.)

Watching a DVD in Media Player

1 Find the button on the PC's tower, keyboard or laptop that opens the DVD drive door. Press it.

2 Place the DVD in the door and press the button again to close it. (Often you can lightly push the door, but not always, so it's best to use the button.)

3 When prompted, choose Play DVD movie using Windows Media Player. If you are not prompted, and the DVD opens in another application, that's fine if that's what you want to use. If it is not what you want to use:

a. Press the Stop button in the application, the Esc key on the keyboard, and/or click the x in the right corner of the window to close the application. There may also be a File menu, where you can select Close.

b. Click the Start button.

c. Click Computer.

d. Right-click the DVD drive icon and click Open AutoPlay.

14

Watch DVDs (cont.)

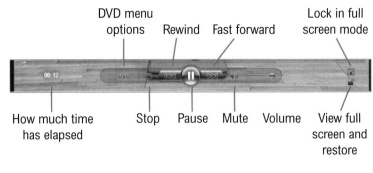

DVD menu options   Rewind   Fast forward   Lock in full screen mode

How much time has elapsed   Stop   Pause   Mute   Volume   View full screen and restore

e. When prompted, choose Play DVD movie using Windows Media Player.

4 The movie may start automatically, or you may be prompted to choose from a menu. Options may include Play Movie, View Special Features, or other options. Use the controls to manage the movie. Windows Media Player controls are outlined here.

5 To return to the Title menu, or the menu shown when you input the DVD, click DVD and choose Title Menu.

6 To skip around in the DVD, either move the slider or choose a title from the Media Guide pane.

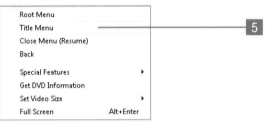

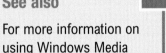

See also

For more information on using Windows Media Player, refer to Chapter 12.

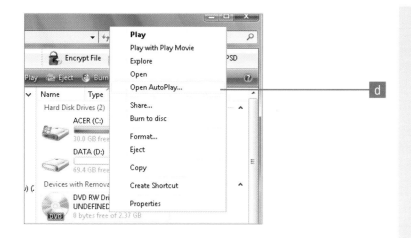

Watching a DVD in Media Center

1 Find the button on the PC's tower, keyboard or laptop that opens the DVD drive door. Press it.

2 Place the DVD in the door and press the button again to close it. (Often you can lightly push the door, but not always, so it's best to use the button.)

3 When prompted, choose Play DVD movie using Windows Media Center. If you are not prompted, and the DVD opens in another application, that's fine if that's what you want to use. If it is not what you want to use:

a. Press the Stop button in the application, the Esc key on the keyboard, and/or click the x in the right corner of the window to close the application. There may also be a File menu, where you can select Close.

b. Click the Start button.

c. Click Computer.

d. Right-click the DVD drive icon and click Open AutoPlay.

14

For your information

If you have additional media player options, you may be prompted to make a choice before starting the DVD. Choose Windows Media Center.

Watch DVDs (cont.)

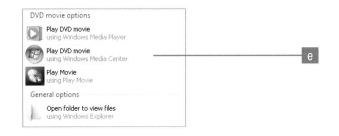

e. When prompted, choose Play DVD movie using Windows Media Center.

4 The movie will start automatically. Use the controls to manage the movie. The Windows Media Center controls that you need to understand to manage DVD playback are outlined here.

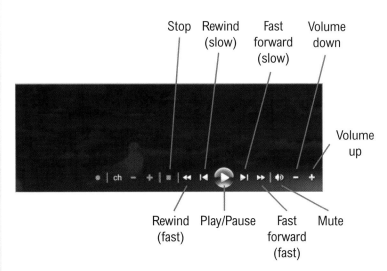

Stop Rewind (slow) Fast forward (slow) Volume down

Volume up

Rewind (fast) Play/Pause Fast forward (fast) Mute

Burn a data DVD

If you want to copy data from your computer to a DVD, you can do so in virtually any window that contains data. Here is a Pictures folder and you can see the Burn icon on the toolbar. To burn a DVD, simply select the data you want to copy and click this icon. When prompted (and the DVD door will open automatically), insert a blank DVD, type a title for it and click Next. If anything else is required, you'll be prompted.

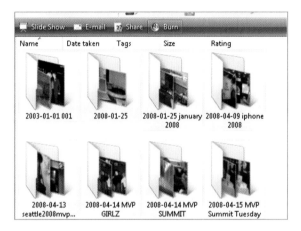

This process is normally reserved for backing up data (as opposed to creating a DVD you will share with others) because there are no options to create menus, scenes or otherwise give the DVD a professional look. If you want to create a DVD for viewing on a TV set using a DVD player, it's best to use Windows DVD Maker. We'll cover that next but, for now, let's use the Burn icon to create a simple data DVD for the purpose of backing up data.

Watch DVDs (cont.)

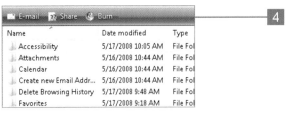

Burning data to a DVD

1 Click Start.

2 Click Documents (or select Pictures, your personal folder or any other folder that contains data you need to back up).

3 Select the data to burn to the DVD. To select contiguous files or folders, hold down the Shift key while selecting. To select non-contiguous files or folders, hold down the Ctrl key while selecting.

4 Click Burn.

5 Insert a writeable disk into your DVD drive.

6 Click the arrow next to Show formatting options.

7 Depending on the type of DVD burner you have and the type of DVD disk you inserted, you may be prompted to select a file system type, as shown here. You'll have to decide what kind of DVD you want to burn. I prefer the default, Live File System, for backing up data if it's offered, because I can add data on the fly to the same disk later. I use Mastered for creating DVDs I'll play using DVD players.

You can also insert a blank, writeable or rewriteable DVD, and wait for a prompt to burn data to it. You can burn data to a disk using Windows Media Player, Windows, Windows DVD Maker and any third-party programs you have installed.

If you choose to burn data to a disk using Windows, you'll work through the same process detailed here. If you choose Media Player, you'll be prompted to drag music from your music, picture or video libraries to the burn list. And if you choose Windows DVD Maker, the application will open where you can select the data to add to the DVD.

See also

Burning a CD using Windows Media Player is covered in Chapter 12. Burning a DVD is the same. Remember though, only music CDs play in car stereos; DVDs do not.

Burn DVDs with Windows DVD Maker

Windows DVD Maker is an application included with Windows Vista Home Premium and Vista Ultimate that guides you through the process of burning a DVD that you or anyone else can watch on a TV using a common DVD player. You can also use the program to create menus, scene selection pages and even slide shows using your favourite songs as a soundtrack. This is an extensive program, and is a much better option when you want to burn a DVD to show others (as opposed to simply backing up data to a DVD). Windows DVD Maker provides a wizard to help you choose what to put on the DVD, to create professional-looking menus and transitions, and to save the data to the DVD so it can be played with a DVD player (not just a DVD drive on a PC). You can find Windows DVD Maker in the Start, All Programs menu.

8 Click Next.

9 For the most part, that's it. If a window pops up and says that files are waiting to be burned to a DVD, click the message and click Burn again. Otherwise, simply wait for the process to finish. (The DVD will automatically eject when the burn is complete.)

Important

Even if you are running Windows Vista Home Premium or Ultimate, it's possible Windows DVD Maker won't run. That's because Windows DVD Maker requires that your PC meets specific video hardware requirements. If your PC doesn't meet the minimum requirements, you won't be able to use the program.

14

Watch DVDs (cont.)

Get started

When you open Windows DVD Maker, you'll see a friendly introduction. Read the introduction and click Choose Photos and Videos to get started.

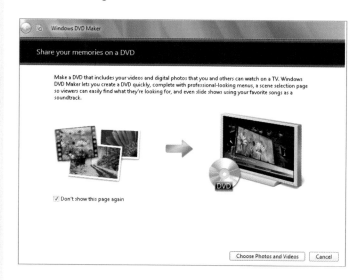

In the second wizard page, you'll add pictures and videos. You can drag and drop these items if you can position the two open windows so that you can access each or you can click the Add items button. When you click Add items, you then browse to and select the data to add. As you add pictures, they are stored in a folder called Slide show. You can add pictures and videos until you've run out of space on the DVD. There's a nice little icon on the bottom to show you how much space you have left.

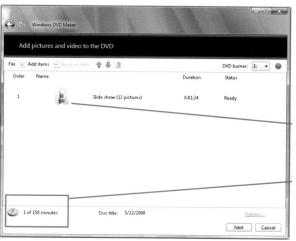

Pictures are stored here

This shows how much space is left on the disk

Once you've added your data, you can reorder them as desired by dragging and dropping, or by selecting the data and using the up and down buttons on the toolbar. After you've added your data, you'll create a disk title.

Configure Options

You may have noticed a small Options link in the lower right corner of the DVD Maker's window. Click this link to open the Options window.

The following options are available:

- Start with DVD menu – select this option to have your DVD perform like most DVDs you've seen, by displaying a DVD menu when inserted.

- Play video and end with DVD menu – select this option to have your DVD play the content first and display the menu after the content is complete.

- Play video in a continuous loop – select this option to have your DVD play in a loop. Users will have to press the Menu button on their DVD remote control or player to access any menus you create.

14

Watch DVDs
(cont.)

- DVD aspect ratio – select a ratio that you think matches what your viewers will use to watch your DVD (or what you will use). A 4:3 aspect is almost square while a 16:9 is 'widescreen' or rectangular.

- Video format – select from NTSC or PAL video format. NTSC format is correct for the USA but PAL is used in the UK, Italy, Ireland, Spain and others.

- Other DVD settings – select the fastest setting. If you have problems during the burn process, choose a slower speed.

Menus, text, foreground and background video, Scenes button, and more

Once you've added your data and clicked Next, you'll have additional options for personalising your DVD. You can skip all of it if you like or you can go crazy, spending hours tweaking menus and such. You can also preview the DVD (always a good idea), add music and change options for the slide show.

At the very least, you should click Preview to see how the movie will look prior to burning it to a DVD. You should also browse through the Menu Styles list. Here I've selected Special Occasion for the Menu Style, and you can see the preview here. This would be a great Menu Style for a DVD for a play or wedding.

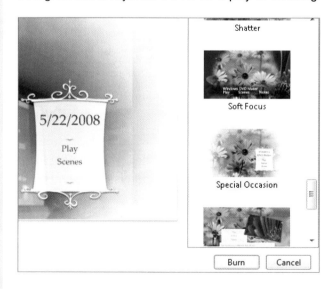

If you want to spend more time here, click the Menu text button. You can change the font and its attributes, the title and the text used for the Play, Scenes and Notes. You can also write your own personalised note! Make changes using the Customize menu toolbar button; add foreground and background video, and even audio; or change the Scenes button style.

Finally, click the Slide show button to change any slide show settings. This includes adding music and animation, as well as choosing how one picture transitions into another.

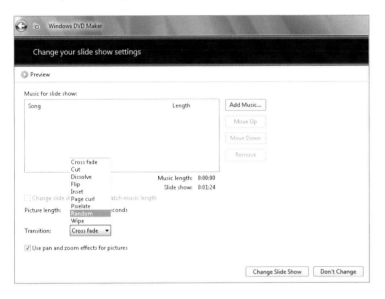

Burning the disk

Once you're ready, and made sure you've previewed your movie, click the Burn button. Insert a blank disk into the drive and wait while the DVD Maker creates the disk.

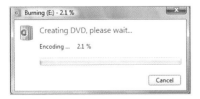

14

Watch DVDs (cont.)

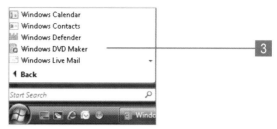

Creating a professional DVD with Windows DVD Maker

1 Click Start.

2 Click All Programs.

3 Click Windows DVD Maker.

4 Click Choose Photos and Videos.

5 Click Add items.

6 Browse to the data you want to add. You might choose the Videos folder, or the Pictures folder, for instance, as shown here.

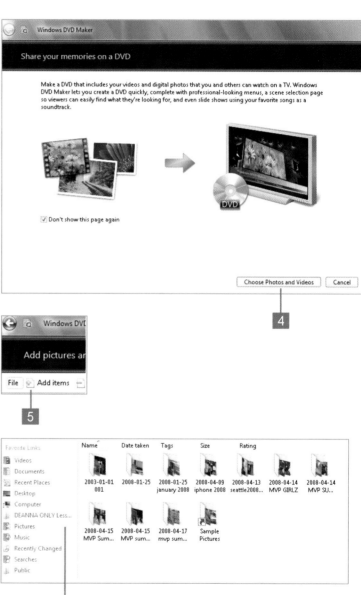

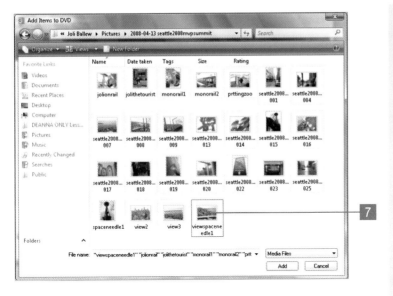

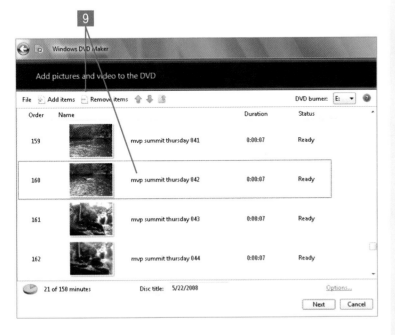

7 Select the items to add, click Add. (Remember, you can select contiguous items by holding down the Shift key or non-contiguous items by holding down the Ctrl key.) You have to choose individual images; you can't choose entire folders. Repeat this step until all data have been added.

8 Double-click the Slide show folder to open it, if you've added images.

9 Select any picture or select multiple pictures and click Remove items if desired.

14

Watch DVDs (cont.)

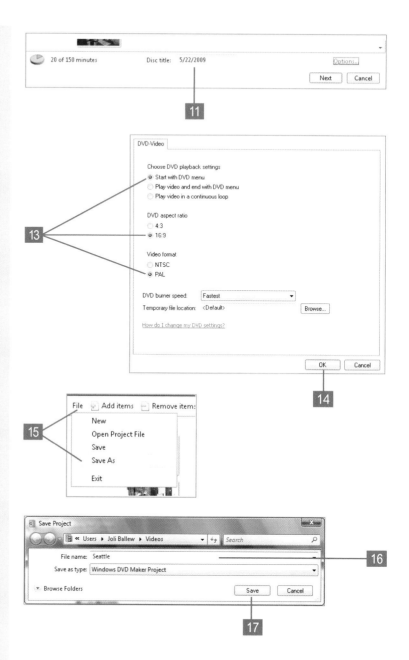

10 Select any picture and use the up- and down-arrow keys to reposition the picture in the list. Remember, pictures will be displayed in the order they appear here. (You can also drag and drop.)

11 Type a name for the disk. By default, it's today's date.

12 Click Options.

13 In the DVD Options window, make changes as desired.

14 Click OK.

15 Click File, and click Save As. (If something happens, you can reopen this file later.)

16 Type a file name.

17 Note that by default, the file will save in the Videos folder of your personal folder. Click Save.

18 Click Next.

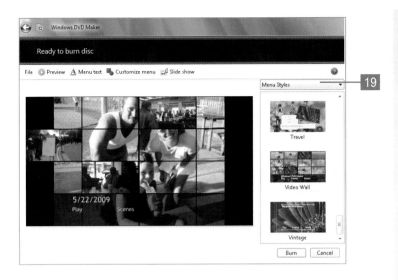

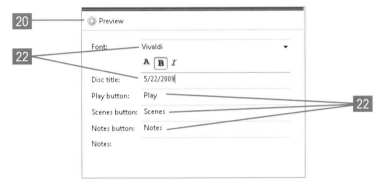

19 Make a selection from the Menu Styles list.

20 Click Preview. Watch the video to see if you like the menu selection. Click OK. Repeat Steps 19 and 20 as desired.

21 Click Menu Text.

22 Select a font from the drop-down list. Change the Disc title and choose a different word to represent Play, Scenes or Notes. (For instance, you might change Notes to Disclaimer or Read This First!)

? 14

Did you know?

At any point, you can click Burn to complete the DVD. You do not have to personalise the DVD.

23 Click Change Text.

24 Click Customize menu.

25 Click Browse to select a foreground video, background video or menu audio if desired. Locate the file and click Open to add it.

Watch DVDs (cont.)

26 Select a new Scenes button style.

27 Click Change Style.

28 Click Slide Show.

29 Click Add Music to add music tracks to the DVD. Browse to the file to add, and click Add.

30 Click how many seconds each picture in the slide show should appear before changing to the next picture.

31 Select a transition.

32 Click Change Slide Show to apply changes.

33 Click Burn.

Networking

Introduction

Windows Vista offers plenty of ways to network (connect) multiple computers. If you have more than one computer in your home, you should consider connecting them. With all of your computers networked, you can share data, printers and an Internet connection.

Vista offers the following to help you get started:

- Network and Sharing Center – a collection of features where you can easily access network connections, sharing options, networked computers and devices, and diagnose and repair features.

- Network (from the Start menu) – the Network window offers links to computers on your network and the Network and Sharing Center. You can also add printers and wireless devices here.

- Network Map – the Network Map details each of your network connections graphically and allows you to distinguish easily among wired, wireless and Internet connections.

- Network Setup Wizard – use this wizard to create a network. You can also tell Vista you want to allow (or block) folder and printer sharing.

What you'll do

Add Vista to an existing network

Enable Network Discovery

Share a dial-up Internet connection

Share a personal folder

Manage network connections

Add Vista to an existing network

When you connect a Vista PC to a wired network or get within range of a wireless one (and you have wireless hardware installed in your computer), Vista will find the network and then ask you what kind of network it is. It's a public network if you're in a coffee shop, library or café, and it's a private network if it's a network you manage, like one already in your home. Connecting to an existing network allows you to access shared features of the network. In a coffee shop that's probably only a connection to the Internet; if it's a home network, it's your personal, shared data (and probably a connection to the Internet too).

When a network is accessible, either because you've connected to it using an 'Ethernet' cable or through a wireless network card inside your PC, the Set Network Location wizard will appear.

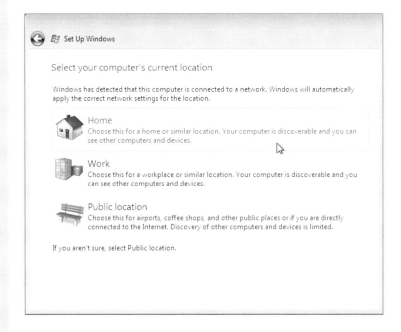

For your information

You might have seen the Set Network Location window if you installed Vista yourself *and* if your network adapter was found by the setup process *and* if a network was in range.

There are three network options, and when you see the Set Network Location dialogue box, you need to select one. Here's how to recognise which one to choose:

- Home – choose this if the network is your home network or a network you trust (like a network at a relative's house). This connection type lets your computer *discover* other PCs, printers and devices on the network and they can see you.

- Work – choose this if you are connecting to a network at work. The settings for Work and Home are the same, only the titles differ so you can tell them apart easily.

- Public location – choose this if the network you want to connect to is open to anyone within range of it, like networks in coffee shops, airports, and libraries. Vista figures that if you choose Public, you only want to connect to the Internet and nothing else. It closes down *discoverability*, so that even your shared data are safe.

After successfully connecting to a network, one of three Network icons will appear in the Notification area of the taskbar:

- Connected with local and Internet access – you are connected to the local network and the Internet. You can access shared data on the local network.

- Connected with local access only – you are connected to the local network and can access shared local resources and data, but you do not have Internet access.

15

Add Vista to an existing network (cont.)

■ Disconnected – you are not connected to the Internet or a local network. This is generally due to a break somewhere in the process, like a router that's been turned off or a disabled wireless network card.

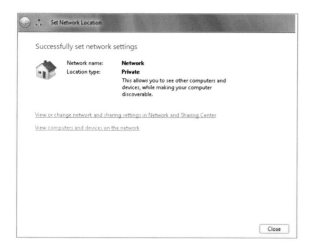

Adding Vista to an existing network

1. Connect physically to a wired network using an Ethernet cable or, if you have wireless hardware installed in your PC, get within range of a wireless network.

2. Select Home, Work, or Public Location. (If necessary input credentials.)

3. You will see that the network was set up, as shown here.

! Important

It isn't always this easy; if you run into problems you'll need to troubleshoot the issue to resolve it. We'll cover a little of that here and in the Troubleshooting section at the end of this book.

15

Types of networks

If you already have a network set up and you've joined your new Vista PC to it, you can skip this section. This section and the section following it are for those readers who do not yet have a network but would like to create one. That said, if you want to create a new network, read on. Otherwise, skip to the section **The Network and Sharing Center**.

While there are many ways to connect two or more PCs, I'll suggest you choose from one of these three: direct connection, Ethernet or wireless. Let's look at each of these in more detail.

Direct connection

If you have only two computers, do not want to purchase expensive equipment, and you trust everyone who has access to the two computers, you may want to consider a direct connection network. This is an older technology though, and thus the connection between the two computers will be much slower than newer alternatives. However, if you don't want to purchase expensive equipment, this is the way to go. Often you only need to purchase one thing: an Ethernet crossover cable.

For this method to work, both computers must be able to connect to an Ethernet cable. That means that each computer must either have a network interface card (NIC) or a USB port for attaching a USB-to-Ethernet converter.

I will venture to say that all computers that come with Vista preinstalled will have the required NIC, but it's possible older computers do not. If you want to use this method but don't have an Ethernet port in one of the PCs, purchase and install an external USB-to-Ethernet converter. (If you don't have a USB port, there are additional options like serial-to-Ethernet adapters.) Once connected, you can share an Internet connection and data, just as you can with any network.

For your information

An Ethernet port looks similar to the port you use to connect your telephone to a wall jack or a phone cord to a modem in the PC; the Ethernet port is just a bit larger.

Did you know?

Another option for connecting two PCs directly is to use a USB-to-USB direct link cable. Microsoft offers the Easy Transfer cable that can be used for this purpose. If both PCs have a USB port, consider this option.

Ethernet

If you have more than two computers to network, consider an Ethernet network. Ethernet networks connect computers through a hardware device like a router. A router is a small piece of external hardware that offers multiple Ethernet ports for plugging in multiple computers and 'routes' the data flowing through the network from PC to PC. Routers come in four-port, six-port and similar varieties. Ethernet networks are fast too, and are a good option when sharing a broadband Internet connection.

The downside here is that you have to purchase a router and cables, and you have to set it up (or pay someone to do it). Often this also entails adding a cable modem to the mix, so you have to know how to position the equipment. While routers come with instructions, it can be a time-consuming and frustrating task. So if you're new to routers, cable modems and networking, have the network professionally installed or call on your children or neighbours to help. If you want to set it up yourself though, no problem. I'll include some generic instructions shortly.

Wireless

Wireless networks are the third option. Wireless networks use radio waves, just like mobile phones and walkie-talkies, and allow you to connect to your networked PCs without cables. If you have a laptop with a built-in wireless card, this is the way to go. If you have older computers that do not have wireless capabilities, you can still make it work. Just get a wireless router that offers a few Ethernet ports. Additionally, you could purchase a USB adapter or PCI card for any computer not wireless-ready. While this network is great once it's set up, like any new network, getting it up and running can be time consuming and frustrating. Instructions that come with the hardware, in my experience at least, are clear, but if you've never done this type of thing before, consider having it professionally installed or getting help from a relative or friend. I'll include some generic instructions shortly if you want to do it yourself though.

15

Physically install new network hardware

Because of the different types of routers, networking hardware and configurations, there's no way I can walk you through physically installing every type of network hardware here. The hardware you purchase will come with specific instructions anyway, and setup is not always the same from manufacturer to manufacturer. However, I can offer information that is generic to specific networks and understanding this may make installing hardware easier.

Direct connection networks

When creating a direct connection network, you first need to connect the two PCs using the desired cable (Easy Transfer or Ethernet Crossover). You may also have to install USB-to-Ethernet converters if your PCs don't have Ethernet ports. Once you make the connection, Vista will attempt to configure it and you'll be prompted when a network is available. Once a network is available, you can tweak it using the Network and Sharing Center. There will be more on that later.

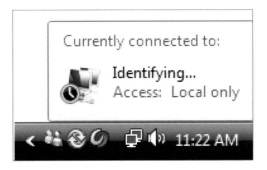

For your information
Computers that are in the same 'workgroup' can communicate more easily than those that are not. By default, Vista names a workgroup WORKGROUP. If you can't see other computers on your network, consider changing their workgroup names to WORKGROUP. (You can do this by right-clicking Computer on Vista or My Computer on Windows XP and choosing Properties.)

Ethernet networks

Direct connection networks generally only require the installation of a single cable, but Ethernet networks require much more setup. Although there's no way to outline how to install the hardware for any Ethernet hardware, the following steps usually need to be performed in the order detailed here.

1 Set up any satellite, cable or broadband modems and connect one of the PCs to the Internet. This may already be done.

2 Set up the router as detailed in the instructions that come with it. For the most part you'll need to:

   a. Install the router software.
   b. Connect the router to the external cable or satellite modem through the router's WAN port.
   c. Connect the PC to an available Ethernet port on the router.
   d. Run the setup wizard provided by the router manufacturer and work through the wizard and/or follow the written directions.
   e. During setup, if prompted regarding how your ISP obtains an IP address, choose *Obtain an IP Address Automatically*. If you have problems with this step, call your ISP.

3 Once the router is configured, turn off the PC, cable or satellite modem, and router.

4 Turn on the modem and wait for all self-tests to complete.

5 Turn on the router and wait for all self-tests to complete.

6 Turn on each PC.

15

Physically install new network hardware (cont.)

Wireless networks

During the process of configuring your wireless router, you'll also set up your wireless network. You'll want to follow the directions that come with your wireless hardware, which often begins with the direction to install the wireless router's software. As with Ethernet networks, you'll need to make sure you have a working connection to the Internet before starting. Once software is installed, you'll be prompted to physically install the hardware.

The hardware you need to install a wireless network includes:

- a wireless router (also called an access point)
- a wireless network adapter for each computer on your network
- an installation CD
- external cable, DSL or satellite modem.

During setup you'll be prompted to create a Wireless Network Name (SSID), passphrase or password, and security settings. Don't worry, there's almost always a wizard to guide you through this. However, just to be on the safe side, here are few terms you should be familiar with:

- SSID – this is the name you create and use for the wireless network during setup.
- Channel – this denotes the operating frequency your wireless network will use. Don't worry, this will probably be configured automatically.
- Mode – this is where you'll tell setup what type of wireless hardware you are using (G, B, A, etc.) but you can simply choose Auto to let the software configure all of that for you.
- Encryption – this is the security you'll apply to your network. You can choose:
  - None – no data encryption
  - WEP – Wired Equivalent Privacy, 64-bit or 128-bit options. 64-bit WEP uses 10 hexadecimal digits (0–9 and A–F) for a password; 128-bit uses 26 hexadecimal digits

- Security Encryption (WPA-PSK, WPA2-PSK, WPA-PSK+WPA2-PSK) – WiFi Protected Access with Pre-Shared Key; the Passphrase is 8–63 characters in length.

This isn't nearly as complicated as it sounds though, for the most part all of this will happen automatically. During setup you'll also be prompted to install the hardware. Again, instructions will be included but generically, you'll perform the following steps:

1. Place the router near the centre of the area where all your PCs will operate. Make sure it's elevated so all PCs have access to its wireless signal. Keep the router away from microwaves and similar devices.

2. Verify a cable modem is installed and connected to the Internet.

3. Connect an Ethernet cable from the Ethernet out jack on the modem to the WAN port on the wireless router.

4. Connect an Ethernet cable from the Vista PC to the wireless router.

5. Complete any additional instructions.

Once the network is set up, all you have to do is wait for Vista to discover the network and prompt you to join. If necessary, reread the section **Add Vista to an existing network** to review how this works.

15

Set up a connection or network

Once your hardware is installed, you'll need to tell Vista you want to set up the network. Often, simply enabling network discovery works, as shown here. Notice the Workgroup name is WORKGROUP. It's best that all computers use the same workgroup name, but it isn't required. Once you've enabled Network Discovery on a network, the network should be configured and working properly.

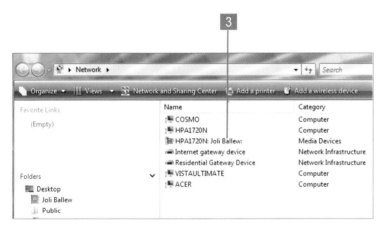

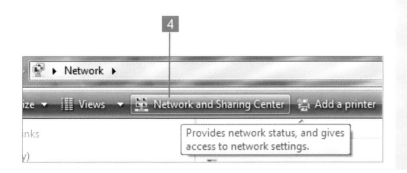

Provides network status, and gives access to network settings.

Set up a connection or network (cont.)

Enable Network Discovery

1 Click Start.

2 Click Network.

3 If you see more than one PC listed in the Network window, the network is already configured. You can skip to the section **The Network and Sharing Center**.

4 Click Network and Sharing Center.

5 Under Sharing and Discovery, click the down-arrow next to Off by Network discovery. It will become an upwards arrow.

15

Set up a connection or network (cont.)

6 Click Turn on network discovery.

7 Click Apply.

8 If you know the name of your workgroup, and the workgroup name shown here is not correct, click Change settings. Otherwise, note the name of the workgroup as configured.

9 Click Change under Computer Name.

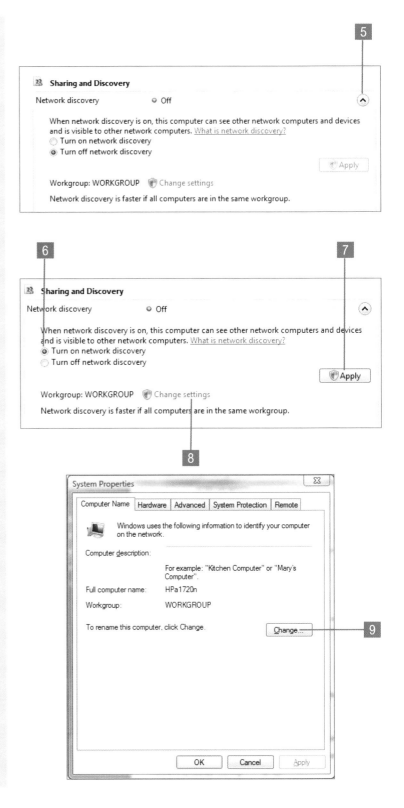

10 Type a new workgroup name.

11 Click OK. Click OK.

15

Set up a connection or network (cont.)

Sharing a dial-up Internet connection

1 After enabling Network Discovery on your Vista PC, click Start.

2 Click Network.

3 Click Network and Sharing Center.

4 Click Manage network connections.

5 Right-click the connection used to connect to the Internet.

6 Click Properties.

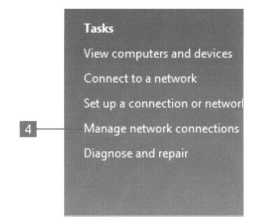

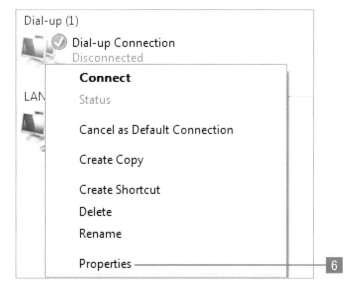

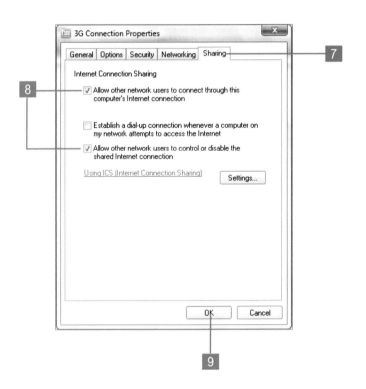

Set up a connection or network (cont.)

7 Click the Sharing tab (if you have a dial-up connection).

8 Select Allow other network users to connect through this computer's Internet connection. If desired, deselect Allow other network users to control or disable the shared Internet connection.

9 Click OK.

15

Share data

The main reasons people create a network is to share data, printers, media and an Internet connection. In this section, we'll talk about sharing data. There are two ways to share data: you can either put the data you want to share in the built-in Public folders or you can share data using personal folders you create. You can use a combination of the two as well. How do you know which to use and when? Here are some things to take into consideration.

Public folder sharing

Public folders are already built into Vista's folder structure. The Public folder contains several subfolders, including Public Downloads, Public Documents, Public Music, Public Pictures, Public Videos and Recorded TV. You can create your own folders here too. To share data using the folders, simply save or place the data there. Then, anyone who has access to the computer or network can access what's in the folders easily.

Use the Public folder for sharing if:

- You want every person with a user account on the computer to be able to access what's in the folder.

- You want to share files and folders from a single location on your PC. If you choose to use your personal folders, shared data will not all be stored in a central location.

- You want to be able to access, view and modify everything you have shared quickly.

- You want everything you are sharing kept separate from the data that you do not want to share.

- You do not need to configure different sharing rules for different people who have access. You are okay with everyone having access to the data and everyone being able to do what they wish with the data.

- You prefer to use the default shared settings and do not want to manually share data, or enable settings in the Network and Sharing Center.

Timesaver tip

You can locate the Public folders by typing Public in the Start Search window. You can also right-click the Public folders icon, as shown on the next page, and choose Send To, and then Desktop to create a shortcut to the folder on your PC's desktop.

Personal folder sharing

Your personal folders and any folders you create yourself can be shared. In contrast to using Public folders for sharing, with personal folder sharing you have much more control over the shared data.

Use any folder for sharing if:

- You want to share data directly from your personal folders, like Documents, Pictures or Music, and do not want to have to resave or move data you want to share to your Public folder.

- You want to allow some users the ability to change the data in the shared folders while at the same time only allowing others to view data. Additionally, you want to completely block others from accessing the data at all. (You can't do this with Public folder sharing.)

- You want to share large files that would be burdensome to copy and manage in a separate shared folder.

15

Share data (cont.)

Permissions for shared folders

When you share a folder, you can configure who can access the folder and what their permission rights are. First, you add users who can access the data and then configure them with the following permission types:

- Owner – the person who creates the folder is the owner. The owner can view, add, edit or delete anything in the folder as well as delete the folder itself.

- Co-owner – users with this permission level can view, add, edit or delete any file in the folder.

- Contributor – users with this permission level can view or add shared files others create, but can only edit or delete files which they themselves added to the folder.

- Reader – users with this permission level can view the files and nothing else.

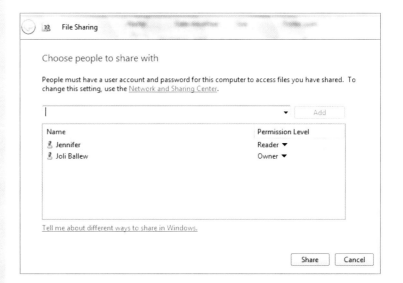

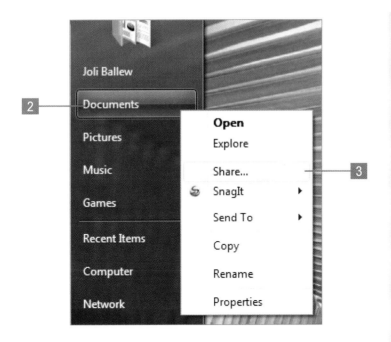

Sharing a personal folder

1. Locate a folder to share. In this example, I'll share my Documents folder.

2. Right-click the folder.

3. Click Share.

4. Click the down-arrow to select a user.

15

Share data
(cont.)

5 Click Add.

6 Click the down-arrow by the new user's name to select a permission level.

7 Click Share.

Manage network connections is an option under the Tasks list in the Network and Sharing Center. This opens the Network Connections window. There, you can view all of the available and/or configured connections, right-click them, and perform network connection-related tasks.

By right-clicking you can access the following:

- Disable – click this to disable the device. If you are connected to a network through this device, you'll be disconnected.

- Diagnose – use this to start the Windows Network Diagnostics wizard.

- Rename – click this to rename a connection.

- View status of this connection. This launches the connection Status window, which was described previously.

- Properties – click this to change the settings of the connection. You probably won't need to be here very often, if at all.

Manage network connections

15

Manage network connections (cont.)

Managing network connections

1. Click the network icon in the Notification area.

2. Click Network and Sharing Center.

3. Click Manage network connections.

4. View the available connections. You may have several including a wireless connection to the local café, a dial-up connection through a connected mobile phone, a broadband Internet connection and an Ethernet connection to a local network.

5. Right-click the connection desired.

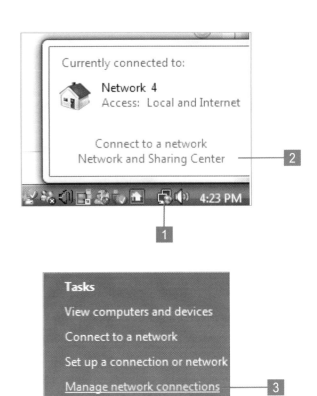

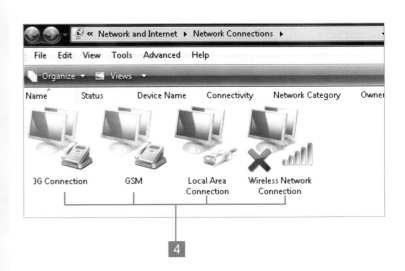

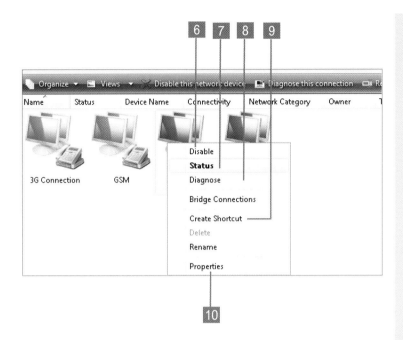

6 7 8 9

Organize ▼ 🖿 Views ▼ ✖ Disable this network device 🖭 Diagnose this connection ⬜ Re

| Name | Status | Device Name | Connectivity | Network Category | Owner | T |

3G Connection   GSM

Disable
Status
Diagnose

Bridge Connections

Create Shortcut
Delete
Rename

Properties

10

Manage network connections (cont.)

6 Click Disable to disable the connection. This does not delete the connection.

7 Click Status to see the status of the connection. You can view activity and bytes sent and received, among other things.

8 Click Diagnose to find and resolve problems with the connection.

9 Click Create Shortcut to create a shortcut for the connection.

10 Click Properties to see the properties for the connection.

Jargon buster

Router – a piece of equipment used to send data from computer to computer on a network. A router 'routes' the data to the correct PC and also rejects data that are harmful or from unknown sources.

Ethernet cable – a cable that is used to connect PCs to routers and cable modems, among other things.

Network Discovery – a state where computers can find other computers on the network. Network Discovery must be on to locate and communicate with network devices.

Network – a group of computers, printers and other devices that communicate via wireless or through wired connections.

Permissions – rules associated with a shared resource, like a folder, file or printer.

15

Appendix A: Windows Easy Transfer

Windows Easy Transfer helps you transfer data to a new Windows Vista PC from an existing PC in your home. It can also help you transfer data when you install Vista on a PC you already own.

When you install Vista yourself using an installation disk you purchase, you have two choices. You can perform an upgrade or a clean installation. If you choose to upgrade an existing PC, Vista will install and keep all of your settings and programs intact, which is certainly a convenience. Unfortunately, it will also keep problems. An upgrade is only recommended if you have not experienced any problems on the PC, including error messages, notifications of missing files or viruses. In most cases you should choose a clean installation. If you choose to upgrade a PC, you won't need to use Windows Easy Transfer.

If you choose to perform a clean installation of Vista on a PC, Vista will first delete everything on that PC. This includes documents, personal files, program settings and e-mail, ISP settings and more. However, a clean installation gives you a fresh start and problems will be erased along with your data. This includes viruses and error messages too. If you perform a clean installation but want to transfer your files and settings during the process of installing, you can use the Windows Easy Transfer wizard to do it.

You can also use Windows Easy Transfer to transfer data from an older PC to a new one running Vista. This means if you bring a brand new PC into your home and want to transfer data from a second PC to it, you can.

With Windows Easy Transfer you will transfer as much or as little of the following as you desire:

- data in the Documents, Pictures, Music, Videos and Shared Documents folders, and any personal folders you've created
- e-mail settings, contacts and messages including Internet account settings
- settings you've configured for security programs, anti-virus programs and other third-party applications: you must manually reinstall programs

- colour schemes, desktop backgrounds, network connections and settings, screen savers, Start menu and taskbar options, folders, files, network printers, accessibility options and more

- Internet connection settings, favourites, and cookies.

Complete pre-Easy Transfer tasks

Windows Easy Transfer moves everything in Documents, Pictures, Music, Videos and Shared Documents folders automatically, so you need to do a little housekeeping before using it. Thus, delete data, pictures, music, videos and any other data you no longer want.

Next, clean up your mail program by deleting unwanted e-mail and e-mail folders. This means you should delete items in the Sent Items folder and Deleted Items folder, at the very least. In Internet Explorer, clean up or delete your Favorites folder, and then use Disk Cleanup to get rid of other unwanted files. Restart the PC and empty the Recycle Bin.

Important

Write down the product activation codes for any software you plan to reinstall on the new or clean Vista PC. If you don't know the activation codes check the Help menu in the program. Often the activation code is listed under Help, and About <this product>.

Easy Transfer scenarios

You have two scenarios when using Windows Easy Transfer. You either have two computers and you want to transfer data from an older PC to a new one running Vista, or you have a single existing PC you want to perform a clean installation of Vista on.

Important

If you want to upgrade an existing computer to Vista and perform an upgrade, you don't need Windows Easy Transfer because your files, folders, settings and personal preferences will remain intact.

Note: in the following process I'll outline how to transfer files from one PC to another. If you are performing a clean installation of Vista on a single, existing PC using a Windows Vista installation disk, you will use the same process detailed here, with a few small changes. Before performing the Vista installation, start Windows Easy Transfer from the Windows Vista installation disk. Then choose *My Old Computer* when prompted (instead of My New Computer) when performing the steps outlined here. Beyond that, the process is virtually the same.

Important

Perform Windows Easy Transfer tasks *before* installing Vista clean on any existing PC.

Using Windows Easy Transfer

As noted, in this example I'll outline how to transfer files and settings from an existing PC to a new PC running Windows Vista. If you are performing a clean installation of Vista on a single, existing PC, see the note above.

To start the process of transferring files and settings from your old PC to your new PC:

1 Sit in front of the new PC. This is the PC running Windows Vista.

2 Click Start.

3 In the Start Search window, type Easy.

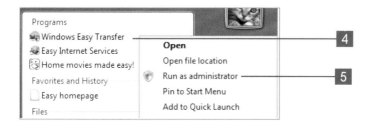

4 Right-click Windows Easy Transfer.

5 Click Run as administrator.

6 Click Next to start Windows Easy Transfer.

7 Select Start A New Transfer.

8 Select My New Computer. (If you're running this on a single PC, click My Old Computer.)

9 If you have an Easy Transfer Cable, select Yes, I Have An Easy Transfer Cable and follow the directions on the following screen to connect it. If you do not have an Easy Transfer Cable, select No, Show Me More Options.

10 Windows Easy Transfer needs to be installed on the old computer. When prompted select from the following:

a. Yes, I installed it

b. Yes, my old computer is running Windows Vista

c. No, I need to install it now.

11 If you chose A or B in the previous step, skip this step. If you chose C, you need to find some way to install Windows Easy Transfer on the older PC. You must select and perform the steps required to choose one of the following options:

a. CD

b. USB Flash Drive

c. External Hard Disk or Shared Network Folder

d. Windows Installation Disk or Windows Easy Transfer CD.

12 When prompted regarding a network connection, select Yes or No as applicable. If you choose Yes, you can save the transfer information to a network drive. If you choose No, you'll need to select from CD, DVD or Removeable Media.

13 When asked if you have a Windows Easy Transfer key, select No, I Need A Key. Write down the key.

14 Continue Windows Easy Transfer at the Old Computer.

15 Sit down in front of your old computer.

16 Using any method you can, start the Windows Easy Transfer on the old computer. You can input the Vista CD or use a CD, USB drive or network drive as configured in Step 11.

17 Click Next to start Windows Easy Transfer.

18 Select Start A New Transfer.

19 Select My Old Computer.

20 If you have an Easy Transfer Cable, select Yes, I Have An Easy Transfer Cable and follow the directions on the following screen to connect it. If you do not have an Easy Transfer Cable, select No, Show Me More Options.

21 You're going to have to wing it now, because there are myriad ways for the process to go. For the most part though, you'll need to do the following:

a. Choose a place to save the data that need to be transferred. You can select a network drive, burn a CD or DVD, or use an external drive. In order of recommended options, choose a network drive first, an external drive second, or a DVD third. Probably a CD won't hold all of the information that needs to be saved.

b. Select what to transfer:

- All User Accounts, Files, and Settings – if the PC has multiple users and accounts.

- My User Account, Files, and Settings – if you're the only person using the PC.

- Advanced Options – choose this if you need to choose what gets transferred and what doesn't, including personal folders and data not stored in default folders like My Pictures, My Documents, etc.

c. If you choose either of the first two, the rest of the process is somewhat automatic. Vista knows what to transfer and where. If you choose Advanced Options, you'll need to select the files, folders and settings to transfer. When that's all done, click Next.

22 Type a user name for the new computer.

23 Click Next.

24 Be patient and wait for the transfer to complete.

25 Click Close on both computers.

26 On the new PC, open Documents, Pictures, Videos and other default folders. You'll find all your data there.

Appendix B: Maintaining your PC

If you never clean your house, never change the filter in the air conditioning unit or the oil in your car, never clean the leaves out of your gutters, and if you never perform routine maintenance on your lawn or garden, problems will begin to appear within weeks (if not days) of neglect. There wouldn't be much left of any of it in a few years and, if there was, you'd have a hard time using it. The same can happen to your PC.

Knowing that, it's important to know how to maintain a computer. You need to know how to delete unwanted files (right-click and choose Delete), how to uninstall programs (use Control Panel), and how to clean up Windows Mail (delete items in the Sent and Deleted Items folders). You also need to know about maintenance tools like Disk Cleanup and how to delete temporary files, cookies and data saved in Internet Explorer. That said, here we'll look at how to maintain your computer in the long term, as well as how to keep it from getting bogged down in the short term.

Get rid of unwanted data and programs

You probably aren't a packrat in your personal life, but in your own computer world there's a good chance you save everything. You may not do this on purpose, but if you look around a bit, you'll see all kinds of data you no longer need. Here are a few places to look and, remember, you can right-click anything and click Delete to get rid of it:

- Check out your personal folder and all of its subfolders. Here you can see a Documents folder with a resumé from 2007, followed by an updated resumé for 2008. It's likely the 2007 resumé is no longer needed.

- Look at any subfolders you've created. You'll probably find lots of data you no longer need.

- Delete any pictures or videos you no longer want.

- Uninstall unwanted programs installed on your PC. (Start, Control Panel, Uninstall a program.) You may find a lot of programs you simply don't use.

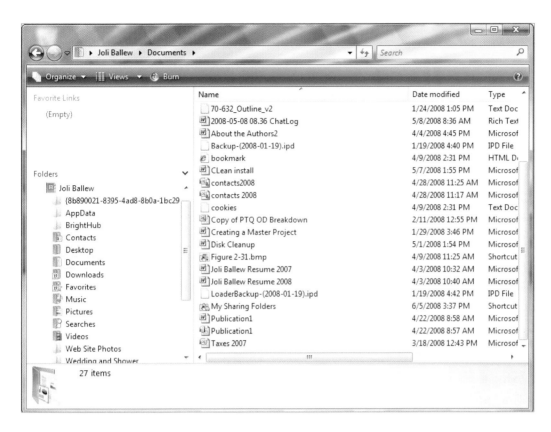

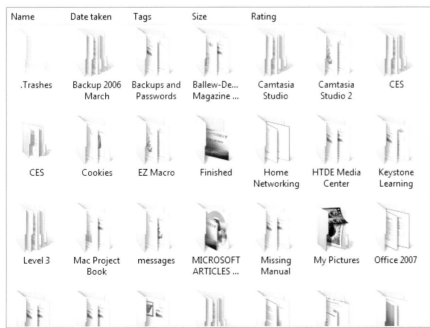

- Remove unwanted items from the desktop (right-click and choose Delete).

- If you use Movie Maker, delete unwanted source and project files. Once you've made your movie, it's likely these files are no longer needed.

Improve or maintain computer performance

There are a few tools you can use to improve computer performance as well as maintain it. You can locate any of these tools from the Start Search menu:

- Disk Cleanup – removes temporary files and unused Windows components.

- Disk Defragmenter – defragments your hard drive. Defragmenting rearranges the data on your hard drive and combines files that should go together.

- Windows Defender – stops unwanted programs from running in the background. (Windows Defender, Tools, Software Explorer.)

- Indexing Options – configures Indexing Options to help you find what you're looking for on your computer more quickly.

- Power Options – lets the computer sleep when not in use.

- Windows Experience Index – run this tool to find out how you can improve the performance of your PC by adding RAM or other hardware.

- Adjust Visual Effects – changes settings to improve performance.

- Advanced Tools – use these tools to perform advanced performance tasks. You can get more information about each by clicking it.

- Security Center – maintain the Security Center by making sure everything is green (i.e everything is running smoothly).

- Windows Update – let it run using recommended settings.

- Windows Mail – monthly, delete unwanted items in your Inbox, delete what's in your Sent Items and then delete what's in the Deleted Items folder. (Right-click, select Delete or Empty.)

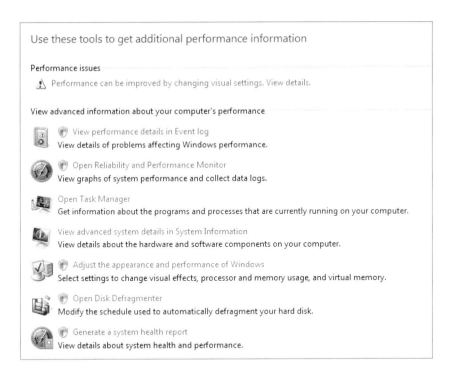

Grow your PC

As time passes and you add more programs and create more data, your PC may start to run more slowly than it did before. You can grow your PC by adding hardware. Some of the best hardware to add includes:

- external hard drives for storing data you do not access often and for saving backups
- RAM inside the PC or use a USB drive for ReadyBoost RAM
- a second monitor for more screen real estate
- a second video card or replace the one you have, especially if you find games are running too slowly.

In addition you can:

- uninstall programs that hang up your computer or keep it from shutting down properly, and replace them with programs created for Windows Vista
- uninstall hardware that hangs up your computer or keeps it from shutting down properly, and replace it with hardware created specifically for Windows Vista. (This includes older cameras, scanners, etc.)

Prepare for a disaster

If you prepare for a computer failure, you'll not only be prepared, but you'll also get yourself organised. Here's how to prepare for a hard drive failure:

- Collect and organise your CDs and DVDs. Use a permanent marker to copy product IDs on the actual disks (on the front of the disk).

- Keep good backups. Store backups on DVDs, network drives or an external drive. Use Windows Backup and Restore tools to create your backups, as well as manually created CDs and DVDs of important data.

- If you have online media, create a backup disk of your music and media if you can.

- Store important data online, such as a website or ISP storage area.

- Keep your tower off the floor and away from where pets congregate, and make sure it's far enough away from anywhere that coffee or cigarette smoke could access.

Jargon buster

Activation – the process you must complete to verify you have a valid copy of Windows Vista including a proper Product ID. You usually activate Vista online, the first time you turn on the PC. This is mandatory.

Address bar – in Internet Explorer or any web browser, this is where you type in Internet addresses, also known as URLs (uniform resource locators). Generally, an Internet address takes the form of *http://www.companyname.com*.

Adware – Internet advertisements (which are also applications) that often include additional code that can be used to track a user's personal information and pass it on to third parties, without the user's authorisation or knowledge.

Aero – Windows Aero builds on the basic Windows Vista interface and offers a high-performing desktop experience that includes (among other things) the translucent effect of Aero Glass.

Aero Glass – added visual reflections and soft animations that are applied when Aero is selected as the display setting.

Applications – software installed on your PC other than the operating system. Some applications come preinstalled, like Windows Calendar, Windows Mail and Internet Explorer. Third-party applications are software you purchase separately and install yourself, like Microsoft Office or Photoshop.

Attachment – an attachment is something you add to an e-mail such as a photograph, a short video, a sound recording, document or other data. There are many ways to attach something to an e-mail.

Backup and Restore Center – this feature lets you perform backups, and in the case of a computer failure, restore them (put them back). However, there are other backup options too, including: copying files to a CD or DVD; copying pictures and media to an external hard drive; USB drive or memory card; or, storing them on an Internet server.

Bandwidth – generally this is used to represent how much data you send and receive on a paid connection, like a smart phone or Internet connection.

BCC – if you want to send the e-mail to someone and you don't want other recipients to know you included them in the e-mail, add them to the BCC line. (You can show this by clicking View, and then clicking All Headers.) BCC stands for blind carbon copy and is a secret copy.

Boot up – when a computer is powered on, it goes through a sequence of tasks before you see the desktop. This process is called the boot-up process. Computers can be rated by many factors, and one of those factors is how long the 'boot-up process' takes.

Browse – browsing for a file, folder or program is the process of drilling down into Vista's folder structure to locate the desired item.

Burn – a term used to describe the process of copying music from a computer to a CD or DVD. Generally music is burned to a CD, since CDs can be played in cars and generic CD players, and videos are burned to DVDs since they require much more space and can be played on DVD players.

CC – if you want to send an e-mail to someone and you don't need them to respond, you can put them in the CC line. CC stands for carbon copy. (BCC is a blind carbon copy; other recipients cannot see the BCC field address.)

Contacts Folder – this folder contains your contacts' information, which includes e-mail addresses, pictures, phone numbers, home and business addresses, and more.

Control Panel – available in all Vista editions, a place where you can change computer settings related to system and maintenance, user accounts, security, appearance, networks and the Internet, the time, language and region, hardware and sounds, visual displays and accessibility options, programs and additional options.

Cookies – these are small text files identifying data establishing your preferences when you visit particular websites. Cookies are what allow you to visit, say, www.amazon.com and be greeted with Hello <your name>, We have recommendations for you! Cookies help a site offer you a personalised web experience.

Copy command – copies the data to Vista's clipboard (a virtual, temporary holding area). The data will not be deleted from their original location even when you 'paste' them somewhere else. Pasting Copy data will copy the data, not move them.

Cut – to remove the selected text, picture or object.

Cut command – copies the data to Vista's clipboard (a virtual, temporary holding area). The data will be deleted from the original location as soon as you 'paste' somewhere else. Pasting cut data moves the data.

Deleted Items – this folder holds e-mail you've deleted.

Desktop Folder – this folder contains links to items for data you created on your desktop. Computer, Network and Recycle Bin aren't listed, but shortcuts to folders you create and data you store on the desktop are.

Dialogue box – a place to make changes to default settings in an application. Clicking File and then Print, for instance, opens the Print dialogue box where you can configure the type of paper you're using, select a printer and more.

Disk Cleanup – an application included with Windows Vista that offers a safe and effective way to reduce unnecessary data on your PC. With Disk Cleanup you can remove temporary files, empty the Recycle Bin, remove setup log files and downloaded program files (among other things), all in a single process.

Disk Defragmenter – an application included with Windows Vista that analyses the data stored on your hard drive and consolidates files that are not stored together. This enhances performance by making data on your hard drive work faster by making data easier to access. Disk Defragmenter runs automatically once a week, in the middle of the night.

Documents Folder – this folder contains documents you've saved, subfolders you created, and folders created by Vista including Fax, My Received Files, Remote Assistance Logs and Scanned Documents.

Domain name – for our use here, a domain name is synonymous with a website name.

Downloaded program files – files that are downloaded automatically when you view certain webpages. They are stored temporarily in a folder on your hard disk, and accessed if and when required.

Downloads Folder – this folder does not contain anything by default. It does offer a place to save items you download from the Internet, like drivers and third-party programs.

DPI – dots per inch refers to how many dots (or pixels) per inch on a computer monitor.

Drafts – this folder holds e-mail messages you've started, but not completed. Click File and click Save to put an e-mail in progress here.

Driver – a driver is a piece of software (or code) that allows the device to communicate with Windows Vista and vice versa.

DV – digital video, generally used as DV camera.

E-mail address – a virtual address you use for sending and receiving email. It often takes this form: *yourname@yourispname.com*.

Enhancements – features in Windows Media Player that you can use to enhance your music, including a graphic equaliser.

Ethernet – a technology that uses Ethernet cables to transmit data and network computers.

Ethernet cable – a cable that is used to connect PCs to routers and cable modems, among other things.

Favorite – a webpage that you've chosen to maintain a shortcut for in the Favorites Center.

Favorites Folder – this folder contains the items in Internet Explorer's Favorites list. It may also include folders created by the computer manufacturer or Microsoft, including Links, Microsoft websites and MSN websites.

Filter Keys – a setting you can configure so that Windows ignores keystrokes that occur in rapid succession, such as when you accidentally leave your finger on a key for too long.

Flip and Flip 3-D – a way to move through open windows graphically instead of clicking the item in the taskbar.

Form data – in Internet Explorer, this is information that's been saved using Internet Explorer's autocomplete form data functionality. If you don't want forms to be filled out automatically by you or someone else who has access to your PC and user account, delete this.

Formatting toolbar – a toolbar in an application window that often sits just below a standard toolbar and offers drop-down lists for the font, font size and language, as well as options to configure the font (or any selected text) as bold, italic or underlined. There's often a Color option for assigning a colour to a font too, as well as alignment tools for Align Left, Center, Align Right, and finally Bullets.

Gadget – in our terms, an icon on the Sidebar like the weather or clock gadget.

GHz – short for gigahertz, this term describes how fast a processor can work. One GHz equals 1 billion cycles per second, so a 2.4 GHz computer chip will execute calculations at 240 billion cycles per second. Again, it's only important to know that the faster the chip, the faster the PC.

GPU – short for graphics processing unit, it's a processor used specifically for rendering graphics. Having a processor just for graphics frees up the main CPU, allowing it to work faster on other tasks.

History – in Internet Explorer, this is the list of websites you've visited and any web addresses you've typed. Anyone who has access to your PC and user account can look at your History list to see where you've been.

Home page – the webpage that opens when you open IE7. You can set the home page and configure additional pages to open as well.

Hot spot – a WiFi hot spot lets you connect to the Internet without having to be tethered to an Ethernet cable or tied down with a high monthly wireless bill. Sometimes this service is free, provided you have the required wireless hardware.

Icon – a visual representation of a file or folder that you can click to open.

Inbox – this folder holds e-mail you've received.

Instant messaging – text and instant messaging require you to type your message and click a Send button. It's similar to e-mail, but it's instantaneous; the recipient gets the message right after you send it. Instant messaging is the term generally reserved for text communications between two or more computers; text messaging is a term generally reserved for communicating between two mobile phones.

Interface – what you see on the screen when working in a window. In Paint's interface, you see the Menu bar, toolbox and Color box.

Internet – a large web of computers that communicate via land lines, satellite and cable for the purpose of sharing information and data. Also called the World Wide Web.

Internet server – a computer that stores data off site. Hotmail offers Internet servers to hold e-mail and data, so that you do not have to store them on your PC. Internet servers allow you to access information from any computer that can access the Internet.

ISP – Internet Service Provider. A company that provides Internet access, usually for a fee.

Junk e-mail – this folder holds e-mail that Windows Mail thinks is spam. You should check this folder occasionally, since Mail may put e-mail in there you want to read.

Link – a shortcut to a webpage. Links are often offered in an e-mail, document or webpage to allow you to access a site without having to actually type in its name. In almost all instances, links are underlined and in a different colour than the page they are configured on.

Links Folder – this folder contains shortcuts to the Documents, Music, Pictures, Public, Recently Changed and Searches folders.

Load – a webpage must 'load' before you can access it. Some pages load instantly while others take a few seconds.

Magnifier – a tool in the Ease of Access suite of applications. You use Magnifier to drastically increase the size of the information shown on the screen.

Mail – Windows Mail is despatched with Microsoft Windows Vista, and is the only thing you need to send and receive e-mail, manage your contacts, manage sent, saved and incoming e-mail, and read newsgroups.

Mail servers – a computer that your ISP configures to allow you to send and receive e-mail. It often includes a POP3 incoming mail server and an SMTP outgoing mail server. Often the server names look something like *pop.yourispnamehere.com* and *smtp.yourispnamehere.com*.

Malware – stands for malicious software. Malware includes viruses, worms, spyware, etc.

Menu – a title on a menu bar (such as File, Edit, View). Clicking this menu button opens a drop-down list with additional choices (Open, Save, Print).

Menu bar – a bar that runs across the top of an application that offers menus. Often, these menus include File, Edit, View, Insert, Format and Help.

Mouse keys – instead of using your mouse, you can use the arrow keys on your keyboard or the numeric keypad to move the mouse pointer on the desktop or inside programs or documents.

Music Folder – this folder contains sample music and music you save to the PC.

Narrator – a basic screen reader included with Windows Vista. This application will read text that appears on the screen to you, while you navigate using the keyboard and mouse.

Navigate – the process of moving from one webpage to another or viewing items on a single webpage. Often the term is used as follows: 'Click the link to navigate to the new web page.'

Network – a group of computers, printers and other devices that communicate wirelessly or through wired connections.

Network – (from the Start menu) the Network window offers links to computers on your network and the Network and Sharing Center. You can also add printers and wireless devices here.

Network adapter – a piece of hardware that lets your computer connect to a network, such as the Internet or a local network.

Network and Sharing Center – a collection of features where you can easily access network connections, sharing options, networked computers and devices, and diagnose and repair features.

Network Discovery – a state where computers can find other computers on the network. Network Discovery must be on to locate and communicate with network devices.

Network Map – this details each of your network connections graphically, and allows you to distinguish easily among wired, wireless and Internet connections.

Newsgroup – an online forum where you can share ideas, post opinions, get help, and meet other people with interests similar to your own.

Notification area – the area of the taskbar that includes the clock and the volume icons, and also holds icons for applications that are running in the background. You may see icons for your anti-virus software, music players, updates or Windows security alerts.

Offline webpages – these are webpages you choose to store on your computer so you can view them without being connected to the Internet. Upon connection, the data are synchronised.

Operating system – in this case, the operating system is Windows Vista. This is what allows *you* to *operate* your computer's *system*. You will use Windows Vista to find things you have stored on your computer, connect to the Internet, send and receive e-mail and surf the Web, among other things.

Outbox – this folder holds e-mail you've written but have not yet sent.

Page Setup button – clicking Page Setup opens the Page Setup dialogue box. Here you can select a paper size and source, and create headers and footers. You can also change orientation and margins, all of which is dependent on what features your printer supports.

Parental Controls – if you have grandchildren, children or even a forgetful or scatterbrained partner who needs imposed computer limitations, you can apply them using Parental Controls. With these controls you are in charge of the hours a user can access the computer, which games they can play and what programs they can run (among other things).

Partition – a hard drive has a certain amount of space to store data, sometimes 40 GB, 80 GB, 120 GB or more. Often, people or computer manufacturers separate this space into two or three distinct spaces, called partitions, drives or volumes. One partition may contain system files, one may contain program files and the other may contain data.

Paste command – copies or moves the cut or copied data to the new location. If the data were Cut, they will be moved. If the data were Copied, they will be copied.

Per user archived Windows Error Reporting – files used for error reporting and solution checking.

Permissions – rules associated with a shared resource, like a folder, file or printer, that define who can use a resource and what they can do once they have access to it.

Phishing – a technique used by computer hackers to get you to divulge personal information like bank account numbers. Phishing filters warn you of potential phishing websites and e-mail, and are included in Vista. In other words, an attempt by an unscrupulous website or hacker to obtain personal data including but not limited to bank account numbers, social security numbers and e-mail addresses.

Pictures Folder – this folder contains sample pictures and pictures you save to the PC.

Pixel – the smallest unit that data can be displayed on a computer. Resolution is defined by how many pixels you choose to display.

Playlist – a group of songs that you can save and then listen to as a group, burn to a CD, copy to a portable music player and more.

Podcast – an online broadcast, similar to a radio show.

POP3 Server Name – the name of the computer that you will use to get your e-mail from your ISP. Your ISP will give you this information when you subscribe.

Power plan – a group of settings that you can configure to tell Windows Vista when and if to turn off the computer monitor or display, and when or if to put the computer to sleep.

Print button – clicking Print opens the Print dialogue box where you can configure the page range, select a printer, change page orientation, change print order and choose a paper type. Additional options include print quality, output bins and more. Of course, the choices offered depend on what your printer offers. If your printer can only print at 300 × 300 dots per inch, you can't configure it to print at a higher quality.

Print Preview button – clicking Print Preview opens a window where you can see, before you print, what the printout will actually look like.

You can switch between portrait and landscape views, access the Page Setup dialogue box and more.

Processor – short for microprocessor, it's the silicon chip that contains the central processing unit (CPU) inside a computer. Generally, the terms CPU and processor are used interchangeably. The CPU does almost all of the computer's calculations and is the most important piece of hardware in a computer system.

Programs – see Applications.

Public Folder – a folder where you can share data. Anyone with an account on the computer can access the data inside these folders. You can also configure the Public folder to share files with people using other computers on your local network.

Publish – in Windows Calendar, a way to distribute a calendar electronically so that it is shared with others. The calendar can be shared via an online source like a webpage or on the user's own network.

RAM – short for random access memory, it's the hardware inside your computer that temporarily stores data that are being used by the operating system or programs. Although there are many types of RAM, all you need to know is that the more RAM you have, the faster your computer will (theoretically) run and perform.

ReadyBoost – a new technology that lets you add more RAM (random access memory) to a PC using a USB flash drive or a secure digital memory card (like the one in your digital camera) as RAM, if it meets certain requirements. Just plug the device into an open slot on your PC and, if it is compatible, choose to use the device as RAM.

Recycle Bin – the Recycle Bin holds deleted files until you decide to empty it. The Recycle Bin serves as a safeguard, allowing you to recover items accidentally deleted or items you thought you no longer wanted but later decide you need. Note that once you empty the Recycle Bin, the items in it are gone for ever.

Registration – a non-mandatory task that you generally perform during the Vista activation process. By registering you can get e-mail about Vista and new products. Registration is not mandatory.

Remote Desktop Connection – a Vista program you can use to access your computer from somewhere else, like an office or hotel room.

Resolution – the number of pixels that are shown on a computer screen. Choosing 800 by 600 pixels means that the desktop is shown to you with 800 pixels across and 600 pixels down. When you increase the resolution, you increase the number of pixels on the screen.

Rip – a term used to describe the process of copying files from a physical CD to your hard drive, and thus your music library.

Router – a piece of equipment used to send data from computer to computer on a network. A router 'routes' the data to the correct PC and also rejects data that are harmful or from unknown sources.

RSS – a new way to access information on the Internet. Also called Really Simple Syndication (and occasionally Rich Site Summary), you can use this technology to 'subscribe' to RSS data, and the information or website you subscribe to will be updated automatically on your PC, and will only acquire information you've yet to view.

Saved Games Folder – this folder contains games that are despatched with Windows Vista and offers a place to save games you acquire otherwise.

Screen saver – a screen saver is a picture or animation that covers your screen and appears after your computer has been idle for a specific amount of time that you set. You can configure your screen saver to require a password on waking up for extra security.

Scroll Up and Scroll Down – a process of using the scroll bars on a webpage or the arrow keys on a keyboard to move up and down the pages of a website or to navigate through open windows.

Searches Folder – this folder contains preconfigured Search folders including Recent Documents, Recent E-Mail, Recent Music, Recent Pictures and Videos, Recently Changed, and Shared By Me. If you need to find something recently accessed or changed and don't know where to look, you can probably locate it here. These folders get updated each time you open them.

Sent Items – this folder stores copies of e-mail messages you've sent.

Setup Log Files – files created by Windows during setup processes.

Sidebar – the Sidebar is a desktop component that lies *on top of* the desktop. It's transparent and offers, by default, a calendar, the weather and a clock. You can delete and add Sidebar items, called gadgets, to show the information you want to see. You can also hide the Sidebar.

SMTP server name – the name of the computer that you will use to send e-mail using your ISP. Your ISP will give you this information when you subscribe.

Snipping Tool – a new feature in Windows Vista that allows you to drag your cursor around any area on the screen to copy and capture it. Once

captured, you can save it, edit it and/or send it to an e-mail recipient.

Sound recorder – a simple tool included with Windows Vista with only three options, Start Recording, Stop Recording and Resume Recording. You can save recorded clips as notes to yourself or insert them into movies or slide shows.

Spam – unwanted e-mail. Compare spam to junk faxes or junk post.

Speech Recognition – a program included with Windows Vista. This program does a good job of allowing you to control your computer with your voice. From the Speech Recognition options you can set up your microphone, take a speech tutorial, train your computer to better understand you and more.

Standard toolbar – a toolbar that is often underneath a menu bar (in an application window) that contains icons, or pictures, of common commands. Common commands include New, Open, Save, Print, Print Preview, Find, Cut, Copy, Paste, Undo and Date/Time.

Status bar – a toolbar that often appears at the bottom of an application window and offers information about what you are doing at the moment. If you aren't doing anything, it often offers the helpful words 'For Help, press F1', otherwise it offers information regarding the tool you've selected from a toolbar, or information about the task you're performing.

Sticky Keys – this setting allows you to configure the keyboard so that you never have to press three keys at once (such as when you must press the CTRL, ALT and DELETE keys together to log on to Windows). With Sticky Keys, you can use one key to perform these tasks. You configure the key to use for three-key tasks.

Subfolder – a folder inside another folder.

Subscribe – using Windows Calendar, a method used to access a calendar created by someone else. The calendar is displayed in Windows Calendar and is updated automatically as changes are made to the original. You can choose how often to update the calendar.

Sync – the process of comparing data in one location to data in another, and performing tasks to match them up. If data have been added or deleted from one device, for instance, synching can also add or delete them from the other.

Sync Center – an application included with Windows Vista that helps you keep your files, music, contacts, pictures and other data in sync between your computer and mobile devices, network files and folders, and compatible programs such as Outlook. Technically, syncing is the process of keeping files matched, when those files are used on more than one device.

System archived Windows Error Reporting – files used for error reporting and solution checking.

System Restore – if enabled, Vista stores 'restore points' on your PC's hard drive. If something goes wrong you can run System Restore, choose one of these points and revert to a pre-problem date. Since System Restore only deals with 'system data', none of your personal data will be affected (not even your last e-mail).

System Restore Point – a snapshot of the computer that Vista keeps in case something happens and you need to revert to it, because of a bad installation or hardware driver.

Tags – data about a particular piece of data, like a photo or a song or album. Tags can be used to group pictures or music in various ways. Some tags are applied automatically when you import pictures from a digital camera, including the date they were uploaded, along with any name you applied to the imported group. You can create your own tags.

Taskbar – the bar that runs horizontally across the bottom of the Vista interface, and contains the Start button, Quick Launch area and Notification area. It also offers a place to view and access open files, folders and applications.

Temporary files – files created and stored by programs for use by the program. Most of these temporary files are deleted when you exit the program, but some do remain.

Temporary Internet files – files that contain copies of webpages you've visited, so that you can view the pages more quickly when visiting the page again.

Text messaging – text and instant messaging require you to type your message and click a Send button. It's similar to e-mail, but it's instantaneous; the recipient gets the message right after you send it. Instant messaging is the term generally reserved for text communications between two or more computers; text messaging is a term generally reserved for communicating between two mobile phones.

Thumbnails – small icons of your pictures, videos and documents. Thumbnails will be recreated as needed should you choose to delete them using Disk Cleanup.

Transition – in Movie Maker, a segue from one clip to another, such as fading in or out.

URL – this stands for uniform resource locator and denotes a location on a network, either the Internet or a local network.

Video messaging – a form of instant messaging where one or both users also offer live video of themselves during the conversation.

Videos Folder – this folder contains sample videos and videos you save to the PC.

Video format – the video file type, such as AVI or WMV.

Virus – a self-replicating program that infects computers with intent to do harm. Viruses often come in the form of an attachment in an e-mail.

Visualisations – produced by Vista and Windows Media Player, these are graphical representations of the music you play.

Web browser – Windows Vista comes with Internet Explorer, an application you can use to surf the Internet. Internet Explorer lets you 'surf the Web', and it has everything you need, including a pop-up blocker, zoom settings and accessibility options, as well as tools you can use to save your favourite webpages, set home pages and sign up to read RSS feeds.

Webcam – a camera that can send live images over the Internet.

Website – a group of webpages that contain related information. Microsoft's website contains information about Microsoft products, for instance.

Window – when you open a program from the Start menu, a document, folder, or a picture, it opens in a 'window'. Window, as it's used in this context, is synonymous with an open program, file or folder and has nothing to do with the word 'Windows', used with Windows Vista.

Windows Calendar – a fully featured calendar application included in Windows Vista that lets you manage your own affairs as well as the affairs of others, using a familiar calendar interface.

Windows Defender – you don't have to do much to Windows Defender except understand that it offers protection against Internet threats. It's enabled by default and it runs in the background. However, if you ever think your computer has been attacked by an internet threat (virus, worm, malware, etc.) you can run a manual scan here.

Windows Firewall – if enabled and configured properly, the firewall will help prevent hackers (people whose job it is to get into your computer and do harm to it) from accessing your PC and data. The firewall blocks most programs from communicating outside the network (or outside your PC). If you want to allow a program to communicate outside your safety zone you can 'allow' a program by adding it to an 'exceptions' list. This is all very easy to do.

Windows Media Center – available in Windows Home Premium and Windows Ultimate editions, an application that allows you to: watch, pause and record live television; locate, download and/or listen to music and radio; view, edit and share photos and videos; and play DVDs (among other things).

Windows Mobility Center – an application that lets you adjust your mobile PC, tablet PC, or laptop computer settings quickly, including things like volume, wireless and brightness.

Windows Update – if enabled and configured properly, when you are online, Vista will check for security updates automatically, and install them. You don't have to do anything, and your PC is always updated with the latest security patches and features.

Worm – a self-replicating program that infects computers with intent to do harm. However, unlike a virus, it does not need to attach itself to a running program.

Troubleshooting guide